The Esthetics of Negligence:
La Fontaine's Contes

The Esthetics of Negligence: La Fontaine's Contes

JOHN C. LAPP

Professor of French
Stanford University

CAMBRIDGE
AT THE UNIVERSITY PRESS
1971

Published by the Syndics of the Cambridge University Press
Bentley House, 200 Euston Road, London NW1 2DB
American Branch: 32 East 57th Street, New York, N.Y.10022

Library of Congress Catalogue Card Number: 72–142130

ISBN: 0 521 08067 3

Printed in Great Britain
by W & J Mackay & Co Ltd, Chatham

Contents

CONTENTS

Preface

In general La Fontaine's *Contes* have fared ill at the hands of critics. They delighted his contemporaries, the staid Chapelain as well as the ebullient Mme de Sévigné, and later found admirers in writers as different in their tastes as Diderot, Musset, Stendhal and Flaubert. But Sainte-Beuve's judgment has had a greater impact than the lesser known applause of the creative writers. Praising Boileau's influence, he declared: 'Sans Boileau…Racine, je le crains, aurait fait plus souvent des *Bérénice*, La Fontaine moins de *Fables* et plus de *Contes*, Molière aurait donné davantage dans les Scapins, et n'aurait peut-être pas atteint aux hauteurs sévères du *Misanthrope*. En un mot, chacun de ces beaux génies aurait abondé dans ses défauts.'[1]

The greatest of modern French critics echoes Sainte-Beuve's judgment, and pronounced an anathema from which the *contes* have not recovered:

Je regrette toutes les heures dépensées par La Fontaine à cette quantité de contes qu'il nous a laissés et dont je ne puis souffrir le ton rustique et faux, les vers d'une facilité répugnante, leur bassesse générale, et tout l'ennui que respire un libertinage si contraire à la volupté et si mortel à la poésie. Et je regrette plus encore les quelques Adonis qu'il eût pu faire au lieu de ces contes assommants.[2]

Most adverse criticism since Valéry has been somewhat more measured, and Pierre Clarac has conceded the *contes* a certain ease and grace in the telling, though labelling them 'monotones polissonneries'. Defenders have not been wanting: Erich Auerbach[3] and Vittorio Lugli;[4] Philip Wadsworth[5] and Renée Kohn[6] have praised their narrative technique and singled out certain of them for special praise. But a recent editor's resigned tones recall Sainte-Beuve and

---

[1] Sainte-Beuve, *Causeries du lundi*, VI, 294.

[2] Paul Valéry, *Œuvres complètes*, ed. J. Hytier (Paris: Bibliothèque de la Pléiade, 1959–60), I, 493–4.

[3] Erich Auerbach, *Mimesis: The Representation of Reality in Western Literature*, tr. W. Trask (New York: Doubleday, 1957), pp. 185 and 358.

[4] Vittorio Lugli, *Il Prodigio di La Fontaine* (Messina-Milan: Principato, 1939).

[5] Philip Wadsworth, *Young La Fontaine: A Study of his Artistic Growth in his Early Poetry and First Fables* (Evanston, Ill.: Northwestern University Press, 1952).

[6] Renée Kohn, *Le Goût de La Fontaine* (Paris: Presses Universitaires de France, 1962).

Valéry: 'Regrettons...tout ce temps perdu à des histoires galantes: quelques fables de plus feraient mieux notre affaire. Mais voilà; nous avons les *Contes*.'[1] And one eloquent voice has resolutely supported Valéry's condemnation: 'Je ne crois pas qu'on puisse revenir sur le dur jugement que Paul Valéry a prononcé sur ces *Contes*. Ils sont froids et ennuyeux.'[2] My writing this book proves my profound disagreement with this view. I hope to show that far from being monotonous, facile or boring, the *contes* sustain the judgment of Stendhal and Flaubert. Mme de Mourgues attributes their failure to *préciosité*, and finds that they demonstrate 'l'impuissance poétique à laquelle les conventions du genre réduisent un écrivain'. Although definitions of *préciosité* still remain somewhat Protean, I hope to show that on two points in particular the *contes* have nothing *précieux* about them: they are extremely inventive, in both content and form, and they almost always resound with the author's vigorous presence.

This presence I shall relate to what I have called the 'esthetics of negligence'. The word has been frequently pronounced in connection with La Fontaine's works; it has been less frequently defined. I shall use it as a synonym of 'nonchalance', although today it has a pejorative connotation that nonchalance has not. My aim is to find how La Fontaine's negligence becomes an esthetic; how it realizes itself in various devices and techniques that combine to make the *contes* unique in themselves.

For they were unique in their time, or in any time. Nothing like them had been seen before the first slim volume appeared in 1664, and none of La Fontaine's imitators ever succeeded in approaching their enchanting combination of wit, eroticism, lyricism and charm. At first glance they seem less original than the *fables*; there is more direct imitation; there is almost no profundity; the formula appears simple: a licentious tale, usually by Boccaccio, is put into verse, usually decasyllabic. But one has only to read Boccaccio or the other sources to be struck by the difference.

This book, the first to be devoted to the *contes*, attempts an exploration of the nature of that difference, and that is why I have devoted its bulk to comparisons between the originals and the *contes* La Fontaine derived from them, always with the idea of esthetic

---

[1] La Fontaine, *Contes et nouvelles en vers*, ed. Georges Couton (Paris: Garnier, 1961), p. i.
[2] Odette de Mourgues, *O muse, fuyante proie...Essai sur la poésie de La Fontaine* (Paris: Corti, 1962), p. 85.

negligence in mind. I begin with a study of two forebears, Rabelais and Montaigne, whose affinity with La Fontaine is clear and whose own particular negligence helps us to approach that of the *contes*.

Portions of this book have appeared, in considerably different form, in *L'Esprit créateur*, *Romanic Review*, and *Studies in Seventeenth-Century French Literature Presented to Morris Bishop* (Ithaca, N.Y.: Cornell University Press, 1963). I am grateful to the editors of these publications for permission to reproduce them here.

I acknowledge with gratitude a Guggenheim Fellowship and a Fulbright Research Grant which enabled me, in 1967, to devote several months in France to the writing of this book.

March 1971

1

The Esthetics of Negligence

In the course of one of the most urbane and gracious conversations ever recorded or imagined, its scene the beautiful palace of Urbino with its wall-hangings of cloth of gold and silk, its marble and bronze statues and rare paintings, one speaker, discoursing upon the quality of grace requisite to the ideal courtier, declares that he should

> practice in all things a certain *sprezzatura* (nonchalance), so as to conceal all art and make whatever is done or said appear to be without effort and almost without any thought about it. And I believe much grace comes of this: because everyone knows the difficulty of things that are rare and well done; wherefor facility in such things causes the greatest wonder; yet on the other hand, to labor and as we say, drag forth by the hair of the head shows an extreme want of grace, and causes everything, no matter how great, to be held of little account.[1]

Count Lodovico da Canossa's formulation in Castiglione's *Book of the Courtier* is one of the earliest modern statements of an attitude I have found in a number of French writers from the sixteenth century on, and one which seems to follow a distinct pattern. These writers, against a social or artistic background which in some way or another would impose upon them a specific set of conventions or rules, proclaim their *sprezzatura*: their nonchalance, negligence, or indifference concerning their art. They do so in some kind of intimate aside to the reader, which usually takes the form of a preface or foreword, and their declarations of independence generally develop in three main categories, all of them related: *Irresponsibility* – The author denies that his work has any special purpose, moral or otherwise, excepting pleasure. *Spontaneity* – He rejects all rules, past or present, claiming to write without preparation or preconceived pattern. His favorite word is 'naturally'. *Consubstantiality* – The writer assures us that he

---

[1] Castiglione, *The Book of the Courtier*, tr. Charles Singleton (New York: Anchor Books, 1959), p. 43.

1

and his work are one; his book is the result of chance or pastime, and so it is indistinguishable from its author, reflecting his own strengths and weaknesses. The words of St John: 'and the word was made flesh', or Buffon: 'Le style c'est de l'homme même', apply equally well to this last category.

I have singled out as three eminent exemplars of 'negligence' Rabelais, Montaigne and La Fontaine, and my study of this aspect of the latter has led to the present book on the *contes*. But I am not suggesting that these writers were alone in adopting the negligent style endorsed by Horace, Quintilian, Terence and Castiglione. One frequently encounters an attitude similar to the one I have described in baroque writers of the seventeenth century. A predecessor and contemporary that La Fontaine certainly read and admired, Théophile de Viau, struck the pose of negligence in voicing his opposition to Malherbe, and we shall see that despite his reverence for Théophile's adversary, La Fontaine on at least one occasion echoes the truculent lines of the *Elégie à une dame*. Here Théophile vaunts his lack of direction and unity:

> Je ne veux point unir le fil de mon sujet,
> Diversement je laisse et reprens mon object.

He refuses to follow rules and admires only ease in execution:

> Mon ame imaginant n'a point la patience,
> De bien polir les vers et ranger la science:
> La reigle me deplaist, j'escris confusément,
> Jamais un bon esprit ne faict rien qu'aisément.
> ....
> Je veux faire des vers qui ne soient pas contraincts . . .[1]

One recognizes the self-deprecatory attitude of the negligent writer in Théophile's assertion that 'ceste publication est plutost de l'humilité de mon ame, que de la vanité de mon esprit'. The impromptu quality he seeks may be linked to the setting and to his desire

> Ecrire dans les bois, m'interrompre, me taire,
> Composer un quatrain sans songer à le faire.

Obviously the strongest element of negligence in Théophile is his reaction against critics and theoreticians. His contemporary Charles

[1] Théophile de Viau, *Œuvres poétiques*, ed. J. Streicher (Paris: Droz, 1951), pp. 11–12.

Sorel, who admits freely to both *nonchalance* and *négligence*, comes somewhat closer to one of our categories by stressing the importance of prefaces, specifically attributing his nonchalance to his disdain for glory and suggesting 'consubstantiality' through his emphasis on the ease and even indolence with which he composes. He neither corrects nor rereads his work, and what is more:

Je n'ai pas composé moins de trente deux pages d'impression en un jour et si, encore a ce esté, avec un esprit incessamment diverty à d'autres pensées ausquelles il ne s'en faloit guere que je ne me donnasse entierement. Aucunes fois, j'estois assoupy et à moitié endormy, et n'avois point d'autre mouvement que celuy de ma main droite.[1]

Scarron's formulation, however, seems particularly self-centred – almost a character-sketch of the author – as indeed does Théophile's. One finds little concern in either writer for the nature of negligence or its effect on the reader. But another anti-Malherbian, the satiric Mathurin Régnier, does allude more specifically to some of the concepts we have noted in *The Courtier*.[2] He defines the truly great poet in terms of inspiration, grace, and naturalness:

> ces divins esprits, hautains et relevés,
> Qui des eaux d'Hélicon ont les sens abreuvés,
> De verbe et de fureur leur ouvrage étincelle;
> De leurs vers tout divins la grâce est naturelle.

The poets Régnier scorns spend their time avoiding hiatus, polishing rhymes, and seeking witty, if empty turns of phrase. They resemble women covered with ribbons and ornaments, heavily made-up, and with impeccable coiffures:

> toute leur beauté ne gît qu'en l'ornement;
> Leur visage reluit de céruse et de peautre;
> Propres en leur coiffure, un poil ne passe l'autre.

The perfect beauty, and by extension, the truly accomplished writer, seek for nonchalance in their aspect:

> Rien que le naturel sa grâce n'accompagne;
> Son front, lavé d'eau claire, éclate d'un beau teint;
> De roses et de lys la Nature l'a peint,
> Et laissant là Mercure et toutes ses malices,
> Les nonchalances sont ses plus grands artifices.

---

1 Charles Sorel, *Histoire comique de Francion*, ed. E. Roy (Paris: Hachette, 1924), I, v–vi. E.g.: 'à quel sujet me fussé-je abstenu de ceste nonchalance?...Il est donc aysé à cognoistre par la negligence que j'advoüe'.
2 Régnier, *Œuvres complètes*, ed. G. Raibaud (Paris: Didier, 1958), Satire IX.

This particular ramification of nonchalance, its extension to dress or bearing in man or woman in order to symbolize the poet's concept of his art and even of humanity itself, appears to have become very early a part of the tradition. Cicero suggested that negligence could be attractive: a *non ingrata neglegentia*.[1] Ovid admired as *neglecta decens*[2] a girl still disheveled in the morning. The same poet makes what was to become a familiar link between negligence and order when the sight of Daphne's *inornatos cappillos*[3] makes Apollo wonder just how beautiful her hair would be if carefully arranged. But most poets prefer their girls with careless tresses; Venus first appears to Aeneas wind-blown: *dederatque comam diffundere*.[4] The negligent in hair or dress can also appeal more urgently to the imagination, and Apollo's *siqua latent, meliora putant*, in the writers we shall study, and particularly in La Fontaine, will have a wide application.

Discussing Yeats' 'careless Muse', one critic has made four suggestions as to why negligence is dear to poets: 'it is pleasing in itself, it is magnanimous, it is true to nature, and it is characteristic of passion'.[5] These reasons undoubtedly hold true for poets in general. In the case of the three writers I shall discuss in this chapter, other motives, other effects should become apparent, including those I have suggested in the first of my three categories.

Rabelais' Prologues: oil or wine?

On opening Rabelais' great book, one's first impression is that of a monumental disorder. Although the work is in some sense a novel, one encounters none of the consistency of plot or character that until fairly recently has characterized the genre. The author, not content with flattering, hectoring and even insulting his reader in the prologues to each book, moves freely in and out of the work itself; the chief characters, if they are giants, on occasion assume normal stature, and if they are not, can change radically and unexpectedly in other respects from one book to the other. The action can come abruptly to a halt, and never begin again. The tone can range from frenzied buffoonery to the gravest solemnity, and one is not always sure why. A recent editor concludes that the work was composed without any

---

[1] *De oratore*, 23, 78. [2] *Amores*, I, xiv, 21–2.
[3] *Metamorphoses*, I, 477. [4] *Aeneid*, I, 319.
[5] J. F. Nims, 'Yeats and the Careless Muse', in *Learners and Discerners*, ed. R. E. Scholes (Charlottesville: University Press of Virginia, 1964), pp. 31–60.

preconceived plan.[1] I believe that it would be more correct to say Rabelais composed so that the critic and any other might have that impression. An examination of the prologues, in which the author addresses his chosen audience and in which he continually declares his purpose in various ways, reveals that he was particularly concerned both with method and with the communication of meaning. This becomes even clearer if we read the prologues with the esthetics of negligence in mind.

Prologue I concerns itself particularly with the difficult question of the author's intent, his responsibility for what he writes, and the meaning of his work. The central figure, the famous Erasmian example of the *Sileni* – tiny boxes whose surface was decorated with grotesque figures, yet which contained the most precious objects – stresses the essential dichotomy between appearance and reality, between the seeming disorder of Bacchanalian frivolity and the serene order of divine wisdom. Rabelais carefully assigns the comparison to Alcibiades, speaking at Plato's Banquet, thus placing it squarely in the realm of the Platonic theory of the coincidence of opposites.[2] Analysis reveals the subtlety and complexity of the passage in Rabelais. The first part, almost equally balanced by the second, describes the ornate containers:

Silenes estoient jadis petites boites, telles que voyons de present ès bouticques des apothecaires, pinctes au dessus de figures joyeuses et frivoles, comme de harpies, satyres, oysons bridez, lievres cornuz, canes bastées, boucqs volans, cerfz limmonniers et aultres telles pinctures contrefaictes à plaisir pour exciter le monde à rire (quel fut Silene, maistre du bon Bacchus); mais au dedans l'on reservoit les fines drogues comme baulme, ambre gris, amomon, musc, zivette, pierreries et aultres choses precieuses (I, 5).[3]

Three elements in this passage deserve attention; first, the attempt to familiarize the image: the boxes belong to the past (*jadis*), but they closely resemble those seen nowadays (*de present*) in apothecaries' shops. Second, the figures painted on the outside of the box are calculated to excite laughter through their stupidity as well as their frivolity. Lastly, the explanation of the name of the boxes, as deriving

---

[1] Rabelais, *Œuvres complètes*, ed. Pierre Jourda (Paris: Garnier, 1962), p. xxxviii.
[2] G. Mallory Masters, *Rabelaisian Dialectic and the Platonic–Hermetic Tradition* (Albany State University of New York Press, 1969).
[3] References in the text are to the Jourda edition of Rabelais' *Œuvres* cited in footnote 1, above.

from Silenus, the aged satyr and preceptor of Bacchus–Dionysos, introduces and links to the joyful exterior that conceals wisdom, the theme of wine. Silenus also prepares us for the description of Socrates, for it is the traditional portrait of the drunken old satyr that Rabelais applies to the philosopher:

Tel disoit estre Socrates, parce que, le voyans au dehors et l'estimans par l'exteriore apparence, n'en eussiez donné un coupeau d'oignon, tant laid il estoit de corps et ridicule en son maintien, le nez pointu, le reguard d'un taureau, le visaige d'un fol, simple en meurs, rustiq en vestimens, pauvre de fortune, infortuné en femmes, inepte à tous offices de la republique, tousjours riant, tousjours beuvant d'autant à un chascun, tousjours se guabelant, tousjours dissimulant son divin sçavoir; mais, ouvrans ceste boyte, eussiez au dedans trouvé une celeste et impreciable drogue: entendement plus que humain, vertus merveilleuse, couraige invincible, sobresse non pareille, contentement certain, asseurance parfaicte, deprisement incroyable de tout ce pourquoy les humains tant veiglent, courent, travaillent, navigent et bataillent (i, 5–6).

This description of Socrates' appearance varies in one interesting detail from the tradition: his nose is pointed, rather than snub. This divergence may contain a hint, for Rabelais assigned several connotations to the various shapes of noses. The sharp or pointed nose in particular indicates the spirit of mockery of the new generation, and derives from Martial's ' et puerum nasum rhinocerotis'. In a letter to Tiraqueau, denouncing the presumption of false philosophers, Rabelais portrays them as the butt of children, 'qui nunc passim nasum rhinocerotis habent' (ii, 482). Then, in his first portrayal of Panurge, Rabelais lends him 'le nez un peu aquillin, faict à manche de rasouer' and in the same sentence declares him (equivocally it is true) 'fin à dorer comme une dague de plomb' (i, 300). Socrates' 'nez pointu' thus appears as a first hint of the torrent of praise that follows, and reminds us of the definition of Pantagruelism, the 'mepris des choses fortuictes' that clearly relates the 'dissimulation du divin sçavoir' to the concept of nonchalance.

From this point on the reader will encounter multiple variations on the paradox of appearance and reality. With the introduction of the second image, that of the 'substantific marrow', Rabelais introduces the idea of the attentiveness he demands of his reader, which he immediately links with drinking and eating. He first portrays a drinker of wine, not in the act of imbibing, but of opening a bottle in order to provoke a visual memory: 'Reduisez à memoire la contenance qu'aviez.' Similarly, the marrow-bone first arouses in the hungry dog an absorbed attentiveness, before he carefully cracks it and sucks out the contents:

Si veu l'avez, vous avez peu noter de quelle devotion il le guette, de quel soing il le guarde, de quelle ferveur il le tient, de quelle prudence il l'entomme, de quelle affection il le brise, et de quelle diligence il le sugce. Qui le induict à ce faire? Quel est l'espoir de son estude? Quel bien pretend il? Rien plus qu'un peu de mouelle. Vray est que ce peu plus est delicieux que le beaucoup de toutes aultres, pour ce que la mouelle est aliment elabouré à perfection de nature, comme dict *Galen., iij Facu. natural.*, et *xj De usu parti* (I, 7).

In thus presenting the hidden marrow of the work as both pleasing and instructive, Rabelais at the same time places the full burden of comprehension on the reader. In the next breath he surprises us by denying any purpose. The famous palinode which refuses to admit that any recondite meanings in his work are intended, appears linked to the nonchalant writer's refusal of responsibility; if neither Horace nor Ovid thought of all the meanings allegorists have found in their works, then, Rabelais tells us, his reader need not think he intended any hidden sense either. But this is not to say, as some critics contend, that he is urging us to look no farther. His claim to complete nonchalance introduces the idea of consubstantiality, for he makes the writing of the work simultaneous with nourishment of the body: 'A la composition de ce livre seigneurial, je ne perdiz ne emploiay oncques plus, ny aultre temps que celluy qui estoit estably à prendre ma refection corporelle, sçavoir est beuvant et mangeant' (I, 9). Yet at mealtimes, he adds, one produces 'haulte matieres et sciences profundes'. As examples of writers who followed this method he instances once again Homer, and then Horace.

It is through the latter that he introduces the contrast between oil and wine, for of Horace an ignoramus had said, 'ses carmes sentoyent plus le vin que l'huyle'. Once again the author identifies himself with the great of antiquity: 'Autant en dict un turlupin de mes livres...' This keeps prominently in the foreground the question of preparation, for the oil of the lamp signifies the pains that the nonchalant writer rejects. The example of Demosthenes illustrates the point. Accused of depending 'plus en huyle que en vin', according to Plutarch, Demosthenes replied sharply that there was a great difference between what he and his detractor did by lamplight. Rabelais liberally interprets Demosthenes' retort to mean that he was proud of his labors and characteristically reverses the image to declare his preference for wine over oil: 'prendray autant à gloire qu'on die de moy que plus en vin aye despendu que en huyle que fist Demosthenes, quand de luy on disoit que plus en huyle que en vin despendoit' (I, 9).

The theme of wine as the source of inspiration and creativity recurs in the prologue to Book III, when the author pauses in a moment of mock indecision and begs the reader to await 'Que je hume quelque traict de ceste bouteille: c'est mon vray et seul Helicon, c'est ma fontaine caballine, c'est mon unicque enthusiasme' (I, 398). Wine has thus become the Rabelaisian equivalent of the Grecian spring of inspiration. A quarter of ancient writers bolster the idea of the fusion of literary creation with the taking of nourishment, a fusion strikingly emphasized by a technique of repetition in which verbs and participles balance each other in a single phrase: 'Ennius beuvant escrivoit, escrivant beuvoit. Æschylus…beuvoit composant, beuvant composoit' (I, 399).

But this prologue is particularly significant for the role it assigns to another Greek philosopher, Diogenes the Cynic. In Prologue I Socrates had symbolized the wisdom that hides beneath a ludicrous exterior; now there appears a philosopher whose wisdom expresses itself in a manner involving concealment of another sort, the preference for enigmatic gesture over words. If Diogenes indulges in speech at all, he is laconic in the extreme. And since Rabelais presents him in a favorable light, his rejection of speech appears as one more aspect of the nonchalant writer's playing down of eloquence or rhetorically inspired writing. As is frequently the case, a particular theme in the prologue leads us to the work itself. In Book IV we see Diogenes standing with a crowd watching archers shooting at a target. One marksman in particular aims so wildly that whenever he draws his bow the onlookers scatter in alarm. Finally, the impassive Diogenes simply walks forward and stands directly in front of the target. In introducing this eloquent mute in Prologue III, Rabelais appeals to both the visual and auditory senses. He asks us at once not if we have *read* about Diogenes, but if we have *seen* him: 'veistez vous oncques Diogenes, le philosophe cynic? Si l'avez veu, vous n'aviez perdu la veue, ou je suis vrayement forissu d'intelligence et de sens logical' (I, 393). He goes on to praise the gift of sight through reference to the man born blind for whom the greatest boon was vision. A moment later he hopes at least that we have *heard* of the great cynic ('pour le moins avez vous ouy de luy parler') and there follows a somewhat baffling paragraph on the virtues of ears as the vehicles of hearing, in which he makes subtle fun of his readers. French poets had tried to prove their descent from Priam through an imaginary hero, Francus, and therefore that they sprang 'du sang de Phrygie extraictz'; the next moment, however, he links them to the stupid King Midas, also of Phrygia, whom Apollo punished by giving him asses' ears. This learned badinage gives way to the central anecdote, which pursues the theme of the superiority of eyes and ears and introduces the value of gesture, portraying Diogenes at the siege of Corinth as observer (the watcher of gesture), and actor (the performer of gesture). The citizens busily occupy themselves building fortifications, preparing their weapons and watching out for the enemy: 'Les uns polissoient corseletz, vernissoient alecretz, nettoioient bardes, chanfrains, aubergeons...Les autres apprestoient arcs, fondes, arbalestes, glands, catapultes...Esguisoient vouges, picques, rancons, halebards...' (I, 395). The variety of their actions, their 'busyness' appears stylistically in the devices of enumeration, and the multiplicity of types of weapons. After watching this frantic activity for some time 'sans mot dire' Diogenes begins to push his famous barrel up the hill called Cranium, and promptly rolls it down again so that, Rabelais tells us, he should not remain idle in the midst of the busy populace, and all at a breakneck pace through torrential rhyming verbs that carry the reader along at vertiginous speed: 'hersoit, versoit, renversoit, nattoit, grattoit, flattoit, barattoit...' (I, 396).

This apparently aimless act may well satirize the futility and automatism of war; more important to our purposes here, it offers a clear analogue to Rabelais' statements upon his goal or lack of one in the earlier prologues. For he makes certain that the reader knows he identifies himself with the cynic by a phrase prominently placed at the beginning of the paragraph following the story of Diogenes' actions, 'Je pareillement'. His book becomes the barrel in which the philosopher lived, and by a natural transference a wine-cask from which he will draw copious drafts 'du creu de nos passetemps epicenaires', thus reiterating his theme of the fusion of literary creation and nourishment.

In Prologue I we noticed Rabelais' ambivalence as far as his demands upon the reader were concerned. Now in one breath he urges his audience to drink deep, but in the next to refuse the wine, if they prefer. This apparent laxness best suits the particular type of reader he claims to prefer, the carefree bibber and *jouisseur*, as opposed to severe critics 'cerveaux à bourlet, grabeleurs de corrections'. Of his 'tonneau Diogenic' he exclaims, 'je ne l'ay persé que pour vous, Gens de bien, Beuveurs de la prime cuvée, et Goutteux de franc alleu'. In Prologue I, addressing in similar terms 'Beuveurs tres illustres' and 'Verolez tres precieux', he emphasizes: 'à vous, non à aultres, sont dediez mes escriptz'. Thus once again Rabelais attunes his ideal reader to the nonchalance of the work, while maintaining, as in the prologue to *Gargantua*, the promise of hidden treasure, for though the barrel may seem dry, 'Bon espoir y gist au fond, comme en la bouteille de Pandora'.

Such a promise suggests the reader's responsibility to find the reward on his own. Prologue II (actually the first and the least complex of all) had revealed somewhat more insistently the author's demands on his public. His readers must neglect all activities save the reading of the work: 'que chacun laissast sa propre besoigne, ne se souciast de son mestier et mist ses affaires propres en oubly, pour y vacquer entierement sans que son esperit feust de ailleurs distraict ny empesché'. Rabelais even urges his readers to commit the work to memory in case printing should cease or all books perish. At this point we glimpse, though briefly, the familiar theme of hidden meaning: the book must be preserved orally, like the Cabbala, 'car il y a plus de fruict que par adventure ne pense un tas de gros talvassiers tous croustelevez'. Such remarks constitute an oblique praise, since Rabelais has been heaping encomiums not upon his own work but upon the anonymous *Grandes Croniques* that he is imitating. We discern a hint of the palinode in Prologue I, the refusal of moral or didactic quality in the author's declaration that the chief virtue of his work lies in its therapeutic function: it disperses melancholy, relieves toothache, and if it fails to cure venereal disease it at least assuages the discomfort of the malady. By this praise of the *Croniques* he can announce that the *Pantagruel*, as their successor, will prove 'plus equitable et digne de foy'. Yet the exaggerated claims he now proceeds to make seem calculated to produce more disbelief than belief. Later, in Prologue III, he will cover with anathema critics and priests; here he threatens with horrendous maladies those who 'refuse to believe' the new book's contents. If one can see in this bombastic plugging a fundamental irony, since he loudly declares the value of the work to be remedial rather than instructive, then this prologue follows the negligent esthetic that denies responsibility for the book's contents.

The theme of curative powers at the expense of instructive content recurs in Prologue IV as Rabelais, after saluting in his now familiar manner the 'Gens de bien' who read him, expresses delight in their healthy looks, confiding that he also enjoys good health thanks to his practice of Pantagruelism, here defined for the first time as 'gayeté d'esprit conficte en mespris des choses fortuites'. In this prologue, and in two related works, the dedicatory epistle to Odet de Châtillon and the prologue to the partial edition of 1548, Rabelais combines and fuses the concept of the curative work, the gaiety and joy essential to the nonchalant writer, and the identification of the writer and his book.

He has already instanced Galen and Esculapius as doctors who could not practice without being themselves in good health; this identity between the state of the practitioner and the one he would confer on his patient appears related to the writer's condition and the effect his work produces. These two opuscules go even farther into the question, stressing that in his relationship with the patient the doctor, following Hippocrates, should always display 'la face joyeuse et seraine' (II, 5). Stressing the familiar theme of the curative book, the beginning of the letter to Odet once again sees the work as the writer's pastime:

j'ay esté et suis journellement stipulé, requis et importuné pour la continuation des mythologies Pantagruelicques: alleguans que plusieurs gens languoureux, malades, ou autrement faschez et desolez, avoient, à la lecture d'icelles trompé leurs ennuictz, temps joyeusement passé, et repceu alaigresse et consolation nouvelles. Es quelz je suis coustumier de respondre que, icelles par esbat composant, ne pretendois gloire ne louange aulcune; seulement avois esguard et intention par escript donner ce peu de soulaigement que povois es affligez et malades absens, lequel voluntiers, quand besoing est, je fays es presens qui soy aident de mon art et service (II, 3).

'Temps joyeusement passé', the effect on the reader, results from the method, 'par esbat composant', and this modest concept of the writer's endeavor as no more than relaxation leads us to the central concern of Prologue IV, the praise of *mediocritas*. Two brief biblical allusions illustrate the virtues of this moderation, first the humble wish of the publican Zacchaeus, who climbed up into a sycamore tree in order to see Jesus on his way into Jericho, and the story of the prophet Elisha, who by throwing a stick upon the water made a woodcutter's axe rise to the surface. Rabelais alters the biblical

11

story to make the miracle more wondrous, so that 'le fer se leva du profond de l'eaue, et se adapta au manche' (II, 15).[1] This adaptation, with its echo of Excalibur, permits the author a burlesque transition, an element of orderly rhetoric mockingly employed in the phrase, 'à propos de souhaits mediocres en matiere de coignée...'

Underlying and counterpointing the central story of 'Mercury and the Woodcutter', to which this transition leads, is the sexual symbolism of axe and handle, illustrated later on in the landing at the island of Alliances, when an inhabitant salutes his wife, 'Bon di, ma coignée', and she answers, 'Et à vous, mon manche'. The story of the woodcutter who loses his axe and to whom Mercury offers a choice of three, one of gold, one of silver and one of wood, and who modestly selects his own wooden one and receives as a reward the gift of the two others, is counterpointed by a dialogue between Jupiter and Priapus in the course of which the god of virility entertains the assembled gods by elaborating upon the axe and handle symbolism. In concluding, Rabelais returns to the idea of health as exemplifying this type of modest wish, and thus within the reach of his readers: 'C'est, goutteux, sus quoy je fonde mon esperance, et croy fermement que, s'il plaist au bon Dieu, vous obtiendrez santé, veu que rien plus que santé pour le present ne demandez.'

As we have already noted in one or two instances, the various manifestations in the prologues of Rabelaisian nonchalance: the ambivalence concerning the work's significance, suggested through the contrasts between appearance and reality; the transference of its effect from the intellectual to the physical; the praise of gesture at the expense of speech; the concept of the book as pastime, reach out into the work itself. For one thing, Rabelais refuses to confine the meeting-place of author and reader to the prologues. His presence in the book as he interpellates the reader, or plays the character Alcofribas, presents another aspect of consubstantiality. One type of intervention finds Rabelais engaging the reader in dialogue, which often takes the truculent tone of the author who refuses responsibility for what he writes. In the curious chapter on young Gargantua's colors, he expostulates with the reader-as-critic, blasting his imagined ideas on color symbolism:

[1] In the Bible story (II Kings 6. 5–7) as a man 'was felling a beam, the axe head fell into the water: and he cried, and said, Alas, master! for it was borrowed. And the man of God said where fell it? And he shewed him the place. And he cut down a stick and cast it in thither; and the iron did swim. Therefore said he, Take it up to thee. And he put out his hand, and took it.'

J'entends bien que, lisans ces motz, vous mocquez du vieil beuveur et
reputez l'exposition des couleurs par trop indague et abhorrente, et dictes
que blanc signifie foy et bleu fermeté. Mais, sans vous mouvoir, courroucer,
eschaufer ny alterer (car le temps est dangereux), respondez moy, si bon
vous semble. D'aultre contraincte ne useray avec vous, ny aultres, quelz
qu'ilz soient; seulement vous diray un mot de la bouteille.

Qui vous meut? qui vous poinct? Qui vous dict que blanc signifie foy
et bleu fermeté? (I, 40).

A similar type of direct intervention involves deprecating the audience's knowledge, in order to stress the exceptional quality of a
given episode. Before Pantagruel harpoons the mighty whale, Rabelais seems to hear us measuring his hero's exploit against numerous
feats by champions of antiquity: 'Vous dictes, et est escript, que le
truant Commodus...tant dextrement tiroit de l'arc que de bien loing
il passoit les fleches entre les doigts des jeunes enfans levans la main
en l'air, sans aulcunement les ferir.' A number of paragraphs, introduced in the same manner, follow: 'vous nous racontez...'; 'Vous
nous dictez aussi merveilles...'; 'Vous faictez pareillement narré des
Parthes...'; 'Aussi celebrez vous les Scythes...' Finally the conclusion is brought home: 'Le noble Pantagruel en l'art de jecter et
darder estoit sans comparaison plus admirable' (II, 140–1). He can on
occasion drop this defensive tone for one of complicity as he asks the
reader why Picrochole's soldiers never caught the disease when they
were sacking the houses of sufferers from the plague: 'Dont vient
cela, Messieurs? Pensez-y, je vous prie' (I, 106). The chapter on the
Andouilles begins with a confidential remark in which the imperious
summons to believe of Prologue II is attenuated by the alternative of
'see for yourself'. 'Vous truphez ici, beuveurs, et ne croyez que ainsi
doit en verité comme je vous raconte. Je ne sçaurois que vous en faire.
Croyez le, si voulez; si ne voulez, allez y veoir' (II, 152).

Such an attitude is much closer to 'le mespris des choses fortuites'.
The scorn of fortune, on the other hand, gives way to an emphasis
on the role of chance, the unexpected, the spontaneous, that characterizes the negligent writer. Gargantua's education, we recall, is a
'joyeux passetemps', and his games improvised: 'tout leur jeu
n'étaient qu'en liberté' (I, 89). Chance provides the subject of a
number of chapters, notably those that treat Homeric and Virgilian
chance, the results of a fling of the dice, or prediction by dreams. One
of the third book's most lively characters, Bridoye, judges his cases by
throwing the dice, but even more striking than this reliance on

chance, he describes the increase of documents concerning lawsuits due to the delays of justice in terms of animal growth. The sacks containing legal documents recall a bear cub, 'informe et imparfaict. Comme un ours naissant n'a pieds, ne mains, peau, poil, ne teste: ce n'est qu'une piece de chair, rude et informe; l'ourse, à force de leicher, la mect en perfection des membres' (I, 577). This Boschian invention once again relates the world of letters to the world of spontaneous generation. Similarly, the instantaneous creation of Rabelais' style – what Leo Spitzer has so happily called *Augenblicksbildung* – creates the impression of spontaneous growth, not only in such well-known phrases as the description of Frere Jean as a 'vray moyne si oncques en feut depuis que le monde moynant moyna de moynerie', but also in the remarkable erotic line from the story of the lion, the fox and the hag, 'Un bon esmoucheteur, qui en esmouchetant continuellement, esmouche de son mouchet, par mouches jamais esmouché ne sera' (I, 298).

Charles Sorel, writing almost a hundred years after Rabelais but imbued with his spirit, said of the preface that it was there 'plutôt que dans tout le reste du livre que l'auteur montre de quel esprit il est pourvu'. Certainly Rabelais' spirit, that of the serious fool, but also that of the writer conscious of his art, stands out graphically in the four prologues, one aspect of whose unity is the esthetics of negligence. But contrary to Sorel's suggestion, the four books maintain in many respects the tone of the prologues, since a clear-cut separation between prologue and tale would run counter to the notion of consubstantiality which perhaps of all our three characteristics is the most central in Rabelais.

Montaigne and some lines from Virgil

The third category of the esthetics of negligence[1] I have borrowed from Montaigne, who declared that his book was 'consubstantial' with its author. The *Avis au lecteur*, published in 1580 with the first two books of the *Essais*, proclaimed but one goal, to recall the author to his parents and friends after his death. Nor had he, in his writings, sought either beauty or elegance; at all costs he had avoided 'une marche estudiée'. He wished above all to be seen 'en sa façon *naturelle*, et ordinaire, *sans artifices*'. The foreword ends with the famous sentence, 'je suis moy-mesme la matiere de mon livre'.

[1] See above, pp. 1–2.

Elsewhere he declared that if his work had reached the public this was purely by chance, since he had had it printed only to avoid having to make a number of hand-written copies. Eight years later, after the success of all three volumes, he added the hope that these volumes might prevent a wedge of butter from melting in the market-place (II, xviii, 647).[1] But if his book belonged to no one, it at least belonged to him, it *was* he: 'Je n'ay pas plus faict mon livre que mon livre m'a faict, livre consubstantiel à son autheur, d'une occupation propre, membre de ma vie; non d'une occupation et fin tierce et estrangere comme tous aultres livres.'

Montaigne's foreword and the later remark smack of a certain coquettishness, for rather frequently he speaks contentedly of the fact that he is widely read (especially by women) and he seems extremely conscious of a 'public'.[2] Yet the lines quoted serve to highlight a fundamental paradox of his work: the *Essais* aim to be the exact replica of their author, yet as the product of one of the most omnivorous of readers they are extremely *literary*. In this respect it may be revealing that in the Bordeaux copy the phrase 'je me fusse mieux paré' replaced 'je me fusse paré de beautés empruntées'.[3] As Pierre Villey has shown conclusively, the earlier essays in particular were made up largely of borrowings, beautiful or not. One aspect of Montaigne's development would therefore consist of his progressive liberation from books, at least as sources, or rather his increasing capacity to transform his reading into a lived experience, so that in the end he could say, 'Les livres m'ont servi non tant d'instruction que d'exercitation' (III, xii, 1016).

With this growing consubstantiality there mingles from the beginning the idea of a spontaneity which involves first of all the rejection of books in favor of experience as a guide. In the famous essay on the education of children we find the phrase which inspired Descartes, 'ce grand monde…je veux que ce soit le livre de mon escholier' (I, xxvi, 157). Here also he praises conversation, that most spontaneous of teachers that prevents our having 'la veüe racourcie à la longueur de nostre nez' (156). If the ideal student's teacher prescribes certain books, he ought also to summarize them for his charge and draw forth their essence, as Montaigne declares in a sentence

---

1 References in the text are to Montaigne, *Œuvres complètes*, ed. A. Thibaudet and M. Rat (Paris: Bibliothèque de la Pléiade, 1962). Where more than one quotation is taken from the same page, the reference will be given only after the first quotation.

2 Cf. Hugo Friedrich, *Montaigne* (Paris: Gallimard, 1968), pp. 345–8.

3 *Œuvres complètes*, ed. Thibaudet and Rat, p. 1431.

that recalls Rabelais' 'sustantificque moëlle', and which is linked to the idea of consubstantiality: '[le précepteur] luy en donnera la moelle et la substance toute maschée' (159).

The nonchalant author does not of course reject books – were they not of his 'trois commerces' the favorite? – but he questions their authority and in particular those who would make tyrants of them, the pedants. No one save Rabelais has mocked with greater verve at 'les sçavanteaux', who 'cognoissent bien Galien, mais nullement le malade', who 'vous ont desja rempli la teste de loix, et si n'ont encore conçeu le noeud de la cause. Ils sçavent la theorique de toutes choses, cherchez qui la mette en pratique, (I, xxv, 138). To demonstrate the weakness of bookish learning, he draws an example from his own experience which nevertheless reminds us of Pantagruel and the lawyers who plead their cause in meaningless jargon until the former delivers his judgment in exactly the same language, to the admiration of all concerned:

J'ai veu chez moy un mien amy, par maniere de passetemps, ayant affaire à un de ceux cy, contrefaire un jargon de galimathias, propos sans suite, tissu de pièces rapportées, sauf qu'il estoit souvent entrelardé de mots propres à leur dispute, amuser ainsi tout un jour ce sot à debatre, pensant tousjours responde aux objections qu'on luy faisoit; et si estoit homme de lettres et de reputation, et qui avoit une belle robe.[1]

Montaigne's humor at the expense of pedants corresponds to his emphasis on joy and pleasure in the pursuit of learning. 'La plus expresse marque de la sagesse, c'est une esjouissance constant' (I, xxvi, 160). As for philosophy, customarily portrayed as long-faced and ascetic, 'il n'est rien plus gay, plus gaillard, plus enjoué, et à peu que je ne dise follastre'. From classrooms he demands: 'Ostez-moi la violence et la force!' (165), in them there should reign 'la joye, l'allegresse et Flora et les Graces!' Thus, like Erasmus, to praise folly, to refuse all constraints, to make of learning a joyous game, is evidently to declare a certain independence with regard to established rules of literary composition. For joy and folly evidently ill suit serious application or the lengthy and laborious preparation of a literary work. Montaigne's love for conversation and the impromptu exchange of ideas appears as the antithesis of the science that emphasizes precept and preparation, that is, rhetoric. In another paradox Montaigne

---

[1] Cf. Rabelais, *Œuvres complètes*, ed. P. Jourda, I, Chapters xi–xiii. Pantagruel's accomplishment is not effortless: 'il gehaignoyt comme un asne'.

makes use of his readings in rhetorical literature to discount the value
of rhetorical training.

Rhetoric is the primary source of modern literary criticism, and
its precepts, first applied to oratory, later came to regulate the art of
writing. Following this lead, Montaigne very frequently identifies
speaking and writing in emphasizing an aspect of literature which
underlies the esthetic of negligence; the role of chance, of the impromptu. Many of his examples come from the rhetoricians themselves,
such as the story of the orator whose opponents feared to make him
angry because it increased his eloquence, since 'il disoit mieux sans
y avoir pensé' (I, x 41). He tells us that this is his own case, and contrasts the happy effect of unforeseen stimuli with works too carefully
prepared in terms that recall both Castiglione and Rabelais:

> Nous disons d'aucuns ouvrages qu'ils puent l'huyle et la lampe, pour
> certaine aspreté et rudesse que le travail imprime en ceux où il a grande
> part. Mais, outre cela, la solicitude de bien faire, et cette contention de
> l'ame trop bandée et trop tendue à son entreprise, la met au rouet, la
> rompt et l'empesche, ainsi qu'il advient à l'eau qui par force de se presser
> de sa violence et abondance, ne peut trouver issuë en un goulet ouvert.

In order to achieve the necessary spontaneity, one should never com-
pose without the stimulus of some external circumstance. The
creative mood, writes Montaigne, 'veut estre non pas secouée, mais
solicitée; elle veut estre eschauffée et reveillée par les occasions
estrangeres, presentes et fortuites. Si elle va toute seule, elle ne fait
que trainer et languir. L'agitation est sa vie et sa grace.'

This type of 'agitation' characterizes conversation, which affords
Montaigne an impromptu stimulus: 'L'occasion, la compaignie, le
branle même de ma voix tire plus de mon esprit que je n'y trouve
lors que je le sonde et employe à par moy.' Conversation, or perhaps
more precisely, since Montaigne's term, *conférer* has various shades
of meaning, oral discussion and argument, provides the subject of an
entire essay 'De l'art de conférer', in which he stresses his need for
an intelligence in direct opposition to his own; as he writes in a key
sentence, he is among those who learn 'plus par contrarieté que par
exemple' (III, viii, 899). Books, rhetoric, provide only dead examples,
but debate challenges accepted ideas: his own, and those of others.
In this essay he declares, in apparent contradiction to his dislike for
strict organization in written works, that discussion should follow a
certain order. But this means merely careful adherence to the theme,

and permits digression: 'On ne faict point tort au sujet quand on le quicte pour voir du moyen de le traiter' (904). Furthermore the order in a discussion is conceived in opposition to the order of Rhetoric, which preaches that form serves subject; 'conférer' adopts a form, that of conversation or argument, that outshadows subject-matter. In defense of this particular type of order, he has once again recourse to the theme of 'naturalness', for he tells us even shepherds and shop-boys know how to follow the thread of their argument: 'moyen naturel, d'un sain entendement'. Typical of the vivacious kind of verbal give-and-take Montaigne had in mind, the 'natural' and the 'fortuitous' equally characterize the writing of his essays: 'je ne me trouve pas où je me cherche; et me trouve plus par rencontre que par l'inquisition de mon jugement' (I, x, 41). The role of *hasard* leads Montaigne to consider in turn the task of reader or critic, which is of necessity particularly exacting when the writer disclaims responsibility for what he has written. In his own case he has often forgotten what he intended to say when later he attempts to correct or revise his text: 'J'aurai eslancé quelque subtilité en escrivant...je l'ay si bien perdue que je ne sçay ce que j'ay voulu dire; et l'a l'estranger descouverte par fois avant moy.' That a 'stranger' should discover his meaning more readily than himself leads easily to an attitude of exigence toward the reader, of whom he now demands that peculiar combination of diligence and comprehension he calls 'suffisance'. Such perspicacity is necessary precisely because of the role of chance in all the creative arts:

Or je dy que, non en la medecine seulement, mais en plusieurs arts plus certaines, la fortune y a bonne part. Les saillies poëtiques, qui emportent leur autheur et le ravissent hors de soy, pourquoy ne les attribuerons nous à son bonheur? puisqu'il confesse luy mesme qu'elles surpassent sa suffisance et ses forces, et les reconnoit venir d'ailleurs que de soy, et ne les avoir aucunement en sa puissance; non plus que les orateurs ne disent avoir en la leur ces mouvemens et agitations extraordinaires, qui les poussent au delà de leur dessein. Il en est de mesmes en la peinture, qu'il eschappe par fois des traits de la main du peintre, surpassans sa conception et sa science, qui le tirent luy mesmes en admiration et qui l'estonnent. Mais la fortune montre bien encores plus evidemment la part qu'elle a en tous ces ouvrages, par les graces et beautez qui s'y treuvent, non seulement sans l'intention, mais sans la cognoissance mesme de l'ouvrier. Un suffisant lecteur descouvre souvent ès escrits d'autruy des perfections autres que celles que l'autheur y a mises et apperceües, et y preste des sens et des visages plus riches (I, xxiv, 126).

18

It is to this 'sufficient' reader that the *Essais* are addressed, to the reader who, very much like that of Rabelais, must seek for the substantific marrow whether or not the author intended to put it there. Montaigne makes it clear that he is discussing the matter of his book, and discourages analysis of his language; as to the critic of his style, 'J'aymerois mieux qu'il s'en teust' (I, xl, 245). His anecdotes, his stories contain more than their obvious meanings: 'Et combien y ay-je espandu d'histoires qui ne disent mot, lesquelles qui voudra esplucher un peu ingenieusement, en produira infinis essais.' Thus, his 'histoires' and the quotations and allusions that accompany them may reward ingenious concentration by revealing more than they seem to say: 'Elles portent souvent, hors de mon propos, la sentence d'une matiere plus riche et plus hardie, et sonnent à gauche un ton plus delicat, et pour moy qui n'en veux exprimer d'avantage, et pour ceux qui se rencontreront mon air.' In this sentence, the phrase 'hors de mon propos' sums up both the author's rejection of responsibility for what he writes and his appeal to the reader's unwavering diligence.

The majority of these quotations come from the essay 'Consideration sur Ciceron', in which, as is so often the case, we hear little about the subject indicated in the title. For Montaigne Cicero exemplified the too-careful writer, the proponent of order, the arbiter of form, and the following sentence typifies his attitude toward the eloquence that the Roman orator exemplified: 'Fy de l'eloquence qui nous laisse envie de soy, non des choses' (246). In 'Des livres' he admits that Cicero's 'façon d'escrire me semble ennuyeuse' (II, x, 393) and condemns his sense of order: 'ces ordonnances logiciennes et Aristoteliques ne sont pas à propos'. If Cicero, or rather the traditional Cicero, begins a sentence by a general proposition, followed by a conclusion, Montaigne firmly declares, 'je veux qu'on commence par le dernier point'. If the Roman finds the exordium the most difficult part to write in a philosophical treatise, our author will work hardest on the conclusion (II, xvii, 621).

It is unnecessary to link Montaigne's attitude to the anti-ciceronianism of his day;[1] in jousting with the conventional Cicero and conveniently forgetting the relaxed and even negligent author of the *Letters to Atticus*, he found a way of emphasizing the character of his own style, 'trop serré, desordonné, couppé, particulier' (I, xl, 246)

[1] Cf. Morris W. Croll, 'Juste-Lipse et le mouvement anti-cicéronien à la fin du XVIe et au début du XVIIe siècle', *RSS*, II (1914), 200–42.

in which he sought absolute identity between spoken and written language, 'simple et naïf, tel sur le papier qu'à la bouche; un parler succulent et nerveux, court et serré, non tant delicat et peigné comme vehement et brusque' (I, xxvi, 171).

Two adjectives in the preceding quotation, speaking of style in terms of taste (*succulent*) and human appearance (*peigné*) remind us of the 'consubstantiality' that I have made one of the characteristics of negligent or nonchalant writing. So far we have discussed in Montaigne certain aspects of nonchalance in literature: the preference for experience over learning, the appeal to the reader's diligence, the wilful confusion of spoken and written language. I shall turn now to some instances of his specific use of the term itself. It is immediately apparent that Montaigne approves of nonchalance in almost all human actions. Of fame and glorious deeds, his sentiments coincide with those Castiglione applies to art: 'Ces actions là ont bien plus de grace qui eschapent de la main de l'auteur nonchalamment et sans bruict' (III, x, 1001). We encounter the word *nonchalant* even in connection with habits of dress which he immediately relates to spoken, and by extension, written style:

J'ay volontiers imité cette desbauche qui se voit en nostre jeunesse, au port de leurs vestemens: an manteau en escharpe, la cape sur une espaule, un bas mal tendu, qui represente une fierté desdaigneuse de ces paremens estrangiers et nonchallante de l'art. Mais je la trouve encore mieus employée en la forme du parler. Toute affectation, nomméement en la gayeté et liberté françoise, est mesadvenante au cortisan (I, xxvi, 171).

Following this echo of Castiglione, Montaigne once again emphasizes the parallel between style and clothing: 'Comme aux acoustremens, c'est pusillanimité de se vouloir marquer par quelque façon particuliere et inusitée; de mesmes, au langage, la recherche des frases nouvelles et de mots peu cogneuz vient d'une ambition puerile et pedantesque. Peussé-je ne me servir que de ceux qui servent aux halles à Paris!' To illustrate his lethargy when things go ill, he again uses vestimentary imagery: 'si j'ay un escarpin de travers, je laisse encore de travers ma chemise et ma cappe' (III, ix, 924).

As the book is nonchalant, so is its author; his nonchalance is actually a character trait: 'Je presteroy aussi volontiers mon sang que mon soing' (II, xvii, 626).[1] In his household affairs he prefers that

---

[1] Increasing the effect of this phrase is the rime between *sang* and *soing* if pronounced with Montaigne's accent.

his servants hide his financial losses from him: 'Au chapitre de mes mises, je loge ce que ma nonchalance me couste à nourrir et entretenir' (627). Of business affairs he sighs, '[je] ne cherche qu'à m'anonchalir et avachir' (III, ix, 931). Although brought up in the country, he confesses ignorance of the names of tools, fruits, wines, different cuts of meat, in short everything concerning agriculture, 'soit par faiblesse ou nonchalance' (II, xvii, 636).

One should not be deceived by this seeming identification of nonchalance with weakness, for to Montaigne to espouse nonchalance is to remain faithful to his own idea of his nature: 'Cette publique déclaration m'oblige de me tenir en ma route, et à ne desmentir l'image de mes conditions' (III, ix, 958). Nonchalance may paradoxically be a kind of method in itself, motivated in part by his social status, and involving a constant struggle with the memory of his reading and the attempt to appear independent of it:

Quand je me suis commis et assigné entierement à ma memoire, je prends si fort sur elle que je l'accable: elle s'effraye de sa charge. Autant que je m'en rapporte à elle, je me mets hors de moy, jusques à essaier ma contenance; et me suis veu quelque jour en peine de celer la servitude en laquelle j'estois entravé, là où mon dessein est de representer en parlant une profonde nonchalance et des mouvemens fortuites et impremeditez, comme naissans des occasions presentes: aymant aussi cher ne rien dire qui vaille que de monstrer estre venu preparé pour bien dire, chose messeante, surtout à gens de ma profession (940).

His actual disorder, in the esthetics of nonchalance, takes on a kind of unity: 'Je m'esgare, mais plustost par licence que par mesgarde. Mes fantasies me suyvent, mais par fois c'est de loing, et se regardent, mais d'une veuë oblique' (973). Plato, in his *Phaedrus*, 'mi party d'une fantastique bigarrure, le devant de l'amour, tout le bas à la rhetorique', far from fearing 'muances' or apparent disorder in subject-matter or organization, acquires grace through his seeming nonchalance, 'une marveilleuse grace à se laisser ainsi rouler au vent, ouà le sembler'.

Such nonchalance among the ancients serves to justify in the *Essais* the frequent discrepancy between title and content, and Montaigne cites in support of his practice such plays by Terence as the *Andria*, the *Lives* of his master Plutarch, and in particular one of his *Moralia*, the 'Daemon of Socrates' in which the author 'oublie son theme, ou le propos de son argument ne se trouve que par incident, tout estouffé en matiere estrangere'. It is in this connexion that we encounter perhaps his strongest praise of nonchalance: 'O Dieu, que ces gaillardes escapades, que cette variation a de beauté, et plus lors que plus elle retire au nonchalant et fortuite!' Finally in a pointed declaration of the reader's responsibility, he accuses those who fail to follow the thread of his argument of being 'indiligent', asserts in the same breath the unity of style and thought and once again, like Rabelais and his mentor Erasmus, praises folly: 'Mon style et mon esprit vont vagabondant de mesmes. Il faut avoir un peu de folie, qui ne veut avoir plus de sottise, disent et les preceptes de nos maistres et encore plus leurs exemples.'

In these remarkable paragraphs from 'De la vanité' Montaigne associates all three characteristics of the nonchalant esthetic. I turn now to an essay which I consider one of the best illustrations of the 'merveilleuse grace' Montaigne found in his 'nonchalant' models, 'Sur des vers de Virgile'. Of our three characteristics this essay perhaps best exemplifies that of consubstantiality, because of its subject: love as the central motif of the aging writer's life; past, present and dimly seen future. Though this is probably the most erotic of the essays – it is here that he declares sexual love to be 'le centre de tout' – one could probably demonstrate that Montaigne's entire work is essentially erotic. And insofar as the erotic presents problems of esthetic expression in the face of moral censorship it may be linked to nonchalance as one form of the writer's refusal to adhere to socially imposed artistic norms.

'Sur des vers de Virgile', as we may expect, deals not merely with some lines from the *Aeneid* but with a quotation from Lucretius; marriage and society; male, female and animal jealousy; the relativity of sexual mores: physical and spiritual sensuality; religion, and the nature of esthetic experience. The key sentence of the essay intimately links the author's present condition with the theme: 'Je me deffens de la temperance comme j'ay faict autresfois de la volupte' (III, v, 818). At the age of fifty-three, six years before his death, long a sufferer from kidney-stone, he is too old, too sick for physical excess; he has therefore no need for 'useful thoughts'. Such precepts of discipline and temperance as those his soul or conscience (the reflective element) imposed upon him were necessary as long as his body (the sensual element) was vigorous and sound. Now his enfeebled body, unable to bear excess, replaces the soul as the counsellor of prudence and discipline. The approach of old age thus reverses the former order; the soul must now look backward and, free of its disciplinary functions, replace former physical joys with the contemplation and memory of past pleasures.

This backward glance sets up a temporal conception which orients us toward the commentary on Virgil's and Lucretius' lines that forms the basis of this chapter. It is equally suited to the essay's place in the third book, for while in the first two volumes Montaigne sought to 'peindre le passage', thus fixing his glance on present and future, he now directs his attention toward the past in what amounts to a resistance to time's passage: 'Les ans m'entrainent s'ils veulent, mais à reculons' (819). He symbolizes this posture by an allusion to the two-faced Janus, guardian of the entrance to Roman homes.

From the beginning the central theme, sexual love and its repercussions in man and society, is linked to the problem of expression: 'Je me suis ordonné d'oser dire tout ce que j'ose faire' (822). His daring, which will permit him to mention the unmentionable, increases with age; as he had declared in an earlier essay, 'Je dy vrai, non pas tout mon saoul, mais autant que je l'ose dire, et l'ose un peu plus en vieillissant' (III, ii, 783). Thus age and boldness of expression are related and the author realizes fully that the result may shock his readers: 'ce chapitre me fera du cabinet' (III, v, 825). Yet once again the 'nonchalant' author justifies his work on the basis of the 'natural': 'J'ayme la modestie; et n'est pas par jugement que j'ay choisi cette sorte de parler scandaleux: c'est nature qui l'a choisi pour moy' (867).

The idea of the natural suppressed by convention inspires the same question that Diderot was to put in the mouth of his Jacques le Fataliste: Montaigne writes:

Qu'a faict l'action genitale aux hommes, si naturelle, si necessaire et si juste, pour n'en oser parler sans vergongne et pour l'exclurre des propos serieux et reglez? Nous prononcons hardiment: tuer, desrober, trahir; et cela, nous n'oserions qu'entre les dents? Est-ce à dire que moins nous en exhalons en parole, d'autant nous avons loy d'en grossir la pensée? (825)[1]

Grossir la pensée, to inflate one's thoughts, introduces the theme of imagination, by means of which an old man may relive his past pleasures. Yet if the imagination is forced into action because of censorship, the result may be undesirable distortions, like the obscene drawings on palace walls, monstrously out of proportion to all reality. Censorship may not only distort the truth but nullify its

---

[1] Diderot, *Œuvres*, ed. A. Billy (Paris: Bibliothèque de la Pléiade, 1962), p. 656.

object: 'N'en va-t-il pas comme en matiere de livres, qui se rendent d'autant plus venaux et publiques de ce qu'ils sont supprimez?' Personal experience affords an example of the futility of censorship. His daughter had been reading aloud in his presence, under the watchful supervision of her governess, when she came upon the word *fouteau*, a dialectal word for beech-tree, but one whose first syllable may suggest the obscene word *foutre*. The governess in alarm stopped her from continuing, making her skip the passage. As Montaigne sadly reflects, 'le commerce de vingt laquays n'eust sçeu imprimer en sa fantasie, de six moys, l'intelligence et usage et toutes les consequences du son de ces syllabes scelerées, comme fit cette bonne vieille par sa reprimande et interdiction' (834).

In the *Essais*, the lackey or the page may exemplify a certain rudeness or naturalness, as in this comment rejecting the refining tendency of such subtle Platonicians as Leo Hebraeus, Ficino and Equicola: 'Mon page faict l'amour et l'entend. Lisez-lui Leon Hebreu et Ficin: on parle de luy, de ses pensées et de ses actions, et si, il n'y entend rien' (852). Here a secondary, but essential theme of the essay, one that bears upon the esthetics of negligence, arises: the relationship between art and nature.[1] Montaigne who elsewhere calls himself a 'naturaliste' (III, xii, 1034) sees the need for reversing the neo-Platonistic trend: 'Si j'estois du mestier, je naturaliserois l'art autant comme ils artialisent la nature' (III, v, 852). The principal, the most glorious subject with which nature provides the artist is love, and Montaigne's ideal is a harmonious relationship in which neither 'nature' nor 'poetry' – that is the actual act of love and its expression – has the priority. If he would 'naturalize' art, it is because the balance needs to be restored in order to attain that harmony: 'Qui ostera aux Muses les imaginations amoureuses, leur desrobera le plus bel entretien qu'elles ayent et la plus noble matiere de leur ouvrage; et qui fera perdre à l'amour la communication et service de la poësie, l'affoiblira de ses meilleures armes' (826).

The problem, then, concerns imagination – 'les imaginations amoureuses' – with love as its 'matiere', and its translation into poetry. The two sturdy columns of the essay, the quotations from Virgil and Lucretius, provide examples of how poetry conveys the experience of love with the arms of imagination. It is no accident that Montaigne should choose Virgil. He considers him, as he says in

[1] On nature versus art in Montaigne's concept of humanity, see D. M. Frame, *Montaigne's Discovery of Man* (New York: Columbia University Press, 1955), pp. 96–109.

an earlier essay comparing various poetic treatments of a single theme
– the importance of Cato the Younger – as 'maistre du coeur' (I,
xxxvii, 228). Now he quotes from the eighth book of the *Aeneid*,
where Venus asks her husband Vulcan to forge armor for Aeneas:

> Dixerat et niveis hinc atque hinc diva lacertis
> cunctantem amplexu molli fovet. ille repente
> accepit solitam flammam, notusque medullas
> intravit calor et labefacta per ossa cucurrit,
> non secus atque olim, tonitru cum rupta corusco
> ignea rima micans percurrit lumine nimbos.
> ...ea verba locutus
> optatos dedit amplexus placidumque petivit
> coniugis infusus gremio per membra soporem.[1]

Having presented this quotation, Montaigne makes a significant statement concerning the relationship of art and nature, which is that
reality as depicted by poetry is more exquisite than reality itself.
'Les forces et valeurs de ce Dieu se trouvent plus vives et plus animées
en la peinture de la poësie qu'en leur propre essence' (III, v, 826).
This idea is so important to him that he repeats it twice, once with
regard to love and once with regard to the beauty of nude woman:
'Elle represente je ne sçay quel air plus amoureux que l'amour mesme.
Venus n'est pas si belle toute nue, et vive, et haletante, comme
elle est icy chez Virgile.'
It is at this stage that the particular nature of consubstantiality in
this essay becomes apparent. For its basic analogue is that between
the writer of the *Essais* and the poet of love. The first and essential
element in this analogue is freedom; the freedom to discuss the unmentionable. The curtain of censorship stimulates the imagination to
produce only the distortion of truth, a monstrous perversion. With
freedom of discussion, however, the imagination untrammeled by
restriction may induce a pleasure greater than sexuality itself, and
one which in the case of the ill and aging essayist constitutes a defense against decrepitude and death. This life-giving quality clearly

---

1 'The goddess ceased, and, as he falters, throws her snowy arms about him and fondles
him in soft embrace. At once he caught the wonted flame; the familiar warmth passed
into his marrow and ran through his melting frame: even as when at times, bursting
amid the thunder's peal, a sparkling streak of fire courses through the storm clouds
with dazzling light...Thus speaking, he gave the desired embrace, and, sinking on
the bosom of his spouse, wooed calm slumber in every limb': *Aeneid*, tr. H. R.
Fairclough (Cambridge, Mass.: Harvard University Press, 1966), VIII, 387–92, 404–6.

THE ESTHETICS OF NEGLIGENCE

corresponds to the eternity of art that Montaigne ascribes to Latin poetry.

One might argue that despite such correspondences there is a contradiction between his opposition to censorship and his dislike for the too-literal description of female nudity or sex; between his rejection of *la superstition verbale* and his belief in the necessity of the 'veil'. But this is to forget that the restrictions against speaking and writing freely of forbidden subjects must first be removed before the artist can bring his resources into play. His imagery will then be analogous to the imaginings of the aging sensualist, and on the social level, to the 'cérémonie', the ritual, the 'difficulté' that both precede and heighten the pleasures of physical love. A better example of the fusion between man and esthetic, of what he called 'consubstantiality' could scarcely be found. How does art present female nudity, a participant in an act of love more beautiful and palpitating than life itself? The poet must avoid literalness, as he suggests by his reaction to an over-explicit line of Ovid which, far from stimulating his erotic imagination, has the effect, he says picturesquely, of 'caponizing him'. He must interpose between the object or the act described some device of indirection, a veil of imagery which will have the paradoxical effect of heightening the reader's pleasure:

Les vers de ces deux poetes, traitant ainsi reservéement et discrettement de la lasciveté comme ils font, me semblent la descouvrir et esclairer de plus près. Les dames couvrent leur sein d'un reseu, les prestres plusieurs choses sacrées; les peintres ombragent leur ouvrage, pour luy donner plus de lustre; et dict-on que le coup du Soleil et du vent est plus poisant par reflexion qu'à droit fil (858).

The veil, the 'reseu' thus becomes, on the sexual, artistic, religious and natural levels, an essential factor in the effect of all these elements.

The quotation from Lucretius, like the one from Virgil, also embodies this discretion and reserve, even though this time, it presents Venus and Mars; the goddess with a lover rather than a husband. Montaigne's comment on the first quotation, that the poet 'la peint un peu bien esmeue pour une Venus maritale', artfully failed to notice that Venus' ardor was chiefly calculating, since as Montaigne certainly realized, she was asking her husband to do a favor to Aeneas, her son by a lover.[1] He actually quotes later the passage he

---

[1] It is an interesting coincidence that Ronsard mentions the same passage as one that makes the reader's hair stand on end with admiration: *Œuvres*, ed. G. Cohen (Paris: Bibliothèque de la Pléiade, 1950), II, 1019.

had omitted from the long quotation, in which Vulcan accedes to her request, as a most unusual and, he hints, unrealistic and naive example of generosity in a husband. The lengthy digression on marriage that directly follows the Virgil quotation may seem wide of the mark. But its central idea, that love has no place in marriage, while a medieval truism, is linked to the nonchalant writer's quest for the natural. Marriage is made for every reason but love: it possesses solid attributes: 'L'utilité, la justice, l'honneur et la constance', even a kind of pleasure: 'plaisir plat, mais plus universel' (831). Since 'l'amour se fonde au seul plaisir', the clear suggestion is that premarital or adulterous love is the only natural subject for erotic poetry.

Thus, when Montaigne turns to his second quotation, from the familiar invocation to Venus in Lucretius' *De rerum natura* showing Mars in the goddess' arms, he can call it a more *appropriate* example: 'ce que Virgile dict de Venus et de Vulcan, Lucrece l'avoit dict plus *sortablement* d'une jouissance desrobée d'elle et de Mars'. Once again Montaigne adapts the lines to his particular purpose, since in Lucretius they are didactic rather than descriptive, illustrating the far-reaching power of love, ruler of the universe. Not only does Montaigne present them as a 'jouissance desrobée' but he omits a significant line:

> belli fera moenera Mavors
> armipotens regit, in gremium qui saepe tuum se
> reicit aeterno devictus vulnere amoris.
> ....
> pascit amore avidos inhians in te, dea, visus,
> eque tuo pendet resupini spiritus ore.
> hunc tu, diva, tuo recubantem corpore sancto
> circumfusa super, suavis ex ore loquellas
> funde.[1]

Only now does Montaigne launch into specific literary criticism, linking the two quotations by singling out certain words in both.

---

[1] 'Mars, mighty in battle, rules the savage works of war, who often casts himself upon thy lap, vanquished by the ever-living wound of love...feeds his eager eyes with love, gaping upon thee, goddess, and as he lies back, his breath hangs upon thy lips. There, as he reclines, goddess, upon thy sacred body, do thou, bending around him from above, pour from thy lips sweet coaxings': *De rerum natura*, tr. W. H. D. Rouse (Cambridge, Mass.: Harvard University Press, 1959), I, 32–4, 36–9. The omission of line 35 (*Atque ita suspiciens tereti cervice*, 'And thus looking upward, with shapely head thrown back') has not, so far as I know, been indicated by Montaigne's editors.

His delectation, emphasized by the verb *ruminer*, seems at first to be that of the impressionist critic he once had scorned: 'Quand je rumine ce *"rejicit, pascit, inhians, molli, fovet, medullas, labefacta, pendet, percurrit"*, et cette noble *"circunfusa"*, mere du gentil *"infusus"*, j'ay desdain de ces menues pointes et allusions verballes qui nasquirent depuis.' There are two points one may make concerning this comment on selected Latin words. We know that the love of the Latin language was very strong in Montaigne. He spoke the language before French, having learned it from a tutor by the 'direct method', his parents and servants cooperating by speaking to him only in that tongue. He tells us that he understands it better than French, and that although he hasn't written or spoken it in forty years, in a moment of excitement Latin, not French words spurt from his mouth. (III, ii, 788). Latin, in a manner of speaking, is thus more 'natural' to Montaigne. The second point is more closely related to the esthetics of negligence. In 'ruminating' – savoring, and almost tasting the Latin words of the quotations – he is suggesting that they have a quality that goes beyond mere meaning, an incantatory power which varies according to the reader. This idea of a richness surpassing the dictionary sense of words he had already expressed concerning Latin, attributing it to prestige: 'le Latin me pippe à sa faveur par sa dignité, au delà de ce qui luy appartient' (II, xviii, 617). Now, recasting the earlier comment, he writes concerning the words in the quotations, 'Elles signifient plus qu'elles ne disent' (III, v, 851). Furthermore this quality evokes in the reader not merely understanding and appreciation, but a kind of ecstasy; it is an eloquence that 'ne plaict pas comme elle remplit et ravit; et ravit les plus forts esprits' (850).[1]

But why did Montaigne choose these particular words to 'ruminate'?[2] How did they fill him with scorn for the French language? One might suggest that each conveys multiple meanings, meanings that could be expressed in French only by using several words. *Pascit* means 'eat' but also suggests sexual fulfillment; *inhians*, 'look at with open mouth', or 'with mouth watering'; *circunfusa*, 'flowed around', but with the additional idea of 'pouring', 'bending' or 'embracing'. While recognizing that such Latin words, with time,

---

[1] Cf. 'Leurs escrits ne me satisfont pas seulement et me remplissent; mais ils m'estonnent et transissent d'admiration' (II, xvii, 620).

[2] The editor of Montaigne's *Lucretius*, Denys Lambin, comments briefly on *reicit, pascit* and *inhians in te*: Titi Lucretii Cari, *De rerum natura, libri sex* (Paris and Lyons: G. Roville, 1563), p. 5.

lose some of their connotative power, Montaigne reasserts their special effect on the discriminating reader:

Comme en nostre commun, il s'y rencontre des frases excellentes et des metaphores desquelles la beauté flestrit de vieillesse, et la couleur s'est ternie par maniement trop ordinaire. Mais cela n'oste rien du goust à ceux qui ont bon nez, ni ne desroge à la gloire de ces anciens autheurs, qui comme il est vray semblable, mirent premierement ces mots en ce lustre (852).

Evidently Montaigne numbers himself and his ideal 'suffisant lecteur' among 'ceux qui ont bon nez'. His emphasis on connotation, upon the inexplicable delight certain words or phrases may evoke in the reader, constitutes a declaration of independence typical of the negligent writer. For how can rhetoricians prescribe rules of language and composition when the deepest beauties of a work may be due to a subjective reaction?

Montaigne's praise of Latin writers, of their 'vigor' which he praises in terms of consubstantiality – for they are 'tout epigramme, non la queue seulement, mais la teste, l'estomac et les pieds' – brings in its wake the denigration of the French language, with its 'pointes et allusions verbales', its 'miserable affectation d'estrangeté', its 'desguisements froids et absurdes', that prevent it from handling 'une puissante conception'. He pointedly discounts the value of the Pléiade's suggested ways to improve and enrich the language, in particular 'provignement', finding once again in favor of Latin writers over French: 'ils n'y apportent point des mots, mais ils enrichissent les leurs, appesantissent et enfoncent leur signification et leur usage, luy aprenent des mouvements inaccoustumés, mais prudemment et ingenieusement' (851).

The negligent writer thus asserting his independence of his own language refuses to heed stylistic or linguistic criteria. In his criticism of French, emphasizing its 'affectation', its 'estrangeté', we discern again Montaigne's search for the 'naturel'. In this key he stoutly defends his use of Gasconisms in one of those dialogues with his reader, his critic, or himself, typical of the negligent author from Rabelais to Diderot:

Quand on m'a dit ou que moy-mesme me suis dict: 'Tu es trop espais en figures. Voilà un mot du creu de Gascoigne. Voilà une frase dangereuse (je n'en refuis aucune de celles qui s'usent emmy les rues françoises; ceux qui veulent combattre l'usage par la grammaire se moquent). Voilà un discours ignorant. Voilà un discours paradoxe. En voilà un trop fol.

Tu te joues souvent; on estimera que tu dies à droit ce que tu dis à feinte. – Oui, fais-je; mais je corrige les fautes d'inadvertence, non celles de coustume. Est-ce pas ainsi que je parle par tout? me represente-je pas vivement? suffit! J'ay faict ce que j'ay voulu: tout le monde me reconnoit en mon livre, et mon livre en moy (853).

This resounding declaration of independence reiterates once again the negligent writer's concern for consubstantiality. 'Sur des vers de Virgile' fuses the author, the work and his theme, as the writer contemplating his sexuality becomes at the same time the reader of erotic poetry and the poet depicting the act of love. What he would have us believe to be merely a 'notable commentaire qui m'est eschappé d'un flux de caquet' (875) possesses on the contrary a very particular type of order, the order of negligence. Of this essay Montaigne might well have said, 'la nonchalance et la lâcheté, elles nous menent aussi aucunement à la résolution' (III, ix, 949).

La Fontaine: the difficulty of negligence

On the level of biography, it was for many years traditional to speak of La Fontaine as a nonchalant or negligent poet. The cosy picture of the 'bonhomme', the lazy writer scribbling in a shady glen, or lulled by a rippling brook, so frequently presented by critics and biographers, has long since been definitively contested and refuted by Paul Valéry in his famous article on 'Adonis'. In a discussion of versification, in the course of which he demonstrates the poet's painstaking skill, Valéry associates two significant concepts with the problem of negligence – freedom and regularity: 'peut-on même répondre', he asks, 'à cette charmeresse (la liberté) qu'elle favorise dangereusement la négligence, quand elle peut si aisément nous remontrer une quantité accablante de vers très mauvais, très faciles, et terriblement réguliers'.[1] To oppose in this way negligence and regularity is not to express a preference for the former, but in defending the poet's freedom to treat the rules as he pleases at the risk of negligence, Valéry leans in that direction. La Fontaine himself frequently declared his aversion to 'regularity' in art. In the *Relation d'un voyage en Limousin*, describing his visit to the castle at Blois, he comments on its three different architectural styles which result in a desirable lack of symmetry: 'Toutes ces trois pièces ne font, Dieu merci, nulle symétrie.' Of the three, he prefers the architecture of

[1] Paul Valéry, *Œuvres*, ed. J. Hytier (Paris: Bibliothèque de la Pléiade, 1959–60), I, 477.

François Ier, both for its variety and its irregularity, and admires its 'force petites galéries, petites fenêtres, petits balcons, petits ornements sans régularité et sans ordre' (OD, 544).[1] In his *Amours de Psyché et de Cupidon*, he adopts as his basic structure an informal conversation between friends, one which rejects 'les conversations réglées et tout ce qui sent la conférence académique'. Chance alone will dictate the subjects these friends discuss, and to describe their manner of treating them he uses the well-worn Platonic metaphor that Montaigne had applied to Ariosto: the bees as they fly from flower to flower.[2] Indeed La Fontaine's remarks on his friends' discourse remind us of 'De l'art de conferer' when Montaigne emphasizes that conversation should aim at 'l'exercice des ames sans autre fruit', and not only shun all practical goals but follow 'pour la plus part la conduicte du hazard'.[3]

But it is chiefly in the *contes* that the esthetics of negligence predominates. True, in the *fables* a certain playfulness of tone, a refusal to be serious, a wilful confusion of author and subject-matter, the subtly wayward transitions Leo Spitzer has studied so expertly,[4] on occasion suggest this poetic attitude. But by my definition, the moral goal of the *fables* by and large excludes them from the esthetics of negligence since they must instruct as well as please:

> En ces sortes de feinte il faut instruire et plaire,
> Et conter pour conter me semble peu d'affaire (132).[5]

The *contes* espouse form, and have no moral aim but to delight:

> Contons, mais contons bien, c'est le point principal;
> C'est tout (477).

In addition, they reject all responsibility for their content. La Fontaine makes this point in the preamble to 'Les Oies de Frère Philippe'

---

[1] La Fontaine, *Œuvres diverses*, ed. P. Clarac (Paris: Bibliothèque de la Pléiade, 1948), p. 544. Page references in the text to miscellaneous works (preceded by the initials OD) will henceforth be to this edition.

[2] His best-known use of the image is in his 'Discours à Mme de la Sablière', where he declares himself 'Papillon du Parnasse, et semblable aux abeilles /A qui le bon Platon compare nos merveilles'.

[3] Montaigne, *Œuvres complètes*, III, iii, 802; viii, 912.

[4] Leo Spitzer, 'Die Kunst des Übergangs bei La Fontaine', *PMLA*, LIII (1938), 393–433.

[5] La Fontaine, *Fables, contes et nouvelles*, ed. René Groos and Jacques Schiffrin (Paris: Bibliothèque de la Pléiade, 1954), p. 132. Page references in the text to *contes* and *fables* will henceforth be to this edition. In the case of extended quotations interrupted by the text, only one page reference will be given.

when, following Boccaccio he defends himself against the accusation of misogyny. 'Ce que mon livre a dit', he declares, 'doit passer pour chansons', repeating a phrase from his second preface: 'Qui ne voit que cela est jeu, et par conséquent ne peut porter coup?' (347) The beginning lines of this *conte* offer an excellent example of the poet's refusal of responsibility. He begs his female readers ('le beau sexe') to laugh at the story, at his 'tours', his ingenious tricks:

> Quelque aventure qu'il y trouve
> S'ils sont faux, ce sont vains discours;
> S'ils sont vrais, il les désapprouve.

There follows a rather perfidious series of compliments, in the course of which he manages to say that everyone knows women's morals are not loose, and that although there is no lack of fortunate lovers these nevertheless are not numbered in thousands. This skilful casuistry concludes with the lines already quoted concerning the preeminence of narrative quality. The critic may object to his 'méchants vers et phrases méchantes', but he must not attack 'les bons tours', the humorous elements of narrative. As for 'méchants vers', these fall into the category of 'necessary negligence' a part of 'les hardiesses et les licences qu'il s'est données':

Nous ne parlons point des mauvaises rimes, des vers qui enjambent, des deux voyelles sans élision; ni en général de ces sortes de négligences que l'auteur ne se pardonnerait pas lui-même en un autre genre de poésie; mais qui sont inséparables, pour ainsi dire, de celui-ci. Le trop grand soin de les éviter jetterait un faiseur de contes en de longs détours, en des récits aussi froids que beaux, en des contraintes fort inutiles; et lui ferait négliger le plaisir du coeur pour travailler à la satisfaction de l'oreille (385).

Despite this proclamation of the necessity for negligence, the problem of versification evidently preoccupied our *conteur*, in fact it seems at one point to have taken precedence over all others, since in the foreword to the first edition he confesses his inability to chose between various metrical forms:

L'auteur a voulu éprouver lequel caractère est le plus propre pour rimer des contes. Il a cru que les vers irréguliers ayant un air qui tient beaucoup de la prose, cette manière pourrait sembler la plus naturelle, et par conséquent la meilleure. D'autre part aussi le vieux langage, pour les choses de cette nature, a des grâces que celui de notre siècle n'a pas...l'auteur a donc tenté ces deux voies sans être encore certain laquelle est la bonne (345).

One notes the identification between *irregular* and *natural*, in which La Fontaine follows Corneille, who had declared, in the 1650 *Examen* of *Andromède*, that *vers libres* (the usual term for what La Fontaine calls *vers irréguliers*) are closer to prose than rhyming Alexandrines because their 'unexpected changes of rhythm' produce effects of 'pleasant surprise'.[1] By using the term *caractère* in its wider Greek sense, which includes style, versification and tone, La Fontaine deliberately suggests that the archaic language in the *contes* he imitated from Boccaccio, Rabelais or Marguerite de Navarre calls for the poetic line of earlier forms of poetry, the decasyllabic or the octosyllabic.

No doubt as well, the peculiar grace he found in the 'vieux langage' of the older poets stemmed in part from their irregularity. For, as he tells us in the second preface, 'le secret de plaire ne consiste pas toujours en l'ajustement, ni même en la régularité; il faut du piquant et de l'agréable si l'on veut toucher'. Modern poets, he goes on, may well have discovered 'le beau tour de vers, le beau langage, la justesse, les bonnes rimes'; a Marot, or a Saint-Gelais, despite their faults display a charm and grace lacking in his contemporaries. And it is of these two poets that he declares in Terence's words that he would rather 'equal their negligence than the obscure diligence of others'.[2]

It seems evident then that whether in *vers libres* or decasyllabics the author places the versification of the *contes* squarely in the domain of the esthetics of negligence. Their content is another matter. There is no gainsaying that they are scabrous; can the poet deny the responsibility for this? Of course; he has only to shelter behind his sources, ancient or modern: 'L'on ne me saurait condamner', he writes, 'que l'on ne condamne aussi l'Arioste devant moi, et les Anciens devant l'Arioste' (346). With considerable skill he succeeds in turning the critics' own arguments against them. If they claim he has offended against the famous *bienséances* or moral standards in art, he answers by shifting the critical basis and enlarging the concept of *bienséance* to include esthetic standards: 'Qui voudrait réduire Boccace à la même pudeur que Virgile ne ferait assurément rien qui vaille, et pêcherait contre les lois de la bienséance en prenant à tâche de les observer.' Thus, to remove from Boccaccio the

---

[1] On the vexed question of *vers libres*, see R. Bray, 'L'Introduction des vers mêlés sur la scène classique', *PMLA*, LXVI (1951), 456–84.

[2] 'Quorum in hac re imitari neglegentiam exoptat potius quam istorum diligentiam.' La Fontaine misquotes Terence, *Andria*, Prol. 20–1: 'Quorum aemulari exoptat neglegentiam / Potius quam istorum obscuram diligentiam.'

erotic element would disfigure his work; *pudeur* or lack of it becomes a question of art alone, an inherent part of a given poem.

Yet the poet knows he must take into account the social attitude that imposes certain rules concerning the expression of sexual matters, which so often culminates in what Montaigne called 'la superstition verbale'. Like Montaigne he sees such expression as an esthetic problem, calling not for censorship but for the special powers of his art. Montaigne compared the effect of Virgil's lines on Venus' and Vulcan's love-making to a veil,[1] and La Fontaine in his most licentious *conte*, 'Le Tableau', employs the same metaphor. The subject, he tells us, is like the painting of a forbidden scene over which the censor drapes a curtain. The poet intends not to remove it, but to replace it by the diaphanous covering of poetic language: 'Tout y sera voilé, mais de gaze', and this veil will consist, he adds, repeating the terms of his preface, 'En nombre de traits nouveaux piquants et délicats,/Qui disent et ne disent pas'. At first glance this esthetic of the veil might seem the effect of care rather than negligence, yet La Fontaine's lines reveal that its practice aims at spontaneity, at the unexpected quality implicit in the esthetics of negligence. The veil as the metaphorical designation of a particular poetic method and as an actual garment artlessly enhancing beauty are fused in the *contes*; in the latter case the element of the unexpected recurs frequently. We see through the eyes of Chimon in 'Le Fleuve Scamandre' how the veil augments the beauty of a lovely bather:

> Son voile au gré des vents va flottant dans les airs;
> Sa parure est sans art (624).

In almost the same terms Venus' scarf in 'Adonis' 'vole au gré' of the winds and 'laisse voir les trésors de sa gorge d'albâtre'. On a less ethereal plane, a handkerchief partially veils the opulent breasts of the merry widow in 'L'Oraison de Saint Julien'; it is 'de deux grands doigts trop court'. Even the eyes, which La Fontaine places in opposition to more fleshly attributes in the curious debate 'Le Différant de Belle Bouche et de Beaux Yeux', are enhanced by the veil, as are the glances of amorous Roman matrons: 'sous leurs voiles brillaient des yeux pleins d'étincelles' (580).

Veiled beauty is frequently accompanied by a dynamic quality: the winds play with veil or scarf; a neckerchief heaves upon an adolescent's budding breasts:

[1] Cf. above, p. 26.

34

La fille crût, se fit: on pouvait déjà voir
Hausser et baisser son mouchoir (497).

By its very nature, which involves dynamism, spontaneity, an essential *contingency*, veiled beauty is linked to the concept of *grâce*, that 'grâce plus belle encore que la beauté', that implies once again a criticism of regular beauty. We recall the poet's rhetorical question in the preface, 'combien voyons-nous de ces beautés régulières qui ne touchent point, et dont personne n'est amoureux?' Grace with its subtle negligence moves us, or in La Fontaine's words, 'touches' us more deeply than mere beauty, because it reaches the 'heart', because it 'pleases'.[1]

One of the most remarkable illustrations of the esthetics of negligent beauty occurs in La Fontaine's portrayal of the sleeping Cupid, in *Les Amours de Psyché et de Cupidon*, which though largely in prose contains, as we have seen, numerous parallels with the *contes*. In particular this portrait admirably conveys the quality of contingency, suggesting despite the subject's immobility its inherent dynamism. La Fontaine achieves this effect by a technique of duplication, describing the sleeper first in poetry then in prose (OD, 170–1), and thus providing a prismatic view that emphasizes the fugitive quality of grace in suspense. The element of contingency appears in the very ambiguity of Cupid's charms,

Non d'un Hercule, ou d'un Atlas,
D'un Pan, d'un Sylvain, ou d'un Faune,
Ni même ceux d'une Amazone;
Mais ceux d'une Vénus, à l'âge de vingt ans.

As is frequently the case, the subject's hair acts as a veil that suggests rather than reveals his beauty:

Ses cheveux épars et flottants
....
Cachaient quelques attraits dignes d'être estimés;
Mais Psyché n'en était qu'à prendre plus facile:
Car, pour un qu'ils cachaient, elle en soupçonnait mille.

In his second description, now in prose, La Fontaine repeats some elements but changes his emphasis as if Psyché's gaze had moved closer. In the poetic portrait he had refused once again 'd'aller par

[1] Cf. Jean Lafon, 'La Beauté et la grâce: l'esthétique "platonicienne" des "Amours de Psyché"', *RHL*, LXXX (1969), 475–90.

ordre en l'affaire', preferring to depict Cupid's complexion and features first. Now he emphasizes the god's posture as he sleeps: 'Il dormait à la manière d'un dieu, c'est à dire profondément, penché nonchalamment sur un oreiller, un bras sur sa tête, l'autre bras tombant sur les bords du lit, couvert à demi d'un voile de gaze, ainsi que sa mère en use, et les Nymphes aussi, et quelquefois les bergères.' The sleeping youth's nonchalance, the arm falling over the edge of the bed, the familiar veil, all emphasize the contingency of his attitude. The association of the veil with Venus, the nymphs and shepherdesses, again suggests sexual ambiguity.

If after this scene of delicate sensuality I turn once again to 'Le Tableau', however brutal the transition may seem, it is because the same esthetic of the veil, so readily adaptable to the loves of Psyche and Cupid, is here put to its severest test, and the contrast should well highlight the poet's mastery of his material. Aretino had portrayed two nuns taking turns in making love to a mule-driver seated on a chair, which in their sexual frenzy they finally overturn.[1] By speaking of this scene as a 'tableau', La Fontaine deliberately stresses its visual quality, which he then underlines by an allusion to some lines from the *Priapeia* commonly attributed to Catullus, the same lines that Montaigne alters in 'Sur des vers de Virgile' to indicate his own inadequacy.[2] The reference serves to emphasize again the direct relationship between the eye and its object. Decorous matrons look with relish upon the male member; then why, asks the poet, almost paraphrasing Montaigne,

> pourquoi plus de scrupule,
> Pourquoi moins de licence aux oreilles qu'aux yeux?

This question, although he does not put it with Montaigne's insistence, suggests the esthetic problem involved, and La Fontaine's explanation of his methods of overcoming conventional restrictions hints at the superiority of the literary over the plastic art. The 'painting's' sexual boldness could not be attenuated by some modification such as painting clothes on the nude figures; the only recourse is to

---

[1] Aretino, *Raggionamenti*, I. The relevant passage may be found in *Œuvres de J. de la Fontaine*, ed. Henri de Régnier (Paris: Hachette, Les Grands Ecrivians de la France), v (1889), 577–8.

[2] *Priapea*, VIII, 4–5: 'Nimirum sapiunt videntque magnam/Matronae quoque mentulam libenter.' Montaigne substituted *parvam* for *magnam* and *illibenter* for *libenter* (III, v, 866).

cover it with a curtain. Yet the poet needs only the diaphanous veil
of his art:

> Nuls traits à découvert n'auront ici de place;
> Tout y sera voilé, mais de gaze, et si bien
>   Que je crois qu'on n'en perdra rien.
> Qui pense finement et s'exprime avec grâce
>   Fait tout passer, car tout passe (613).

Literary analysis can show how La Fontaine weaves the veil he inter-
poses between the reality of the imaginary painting and the reader's
eye. One device is that of postponement; thereby the poet both
creates suspense, and suggests that his esthetic problem is as important a subject as the crucial scene he has eventually to depict. He
obtains an effect of distance through mythological allusions. First of
all, the scene itself is no ordinary convent, it is a suburb of 'la ville
de Cythère', in the land of Love, and Venus has made of it her
'seminary'. Using a favorite device that one might call the 'rhetoric
of incapacity' he appeals for help in his difficulties to the Muses, but
immediately cancels this request because they are virgins, 'Au joli
ieu d'Amour ne sachant A ni B.' At most they can plead his case with
Apollo, who has more experience. Mythology helps him depict the
nuns' beauty, which he compares to Venus':

> A ces soeurs l'enfant de Cythère
> Mille fois le jour s'en venait
> Les bras ouverts, et les prenait
> L'une après l'autre pour sa mère.

Cupid's charming gesture, creating the impression of a crowd of
beauties, has come to La Fontaine's pen via the Greek Anthology and
a *dizain* by his cherished Marot.[1]

When it comes to depicting nudity, mythology affords a certain
idealization both during and after the central scene, as the poet once
again calls on the Greek Anthology, adapting another epigram in
which Venus tells Pallas she needs no armor since she triumphs nude
over her enemies:

> Quoique Bellone ait part ici,
> J'y vois peu de corps de cuirasse.
> Dame Vénus se couvre ainsi
> Quand elle entre en champ clos avec le dieu de Thrace;
>   Cette armure a beaucoup de grace.

---

[1] Marot, Epigramme CIII, 'De Cupido et sa dame'.

Here Venus' 'armor' corresponds to the veil that 'couvre si bien/Que je crois qu'on n'en perdra rien'. The poet maintains his burlesque tone in comparing the nuns' dalliance to the Trojan War, and wishing that Vulcan had engraved 'notre tableau' upon Achilles' shield.

Allusions to Venus and mythology furnish indirect suggestions of sensuality, but more intimate allusions are derived from the fusion of the veil of clothing and the veil of art, of which perhaps the most perfect example may be found in 'L'Oraison de Saint Julien' as the poet describes the hospitable widow's dress:

> La négligence, à mon gré si requise,
> Pour cette fois fut sa dame d'atour,
> Point de clinquant, jupe simple et modeste,
> Ajustement moins superbe que leste (415).

To this negligent attire corresponds almost exactly his call for irregularity in the preface, as he asks, 'Combien voyons-nous de ces beautés régulières qui ne touchent point, et dont personne n'est amoureux?' The attractiveness of the nuns also benefits from concealment by clothing, but in an unusual way. First of all, rather than an 'ajustement leste' that partly reveals, its secretiveness increases ardor:

> Mille secrètes circonstances
> De leurs corps polis et charmants
> Augmentaient l'ardeur des amants.

The ecclesiastical garb, conceived to hide feminine charms as completely as the censor's curtain concealed the painting, only reveals them to greater advantage to the imagination.

> En mille endroits nichait l'Amour,
> Sous une guimpe, un voile, et sous un scapulaire.

One may relate this Cupid, flitting from one layer of clothing to another, to the winds that played with Venus' scarf, imparting once again to the nuns' pulchritude the same quality of contingency we saw in the sleeping Adonis.

Such evocations of female beauty are only one of a number of subterfuges after which the poet finally arrives, trembling with mock anxiety, at the point where he must deal with the scene of sexual dalliance. In vain he calls on Apollo, as if to stall by asking why the loutish object of the nuns' affections remains seated, rather than offer them the chair. The god answers curtly,

> Tout beau! Ces matières
> A fond ne s'examinent guères.

This also sounds like a clever way to make the God of Poetry echo his own theory, for in the preface of 1666 he had declared 'il faut laisser les narrations étudiées pour les grands sujets' (385) – the negligent author may leave details to the reader's imagination. When he finally sets about portraying the amorous trio, he now calls on the God of Love, of whom he makes another divine accomplice:

> l'Amour est un étrange garçon;
> J'ai tort d'ériger un fripon
> En maître de cérémonies.
> Dès qu'il entre en une maison,
> Règles et lois sont bannies;
> Sa fantaisie est sa raison.

La Fontaine or his master of ceremonies divides the 'tableau' into two parts: the fall from the chair and the resultant confusion. Speculations on the reason for the collapse and various euphemisms serve to veil the action:

> Le voilà qui rompt tout; c'est assez sa coutume:
> Ses jeux sont violents. A terre on vit bientôt
> Le galant cathédral. Ou soit par le défaut
> De la chaise un peu faible, ou soit que du pitaud
>   Le corps ne fût pas fait de plume,
> Ou soit que soeur Thérèse eût chargé d'action
> Son discours véhément et plein d'émotion,
> On entendit craquer l'amoureuse tribune:
> Le rustre tombe à terre en cette occasion.

The designations of the participants and their actions oscillating from the grandiose to the ludicrously realistic (doubtless what La Fontaine meant by 'traits...qui disent et ne disent pas) militate against too great visual precision. The bumpkin is both a gallant 'cathédral' – a rare word derived from cathedra, meaning simply 'he who sits' but which the poet certainly chose for its ecclesiastical resonance, and a 'pitaud', a lout. Thérèse's sexual drive is merely a 'discours véhément' that she may have overdone; the 'chaise un peu faible' is also an 'amoureux tribune' and we hear rather than see it break and fall. The poet intervenes in the second part with his stern admonition to the censorious critic and a plea for his readers' (Rabelais' 'gens de bien') complicity:

39

> Censeurs, n'approchez point d'ici votre oeil profane.[1]
> Vous, gens de bien, voyez comme soeur Claude mit
>   Un tel incident à profit.

The following confusion suggests a ship in a storm; Thérèse losing her place 'perdit la tramontane', and Sister Claude pushes her aside, 's'emparant du timon'. Now La Fontaine steps momentarily into the action, warning the victorious Claude that Thérèse is about to come to blows: 'Elle a le poing levé', which elicits the indifferent reply, 'Qu'elle ait'. The poet maintains his presence, approving this answer, by actually answering his own character: 'Quiconque est occupé comme vous ne sent rien', whereupon he withdraws to make the comparisons with the Trojan War that we discussed earlier. The ending is left 'open' as he speculates once again on the esthetic problem posed by the licentious scene. With a self-deprecation that typifies the negligent writer he confesses he has failed: 'La peinture déchet dans ma description.'

He has lost nothing of his truculence concerning 'narrations étudiées', however. He expresses momentary qualms about the nuns' prearranged meeting with their lover:

> Enfin, tout alla bien, hormis qu'en bonne foi
> L'heure du rendez-vous m'embarrasse.

But he recovers rapidly, with an eloquent shrug:

>   Et pourquoi?
> Si l'amant ne vint pas, soeur Claude et soeur Thérèse
> Eurent à tout le moins de quoi se consoler:
> S'il vint, on sut cacher le lourdaud et la chaise;
> L'amant trouva bientôt encore à qui parler.

The saga of Sisters Claude and Thérèse amply illustrates the various aspects of La Fontaine's negligent muse that we shall have occasion to treat in the course of this study. Prominent among them are the veil as a vehicle of spontaneous and dynamic poetic communication, and the consubstantiality that fuses the author and his work. This latter trait appears in such interventions as the one discussed above, in which the poet enters the poem, not merely to make an aside concerning his own *persona* or his esthetic struggle, but actually to converse with one of his own characters.

---

[1] For a similar tone see 'Contre ceux qui ont le goût difficile': 'Maudit censeur, te tairas-tu?' (52).

The complexity of his involvement in his stories is reflected by the range of his interventions, which vary from simple direct address to the reader, commentary on the characters and their creator, hot debate with reader or critic on his artistic method, or a myriad of subjects, to a fusion with the characters that recalls Molière playing himself in the *Impromptu de Versailles*.

A further means of identifying with his work is to suggest that the writing of the *contes* was somehow obsessive. He solemnly declared in his second preface: 'Voici les derniers ouvrages de cette nature qui partiront des mains de l'auteur', yet somehow, untiringly, he continued to turn them out. To emphasize, as he does, the infallibility with which he strays from his promise is to insist on the spontaneity of the *contes*; he writes them, as he says, 'malgré lui'. He apologizes in particular for his satire of nuns, and after 'Mazet de Lamporecchio', 'L'Abbesse' and 'Soeur Jeanne ayant fait un poupon', he vows, his hand on his heart:

> Nonnes, souffrez pour la dernière fois
> Qu'en ce recueil, malgré moi, je vous place (572).

He begins a new story with a false sigh of despair: 'J'avais juré de laisser là les nonnes (598). Once again the hopeless 'J'avais juré...' appears in an aside to the reader that blames his incorrigibility on human inconstancy:

> O combien l'homme est inconstant, divers,
> Faible, léger, tenant mal sa parole!
> J'avais juré hautement en mes vers
> De renoncer à tout conte frivole.

It is not without interest that after his conversion and after denouncing his verse tales as a 'livre abominable', he included in a last book of fables, published in 1693, two *contes* – from among his least scabrous, it is true – 'La Matrone d'Ephèse' and 'Belphégor'.

One senses continually La Fontaine's devotion for, his commitment to, the *contes*. It would perhaps be too simplistic to suggest that they provided a relief from the constraint imposed by the dual form of moral and story, since *conte* and *fable* are two polarities on an indeterminate ground where the two genres may come close to one another, and even, as in the case of 'Tircis et Amaranthe', occasionally fuse.

If one analyses one of the acknowledged masterpieces among the *fables*, 'Les Deux Pigeons', after studying *contes* of comparable beauty, one realizes that the essential difference may be the liberty not only to create exactly as he pleases but to reject any moral aim whatsoever. Imitated from 'Pilpay', this fable illustrates the dangers to love of separation – one of the two alternatives in a hackneyed enough theme: 'l'absence est le plus grand des maux'. But although it never entirely corresponds to the rather rigid distinction set forth in the preface to the *Fables*: 'L'apologue est composé de deux parties, dont on peut appeler l'une le corps, l'autre l'âme. Le corps est la fable; l'âme la moralité' (11), this fable does prove its point. The message is skillfully dissimulated; the three parts blend imperceptibly into one another, and no more specific statement of the moral occurs than two lines of advice to lovers. It is instructive to see how the didactic quality is woven into the fabric.

The first part, a dramatic dialogue between the couple after one has decided to go on a voyage, begins with a clear indication from the author that this plan is folly, for the would-be wanderer is 'assez fou pour entreprendre/Un voyage en lointain pays'. Just as in certain tragedies a dream or an omen heralds the catastrophe, so the stay-at-home pigeon has heard that a crow 'Tout à l'heure annonçait malheur à quelque oiseau'. His dreams, he knows in advance, will prophesy misfortune: 'rencontre funeste,/...faucons...réseaux... Hélas, dirai-je, il pleut...' The second part consists of the detailing of these predictions: the elements, birds of prey, man and his lures and weapons, harass the unhappy wanderer. In addition, La Fontaine illustrates the evil and rapacity of the world outside by his comment on the child who attacks the pigeon ('cet âge est sans pitié') and by the eagle's attack on the vulture who was about to seize his victim, illustrating a hierarchy of malevolence.

The third part, the well-known elegy, far from being moralistic, offers wistful advice from one who envies lovers fortunate enough to be together. The familiar lines, beginning 'Amants, heureux amants', are part of the admirable technique that fuses 'âme' and 'corps', for La Fontaine now speaks clearly of love between man and woman.

Henri de Régnier, and others since, have assumed that in 'Les Deux Pigeons' 'il s'agit d'amitié, non d'amour au sens ordinaire', basing this opinion on the pigeons' use of the word *frère* in addressing one another. Evidently this word need no more be restricted to fraternal sentiments than Baudelaire's 'Mon enfant, ma soeur' to paternal or brotherly feelings, but this scarcely solves the problem of gender. The fact is that La Fontaine's 'amour tendre' encompasses differing modes of love, from the deep friendship between men that is a form of love, with all its mystery, as in Montaigne's 'par ce que c'estoit luy; par ce que c'estoit moy' (I, xxviii, 187), to the passion of man for woman. This range and ambiguity are attained through the use of the word *pigeon* for both birds, and the maintaining of the masculine gender through such words as *voyageurs* and *oiseau*. But after the child's attack, 'le pigeon' becomes 'la volatile malheureuse' – the bedraggled victim acquires femininity and thus the closing lines of the second part relating the pleasure of reunion take on sensual undertones, heightened by the device of refusal to elaborate familiar to readers of the *contes*: 'je laisse à juger':

> Voilà nos gens rejoints; et je laisse à juger
> De combien de plaisirs ils payèrent leurs peines (219).

Sensual pleasures suggested in this way link the second part to the elegiac conclusion. If it is a plea in retrospect for loyalty in love, it is also the yearning for a love long lost, for 'les premiers serments', in which the poet's 'âme inquiète' looks back upon the 'humeur inquiète', now assuaged, of his protagonist.

A more subtle amalgam of narrative and didacticism could scarcely be imagined, yet however far he strays from the formulas of the preface, the poet does point his moral through Pilpay's brief story.[1] A second point may be made in distinguishing *conte* and *fable*. In 'Les Deux Pigeons', as in so many of the *fables*, La Fontaine transforms his source; yet his expressed attitude toward sources differs considerably from his position concerning the origins of his *contes*. Of the changes he makes in the works of Phaedrus, Avienus, Aesop, he says modestly that they are merely compensation for his inability to equal his predecessors' elegance and their concision. As a *conteur*, however, he deals with sources far fuller, and ostensibly much closer to his final product, yet now he emphasizes his creativity, even his originality: 'il retranche, il amplifie, il change les incidents et les circonstances, quelquefois le principal événement et sa suite: enfin, ce n'est plus la même chose, c'est proprement une nouvelle nouvelle.' To determine how this process of re-creation occurred should help us illuminate the poet's genius; we shall begin by studying the tales he imitated from Boccaccio.

---

1 When he moralizes in a *conte* (see pp. 80 and 105) it is incidental; 'nonchalant', not a part of the fabric.

2

The Inspiration of Boccaccio

If we are to believe La Fontaine, Boccaccio was his favorite story-teller. He adapted nineteen of his *contes*, the largest number from any single author, and clearly admitting this preference wrote, 'ce divin esprit/Plus que pas un me donne de pratique'. If for La Fontaine Aesop embodied the fable, Boccaccio was his *conteur* par excellence, as we may gather from his announcement that at one point in his career he had decided to devote himself entirely to the *conte*: 'J'avais laissé Esope/Pour être tout à Boccace.'

The *Decameron* possesses a far wider range than its common reputation as a collection of bawdy stories would suggest. No modern realistic description surpasses Boccaccio's portrayal of the pestilence, its physical symptoms and its effect upon the population; Sigismonde's eloquent plea for her low-born lover, based on the equality of all men before God and urging that virtue and merit, not birth, be the criteria of nobility, startles the reader of Rousseau; the tragic story of Isabel and the pot of basil has inspired poet and novelist alike.

For this reason La Fontaine has been accused of emasculating Boccaccio; of reducing his characters to mere puppets, of suppressing the true feeling that permeates his work. But one should not seek Boccaccio in La Fontaine any more than Ariosto or Machiavelli; he went to his favorite *conteur* for those stories that most closely fitted the Gallic tradition, the straightforward realistic tales of sensual man and woman, and resolutely following Horace, refused to 'faire rire et pleurer dans une même nouvelle' (397).[1] For undeniably, sensuality and the impulses of physical love form one important characteristic of the *Decameron* and a reigning motif is the ingenuity with which such love triumphs over obstacles. This inevitable victory of love constitutes a central theme of the *contes*, and exactly as in Molière, the sensual instinct enlists in its support reason, argument, guile and

[1] Page references in the text to *contes* and *fables* are to the Groos and Schiffrin edition.

44

deception. All the familiar characters are there: the stuffy, near-impotent husband; the dissatisfied young wife; the handsome and enterprising lover; the valet and chambermaid who act as accomplices. Perhaps the chief difference from Molière is that La Fontaine's conspiratorial lovers are also adulterers, and that they revolt against one institution only: that of marriage.

There arises from this central theme one of the principal characteristics of these stories: a particular type of irony, which derives from their Gallic nature, one that we might call the irony of female insatiability. It consists of the interplay of two basic tenets: that which holds that women are basically pure, modest, charitable, even uninterested in sex, and the reverse, that they are inherently lustful and that lust motivates all their actions. La Fontaine creates this type of irony by ascribing to a lustful act a motive drawn from the first tenet. A typical example is Alaciel's yielding out of pity to a suitor who threatens her with suicide:

> Par pitié donc elle condescendit
>   Aux volontés du capitaine;
>   Et cet office lui rendit
> Gaîment, de bonne grâce, et sans montrer de peine;
>   Autrement le remède eût été sans effet (452).

Note that the ironic motive for Alaciel's alacrity is her concern that the remedy be effective. Another type of irony, somewhat less frequent, is that of circumstance, which unlike the irony of fate, has fortunate rather than disastrous consequences.

These types of irony are characteristic of La Fontaine's imitations of Boccaccio. In these *contes*, however, invention, insofar as the creation of new narrative elements are concerned, is minimal; condensation is the rule rather than amplification, and formal changes have nothing like the scope of those in the stories from Ariosto. La Fontaine's primary innovation lies perhaps in his poeticizing these prose tales. It is largely thanks to their new guise that they really become 'nouvelles nouvelles'. Their original character of a leisurely recitation by various members of a group, greeted by laughter and comment after each telling, has no counterpart in the French versions. Their 'singleness' as separate poems, which deprives them of the overall unity of the *Decameron*, leads the poet to seek by other means a unified structure. All these elements will occupy our attention in the present chapter, but we shall pay particular attention to the following characteristics or predominant patterns: amorous ruse, irony, adaptation and invention.

The amorous ruse

In 'Richard Minutolo' (364–9) the amorous ruse involves a confusion of identities. Richard falls in love with the wife of Fighinolfi, but she rebuffs his suit. Learning that she is jealous of her husband, he tells her that the latter plans to visit the baths with a mistress. At Richard's suggestion she herself goes to the baths where she waits in the darkened room that is the supposed place of assignation. She accepts in silence the caresses of the man she assumes to be her husband, and whose ardor she angrily takes to be inspired by the mistress whose part she is playing. Richard reveals his presence only after the couple has made love, and despite her tears the duped wife accepts him as her lover, yielding to his skillful combination of blackmail (what if your husband found out?) and specious logic (the thing is already done, so why stop?).

But it is on such logic that the success of the ruse depends, and the *conte*, in La Fontaine's hands, demonstrates the power of language. Nearly half of the tale is in dialogue, with the wily Richard speaking most of the lines, almost twice as many as Catelle. Through this persuasive dialogue La Fontaine stresses the eloquence of love, of which he wrote elsewhere:

> Je ne connais rhéteur, ni maître ès arts
> Tel que l'Amour, il excelle en bien dire.

Catelle yields because of the trick, yes, but Richard's arguments sway her most, with their eloquent assessment of her situation. Of his hero's first failure La Fontaine writes, 'Minutol n'en sut tirer raison'. The *conte* will demonstrate the final victory of ruse aided by reasoning.

As in Boccaccio, when his suit is unsuccessful Richard pretends no longer to love Catelle, but La Fontaine adds a telling point: his feigned indifference, which permits him to clothe his calumny of Fighinolfi with the appearance of sincerity. 'If I were still your suitor', he tells Catelle, 'I would not speak to you thus, since you would rightly mistrust me and see my speaking ill of your husband as a trick to ingratiate myself with you.' Richard's words almost infallibly impress his victim. After his eloquent description of the plan

to trap her husband has aroused her ire, she sets out, 'de grand
dépit', for the bathhouse. When the stratagem is exposed, she does
not yield at first to his arguments, but the fact that she weeps 'ten-
derly' hints at the final capitulation:

> Tout ce discours n'apaisa point Catelle;
> Elle se mit à pleurer tendrement.

To persuade her to remain silent Richard needs only the suggestion
that if she called for help, she herself would be denounced. La
Fontaine suggests his powers of eloquence, but also Catelle's growing willingness, by dividing the final argument into three parts, the
first, that she is not guilty, which 'n'apaisa point Catelle'; the second,
that if the affair got out she would be blamed – 'à ces raisons enfin
Catella cède'; and the third, that having already made love, they
should continue,

> Tant bien sut dire et prêcher, que la dame,
> Séchant ses yeux, rassérénant son âme,
> Plus doux que miel à la fin l'écouta.

Various other devices lend importance to the seducer's words.
The unfolding of his scheme – the first piece of direct discourse –
reveals the speaker as he steps forth into the spotlight. Boccaccio's
Catella first pleads eloquently with Richard to reveal the name of her
husband's mistress, but La Fontaine reduces this request to four lines,
ending with a remarkable example of his ability to condense an
action into a single verse. Catelle

> Voulut savoir de son défunt amant,
> Qu'elle tira dedans une ruelle,
> De quelles gens il entendait parler,
> Qui, quoi, comment, et ce qu'il voulait dire.

Even the physical victory appears secondary to the conquest by
language. La Fontaine omits, for example, Boccaccio's pointed comparison of Richard's and the husband's sexual prowess, which
Catella unwittingly makes in her denunciation. Her husband, she
cries accusingly in Le Maçon's translation, 'cuydant avoir entre ses
bras une aultre femme, m'a plus faict de caresses et de demonstra-
tions d'amytié en ce peu de temps que j'ay demouré avecques luy,
que en tout l'aultre remanant de temps que j'ay esté sienne!' La
Fontaine dilutes this to three rather pale lines:

47

> C'est donc cela que tu te tiens en mue,
> Fais le malade et te plains tous les jours,
> Te réservant sans doute à tes amours?

La Fontaine makes his presence felt by changing the story to suit his own opinions on marriage and love. In the Italian story Catella's jealousy of her husband suggests she loves him. La Fontaine omits any reference to her jealousy and simply shows her reacting violently to Richard's insinuations. His interventions, at the same time as they state his favorite cynical commonplace about money as the key to love, situate the story in time and place:

> L'argent fait tout: si l'on en prend en France
> Pour obliger en de semblables cas,
> On peut juger avec grande apparence
> Qu'en Italie on n'en refuse pas.

This shift between France and Italy, briefly reminding us that the French writer is adapting the Italian, reappears in his characterization of Richard:

> Il n'était lors de Paris jusqu'à Rome
> Galant qui sut si bien le numéro.

In the amorous ruse of still another Ricciardo, nicknamed 'Le Magnifique' for his fine dress and love of luxury, language again plays a central role. The young man persuades a jealous husband, Francesco, in exchange for a fine trotter, to allow him a brief interview with his wife, in the husband's presence but out of earshot. The husband slyly attempts to counter by forbidding his wife to answer the 'Magnificent'. But Ricciardo rises splendidly to the occasion, improvising the lady's replies which he makes favorable to his suit. La Fontaine's Richard is even more enterprising than his model. He asks only a quarter of an hour with the lady, and no sooner are they seated than he declares his suit:

> Notre galant n'étale
> Un long narré, mais vient d'abord au fait.
> Je n'ai le lieu ni le temps à souhait,
> Commença-t-il; puis je tiens inutile
> De tant tourner; il n'est que d'aller droit (609).

Here the exigencies of time are made to reinforce the impetuosity of young love. In Boccaccio the lady is merely to signal for him to come to her room, but La Fontaine's hero has his plans made to the smallest detail:

Vos douagnas en leur premier sommeil,
Vous descendrez sans nul autre appareil
Que de jeter une robe fourrée
Sur votre dos, et viendrez au jardin.
De mon côté l'échelle est préparée.
Je monterai par la cour du voisin:
Je l'ai gagnée: la rue est trop publique.

This story demonstrates the triumph of love over opposition and counter-ruse. Despite her husband's watchful eye, the lady acquiesces by a nod or a glance so that there is actually no need for Richard to frame her replies. That he should do so illustrates once again the importance of dialogue as a preliminary to love.

In 'La Confidente sans le savoir' a lady, in love with a man she does not know, asks a mutual friend to request that he cease courting her; thus he learns of her passion, and they are united. Such a plot – a more cerebral amorous ruse than usual in the Boccaccian tales – is highly rhetorical and dramatic in nature. In both the French and Italian versions, the lady complains three times about the lover's suit, the second time making him a gift by pretending that she is only returning it to him, and the third, by appearing to quote her presumptuous suitor, giving specific instructions on how to reach her bedroom. The ruse is wholly verbal, again demonstrating the important role of language in amorous conquest. Both authors emphasize this by making it clear that letters should not be included. This is sound instinct. It is true that in *L'Ecole des maris*, where Molière uses the same device, Isabelle contrives to have her guardian transmit a letter from her unopened to Valère. But in the play the letter as object (will Sganarelle open it or not?) adds a dramatic dimension, while in narrative it might have tended to obscure the importance of language.

Aminte's lover takes longer to understand the ruse than his counterpart in Boccaccio, who 'cogneut incontinent, sans trop songer, la sagesse de la dame'. His perplexity invests the device with a somewhat greater subtlety; Aminte has a natural barrier of incredulity and timidity to break down. Thus, after her first complaint, Cléon is simply taken aback:

Il va chez lui songer à cette affaire (628).

After Aminte's second visit to the maiden aunt whom La Fontaine substitutes for Boccaccio's priest, the light begins to dawn:

> Il s'en retourne, il rumine, il repense,
> Il rêve tant, qu'enfin il dit en soi:
> Si c'était là quelque ruse d'Aminte?

Yet even after this awareness, Cléon's passivity emphasizes Aminte's control of the situation through the verbal ruse: 'Laissons-la faire et laissons-nous conduire', he decides after weighing the pros and cons of making an outright declaration of his love.

The entire *conte*, with the exception of the prologue, is given over to Aminte's clever protests to Alis, and the description of their consequence, but at the conclusion, before the lovers meet in the 'cabinet d'amours', three lines suddenly stand forth to evoke the stillness and darkness of their trysting hour:

> Un profond somme occupait tous les yeux;
> Même ceux-là qui brillent dans les cieux
> Etaient voilés par une épaisse nue.

Appropriately in a *conte* that demonstrates so conclusively the power of language in the pursuit of love, consummation is preceded by the lover's compliments 'Sur son esprit, sur ses traits, sur son zèle'. Even the suggestion of physical love depends on the idea of praise, for the poet leaves the story open, the last line a question more eloquent than mere precision: 'Ne fit-il que louer?'

In a number of these *contes*, the amorous ruse is favored by darkness, an aspect La Fontaine almost invariably accentuates. The alliance of love and darkness, which is nevertheless accompanied by suggestions of the illicit, and even a kind of terror inherent in the anonymous, is a central theme of *Psyché*, where love can only be consummated in the dark, and night brings fear in its wake:

> La Nuit vient sur son char conduit par le Silence;
> Il amène avec lui la crainte en l'Univers (OD, 139).[1]

Sexual congress in *Psyché* has thus as its essential preliminary the absence of light. When Psyché unexpectedly meets her husband in the grotto, 'la clarté…lui faillit tout à coup' (148); and as soon as she gets into bed, her servants remove the torches (167). Her first for

---

[1] Cf. my 'Ronsard and La Fontaine: Two Versions of "Adonis"', *L'Esprit créateur*, x (1970), 125–44.

bidden glance at her husband sleeping enraptures her, but he awak-
ens with the pain of a drop of oil from her lamp, and the result is her
banishment.

Numerous variants on this love-in-darkness motif may be found
in the Boccaccian tales. Minutolo preparing for the rendez-vous with
Catelle first makes certain there are no apertures by which light can
enter the room and endanger his love ('par où le jour puisse nuire à
sa flamme'). The suggestion of violence or shock is likewise present:
Richard's pleasure is tinged with feelings of vengeance:

> Premièrement il jouit de la belle;
> En second lieu il trompe une cruelle.

When Catelle, resolving to reveal herself, tiptoes to a window and
throws it open, her amazement is traumatic: 'Elle tomba plus qu'à
demi pâmée.'

Darkness and mistaken identity play a major part in 'Le Berceau'.
At night a cradle, set beside the innkeeper's bed but moved from its
place, causes a series of errors as the lodgers and their hosts use it as a
guide and grope their way to the wrong beds. La Fontaine here
accentuates two elements: the sensual and the fearful. The sexual
act, however pleasureful, involves fatigue and even violence, it is a
game 'Qui, comme on sait, lasse plus qu'il n'ennuie'. Of the vigorous
young friend of Pinuccio, whose bed is mistakenly invaded by the
innkeeper's wife, and who rallies to the occasion, we learn

> Il fit l'époux, mais il le fit trop bien.
> Trop bien! je faux; et c'est tout le contraire:
> Il le fit mal; car qui le veut bien faire
> Doit en besogne aller plus doucement (403).

But this personal reflexion is wittily countered by the goodwife's own
reaction, as she muses delightedly, 'Prenons ceci, puisque Dieu
nous l'envoie'.

When Pinuccio returns from his sweetheart's cot, and mistakenly
gets into his host's bed, his ecstatic description of his delight is
considerably more detailed than in the Italian version:

> C'est bien le cuir plus doux,
> Le corps mieux fait, la taille plus gentille;
> Et des tetons! Je ne te dis pas tout.

The innkeeper's rage at this unexpected revelation far exceeds that of
his Italian counterpart. In Boccaccio he speaks one sentence; in La

Fontaine his voice is 'full of anger', and he fulminates for eleven lines, threatening to kill his daughter, commanding Pinuccio to leave, and hinting bitterly at the abuses of the nobility:

> Prétendez-vous, beau Monsieur que vous êtes,
> En demeurer quitte à si bon marché?
> ....
> Pour vos ébats nous nourrirons nos filles!
> J'en suis d'avis!

La Fontaine underscores the father's fury by the silence that follows. Pinuccio is petrified – 'plus froid qu'une statue' – the daughter is terrified; even the wife is at a loss for words. Only the friend's presence of mind saves the day by suggesting that Pinuccio is a somnambulist. Then the rest chime in and the amorous ruse succeeds with the innkeeper's 'C'est assez, je vous croi'.

Another ruse carried out in darkness occurs in 'Le Muletier'. A groom falls in love with his queen, and one night takes the king's place in her bed. La Fontaine intensifies both darkness and silence. The substitution is easier because the king habitually goes to the queen's room clad only in a long robe and carrying a candle. He always knocks *softly* on the door, which is opened *noiselessly* by a lady-in-waiting, who takes the candle – which, as the poet emphasizes, casts only a small light: 'n'ayant grand'lueur ni grand' flamme'. Again, when the king discovers the ruse, in Boccaccio he goes simply to the 'fort grand corps d'hostel' where his servants sleep. As he begins to feel their chests for a telltale heart beat, the guilty groom sees him, and though frightened, is reassured because the king has no weapon. La Fontaine reduces the suspects to the grooms alone, since the king at once realizes that only a *muletier* would be capable of such an amorous feat. Now the search takes place in complete darkness, incidentally furnishing a better motive for the king's trick of cutting a lock of the culprit's hair so as to recognize him in daylight, an act that Boccaccio ascribes simply to discretion ('comme celuy qui ne vouloit qu'on sçeust rien de ce qu'il prétendoit faire').

La Fontaine also increases the element of *gauloiserie* which is almost entirely absent in the Italian story. The 'palefrenier' of Le Maçon's translation[1] becomes a *muletier*, traditionally renowned for sexual prowess according to Marot:

[1] La Fontaine used this translation. Page references in the text are to Boccaccio, *Le Décaméron*, tr. Le Maçon, ed. Paul Lacroix (Paris: Librairie des Bibliophiles, n.d.), 3 vols.

> Six et sept fois ce n'est point le mestier
> D'homme d'honneur: c'est pour un muletier.[1]

Montaigne suggests that his powers can conquer even the most formidable chastity.[2] La Fontaine wittily develops this traditional prowess into a God-given talent:

> le Ciel est toujours juste:
> Il ne départ à gens de tous états
> Mêmes talents. Un empereur auguste
> A les vertus propres pour commander;
> Un avocat sait les points décider;
> Au jeu d'amour le muletier fait rage:
> Chacun son fait, nul n'a tout en partage (407).

Thus the virile groom appears as the equal of his monarch.

Although Queen Teudelingue remains innocent in both versions – La Fontaine emphasizes simply her wonderment at her 'husband's' new vigor and her concern for his health – *gauloiserie* erupts again when the king, confronted by *all* the grooms with a lock of hair shorn off by the clever culprit, jocularly wonders how his wife could have jousted with all sixteen.

But Queen Teudelingue is exceptional among many of the women of the Boccaccian *contes*, mistresses of female guile and the art of amorous ruse. A number of these stories illustrate the wife's triumph over her husband, although not necessarily in a war of wits, since the baffled spouse is almost always a dupe. The wife's success, indeed, should not be seen as demonstrating the superiority of woman's intelligence, but rather as a proof of the insatiability that goads her. One of the first tales of this type is 'Le Cocu battu et content', in which a young man, hearing of Béatrix's great beauty, enters the service of her husband Engano, declares his love, and becomes her lover through her successful ruse. Béatrix tells her husband she has promised to meet Loys that night in the garden, and at her urging he dons female garb and goes to the rendezvous in her place. As he waits in vain, Loys and Beatrix consummate their love, after which the lady sends her lover with a stick to punish the 'faithless wife'. Engano suffers the blows gladly, overwhelmed by such a demonstration of fidelity, and the lovers settle down to a life of untrammeled bliss.

---

1 Marot, Epigramme CCLXXIV: 'Du ieu d'amours', III, 111.
2 Montaigne, *Œuvres*, ed. Thibaudet and Rat, II, i, 317.

However, in this case La Fontaine somewhat attenuates the power of female guile, in that he changes Boccaccio's lovesick boy into an experienced roué. A striking scene in the Italian version clearly demonstrates the wife's control; she tells her story of rebuffing her lover's advances to her husband, all the while holding tightly to Loys' hand, for he has crept into her bedroom in the dark. La Fontaine sacrifices this highly dramatic moment, and the ruse becomes much more collaborative.

As in 'Richard Minutolo' dialogue adds to the characterization, and the lady's lively account of Loys' bold overtures, her indignation and her setting of the trap demonstrates her skill. La Fontaine subtly exploits the irony of a situation in which a wife makes her husband the accomplice of his own cuckoldry. In particular the wife's mastery is revealed in one delightful line. She is relating to her husband how she told Loys that he never left her side, but the reason she says she gave is also a reassuring aside to Engano:

> Mon mari, dis-je, est toujours avec moi,
> Plus par amour que doutant de ma foi.

Such a line tells us more of her guile than several adjectives. Her final words, which conclude the tale, consecrate, in their ironic double-entendre, her complete victory. When the duped husband commands her to treat the young man in future just as she would himself: 'Pas n'y faudrai, lui repartit la dame.'

A similar self-confidence characterizes the three merry wives of 'La Gageure des trois commères', who wager they can best one another when it comes to tricking their husbands. La Fontaine adds variety by giving each of the duped spouses a different degree of gullibility. One is completely naïve, the second alert and suspicious, and the third falls somewhere in between.

The first victim is the suspicious husband. His wife disguises her lover, who is 'frais, délicat, et sans poil au menton', as a chambermaid, who immediately catches the husband's eye and pretends to yield to his advances. The wife appears in the nick of time, denounces her errant husband and drags the tearful 'maid' off to her own bedroom, the better, so she says, to keep an eye on her.

The most far-fetched of the ruses confounds, appropriately enough, the most gullible of the three husbands. The method employed is that of an enforced illusion; the wife's lover, a servant, climbs into a pear-tree to shake down some fruit to her and her husband standing below. From above he pretends that he sees them engaging in intercourse and begs them to stop for propriety's sake. When he comes down, of course, nothing is amiss, but he sticks to his story. The husband climbs up in turn and, as we might expect, sees his wife and servant embrace, but they in turn indignantly deny his accusations when he descends. The dupe thereupon concludes that the tree is bewitched, and the wife demands it be chopped down.[1]

The third ruse, though influenced by Boccaccio, has been radically changed. In the original, the wife ties to her toe a string which leads out of the bedroom window. When her lover tugs on it, she signals to him whether her husband is sleeping soundly enough so that they can spend the night together. Her mate discovers the string and pursues his rival, who escapes. He returns and beats the person he assumes to be his wife, but who is in reality the chambermaid she has put in her place. When he brings her family to the house to denounce her infidelity, he is confounded by his triumphant spouse, who shows herself to be unscathed and accuses him of betraying her.

La Fontaine has the string device serve as a double ruse. The wife makes sure her husband sees it precisely so that he will follow it to the street and there lie in wait for her lover, who can then enter through the back door and spend the time of her husband's vigil with her, in an alteration that may have been suggested by Boccaccio's seventh tale, on which La Fontaine had already based 'Le Cocu battu'. The clever wife and her paramour triumph three times as the cuckold watches in vain at the wrong door. But not content to deceive the husband with impunity, the rascally pair quite literally 'pull the strings' that once again make him do their bidding like a marion-nette. The lover has one of his servants tug at the string, and the husband seizes him and drags him into the house. At this point La Fontaine introduces the chambermaid-substitute who in Boccaccio has to suffer the husband's blows; here she bears only the blame for the string trick: the manservant protests that he had a rendez-vous with her, whereupon the wife appears and berates the girl for having

---

[1] As the editor of the Grands Ecrivains edition points out (*Œuvres*, ed. Régnier, IV, 308–9), the shade of the pear-tree was traditionally 'propice aux amours'. In 'Le Cocu battu et content' La Fontaine changes Boccaccio's pine to a pear-tree. A curious parallel exists in Zola, *La Fortune du Rougon*, where luscious pear-trees grow in the cemetery of the Aire Saint-Mittre, scene of the lovers' trysts and of the hero's death. See my *Zola before the Rougon-Macquart* (University of Toronto Press, 1964), pp. 44–7.

used the device which she had made her imitate in order to set the trap:

> C'est donc cela, poursuivit la commère,
> En s'adressant à la fille en colère,
> Que l'autre jour je vous vis à l'orteil
> Un brin de fil?

The husband, a perfect dupe, comes to the chambermaid's defense, and she is married off with a handsome dowry to the manservant.

Although in the *contes* such amorous ruses are chiefly a feminine proclivity, masculine guile animates a number of them, with in almost every case the triumphant male a cleric whose success depends not solely on his skill but on his authority as well. The exception is 'A femme avare galant escroc', which illustrates the well-worn theme 'En beaux louis se content les fleurettes'. Boccaccio's Gulphar falls in love with Gasparin's wife, but when she demands money in exchange for her favors, his love turns to hate and he determines to punish her. In the more cynical French version Gulphar offers the two hundred crowns at once. The ruse consists of his borrowing the promised sum from the husband, giving it to the avaricious wife in the presence of witnesses, having his will with her, and then telling the husband, on his return, that he has returned the money to his wife after discovering he did not need it after all.

This rather perfunctory tale fades in comparison with the three that illustrate the guile of enterprising priest and monk. In 'Feronde ou le Purgatoire' a scheming abbé administers a potent sleeping-powder to a jealous husband, thus sending him effectively to 'purgatory' for ten months so he may enjoy his wife at leisure. In La Fontaine's version, Feronde is the abbot's bursar, a function which provides an excuse for his wife to 'consult' his employer; her husband, however, is aware of the liaison, and treats his wife with jealous brutality. La Fontaine points up the clerical satire by clothing his abbot in white, and thus making him a member of one of the newer orders, which permits sly contrasts:

> J'en sais de ce plumage
> Qui valent bien les noirs, à mon avis,
> En fait que d'être aux maris secourables (568).

Thus, one of the false 'angels' who punish the unfortunate Feronde by whipping him, tells him that if he had accused a black-clad priest, e.g. a Jesuit, his punishment would have been less severe, since presumably his allegations would have been closer to the truth. The description of the abbot provides the occasion for thrusts at the clergy: their idleness, gluttony and lechery:

> N'ayant autre oeuvre, autre emploi, penser autre,
> Que de chercher où gisaient les bons vins,
> Les beaux morceaux, et les bonnes commères,
> Sans oublier les gaillardes nonnains.

A definition of a prelate recalls *Tartuffe*:

> Comme prélat qu'il était, partant homme
> Fuyant la peine, aimant le plaisir pur,
> Ainsi que fait tout bon suppôt de Rome.

But the central portion of the story lacks interest, despite La Fontaine's valiant efforts and some examples of dexterous humor. Unlike most of the amorous ruses in these tales, Feronde's mishaps fail to delight the reader, perhaps because the abbot has things too much his own way.

The wily Friar Jean of 'La Jument du compère Pierre', while he does not succeed as completely as Feronde's master, manages nevertheless to have intercourse with a peasant's wife before his eyes, on the pretext that he is thus transforming her into a mare that will earn money by day and become a woman again at night. This ribald tale, one of the few that actually depict the sexual act, nevertheless provides, together with 'La Tableau', an excellent example of La Fontaine's ability to veil the grossest subject with understatement and imagery. The amorous ruse is of the coarsest, closely resembling that of 'Le Faiseur d'oreilles et le raccommodeur de nez', but the thirteen lines describing the incantatory preliminaries, which involve the laying of hands upon all parts of Magdeleine's body, suggests the friar's movements by a skilful use of geographical imagery:

> Puis cette main dans le pays s'avance.
> L'autre s'en va transformer ces deux monts
> Qu'en nos climats les gens nomment tetons;
> Car quant à ceux qui sur l'autre hémisphère
> Sont étendus plus vastes en leur tour,
> Par révérence on ne les nomme guère (593).

The various stages in Magdeleine's disrobing are described indirectly, by the friar's brief approbatory phrases:

Dégrafez-moi cet atour des dimanches;
Fort bien: ôtez ce corset et ces manches;
Encore mieux: défaites ce jupon;
Très bien cela.

As we might expect, her protests when the husband cuts the ceremony short are far shriller than those of her counterpart, and she
gives the friar a pressing invitation to return and complete the
'metamorphosis'.

The ironic muse

Irony is clearly an important ingredient of La Fontaine's humor. In
general the *contes* delineate a situation which subscribes to certain
norms, but which in the course of events is radically altered, although
appearing to remain constant to these norms. To take the commonest
situation of all, a marriage becomes, unknown to the husband, a
ménage à trois. Two of the Boccaccian *contes*, however, project another
type of irony, which I shall call irony of circumstance. In both a
peripeteia, or reversal, provides the basic structure.

Based on the familiar legend of Saint Julian the Hospitable, to
whom medieval travelers prayed for a safe journey and a comfortable
lodging at night, 'L'Oraison de Saint Julien' relates the misadven-
tures and adventures of Renaud, who is robbed by bandits and
abandoned half-naked in the freezing cold, but who finds a haven in
the arms of a beautiful widow, recovers his possessions and sees his
despoilers hanged for their crime.

Irony appears almost immediately when the bandits, asking permission to accompany Renaud on his journey, expatiate hypocritically
on the dangers of traveling alone:

En voyageant, plus la troupe est complète,
Mieux elle vaut: c'est toujours le meilleur.
Tant de brigands infectent la province,
Que l'on ne sait à quoi songe le prince
De le souffrir. Mais, quoi? les malvivants
Seront toujours (409).

La Fontaine also introduces an ironic wager as to who will find the
better lodging, proposed by one of the highwaymen, who asks laugh-
ingly if Renaud has said his prayers that morning. There follow
elaborate details. Renaud takes care to insist that his adversary must

not also invoke the saint, and stipulates that the lodging be in an inn and not the house of a friend. This preamble makes the cynical lines of the bandit all the more telling when he shows his true colors:

> J'en suis d'accord; et gage votre habit,
> Votre cheval, la bourse au préalable;
> Sûr de gagner, comme vous allez voir.

When the brigands take Renaud's boots they assure him that this will make it easier for him to continue on foot.

The eventual reversal of this situation will be the more striking because of the author's skepticism about the efficacy of prayer; he treats as 'recettes frivoles' all 'brevets, oraisons et paroles'. As the travelers journey on, they fall to talking of such prayers, which La Fontaine, unlike Boccaccio, causes to appear ludicrous by detailing their effects:

> Comme de faire aux insectes la guerre,
> Charmer les loups, conjurer le tonnerre,
> ....
> L'on se guérit, l'on guérit sa monture,
> Soit du farcin, soit de la mémarchure.

His ambivalence toward Saint Julian comes out in an aside on fate:

> Le Sort se plaît à dispenser les choses
> De la façon: c'est tout mal out tout bien:
> ....
> ...témoin les aventures
> Qu'eut cette nuit Renaud.

One should not see his rejection of 'brevets, oraisons et paroles' as evidence of anti-clericalism but rather as a skillful way of emphasizing the power of language, for in the game of love the scorned 'paroles', 'charmes' and 'brevets' acquire their full value:

> auprès d'une beauté
> Paroles ont des vertus nonpareilles;
> Paroles font en amour des merveilles
> Tout coeur se laisse à ce charme amollir.
> De tels brevets je veux bien me servir;
> Des autres, non.

These *paroles*, in La Fontaine's rendering, form an essential part of the ceremony of love. Renaud first pays the widow his compliment 'en homme bien appris', then, 'pour l'aider', she makes him an indirect declaration by comparing him with her late husband,

> Plus je vous vois, plus je crois voir aussi
> L'air et le port, les yeux, la remembrance
> De mon époux; que Dieu lui fasse paix:
> Voilà sa bouche, et voilà tous ses traits.

This kind of comparison, which strangely recalls Phèdre's avowal to Hippolyte, provides Renaud with a neat transition, for the literary device serves as an aid to his expression of love:

> Ce m'est beaucoup de gloire:
> Mais vous, Madame, à qui ressemblez-vous?
> A nul objet...

His apostrophe to her beauty reaches its crescendo in La Fontaine's witty reprise of the familiar Petrarchan balancing of love's contradictions which he deftly links to the hero's recent situation:

> Or me voici d'un mal chu dans un autre:
> Je transissais, je brûle maintenant.
> Lequel vaut mieux?

An ironical aspect of the game of love is that thought, reflection or reasoning almost never coincide with actual speech. So it is that the widow, smitten by the handsome Renaud, rejects her scruples:

> Quand je ferai, disait-elle, ce tour,
> Qui l'ira dire? il n'y va rien du nôtre.
> Si le marquis est quelque peu trompé,
> Il le mérite.

Renaud moves from compliment to action, but first the game must be played. When he lauds her beauty she deprecates it, 's'humilia pour être contredite', which gives evidence of her skill, 'une adresse à mon sens non petite'. Her very resistance is part of the game, and the impersonal 'on' suggests that the game is universal:

> On résista tout autant qu'il fallait,
> Ni plus ni moins, ainsi que chaque belle
> Sait pratiquer, pucelle ou non pucelle.

Of the first physical contact La Fontaine makes an instrument of fate, for each kiss bestowed progressively reverses Renaud's earlier misfortunes:

Voilà, disait la veuve charitable,
Pour le chemin, voici pour les brigands,
Puis pour la peur, puis pour le mauvais temps;
Tant que le tout pièce à pièce s'efface.

The conclusion reveals anew La Fontaine's skepticism concerning Saint Julian's powers. He has already declared his disbelief in the efficacy of prayer; yet he had perforce to write a tale illustrating precisely that efficacy. His opening comments, with their grudging *pourtant*, had shown the ambiguity of his attitude:

Voici pourtant un conte
Où l'oraison de Monsieur Saint Julien
A Renaud d'Ast produisit un grand bien.

The final lines maintain this ambiguity. After all this, he writes, how can one doubt the power of prayer? Yet he is careful to show that it is not he who speaks, but 'quelqu'un de ceux/Dont j'ai parlé', in other words, those who already believe in that power. And although at the end, he must pronounce Saint Julian's name, he couples it with that of God, and repeats the reductive 'Monsieur' of the earlier lines: the reversal of Renaud's misfortune is 'grâce à Dieu et Monsieur Saint Julien'.

Were it not for the ironic structure of 'Le Faucon', one would be at a loss to understand why La Fontaine chose as a model the story of Federigo Alberigui, his beloved falcon, and his hopeless love which in the original, despite its happy ending, contains more pathos than comedy. Desperately in love with the wife of a wealthy Florentine, Federigo squanders all of his considerable wealth in courting her, to no avail, and finally has nothing left but a small farm and the precious bird. The lady's husband dies, and her son becomes desperately ill, and begs for the falcon, which he has seen on visits to a property near Federigo's farm. The desperate mother decides to ask her former suitor for this last favor. When she arrives at the farm she asks to dine with him, and since he has nothing to offer her, unaware of the request she plans to make, he kills the falcon and serves it. This sacrifice so moves her that she marries him.

Nowhere in any of this do we discern a favorite theme of La Fontaine's: no amorous ruse, no triumph of nature over constraint, no exquisite game of love. The story actually postulates the contrary of one of his favorite concepts: that money opens all doors, including those to bedrooms, for Giannina, or Clitie as La Fontaine calls her, stoutly resists despite the wealth her suitor lavishes upon her. This does not prevent him from beginning with a reiteration of the theme; Fédéric, he tells us,

> Sachant très bien qu'en amour comme en guerre,
> On ne doit plaindre un métal qui fait tout,
> Renverse murs, jette portes par terre,
> N'entreprend rien dont il ne vient à bout;
> Fait taire chiens; et quand il veut servantes;
> Et quand il veut les rend plus éloquentes
> Que Cicéron, et mieux persuadantes (506).

Note that La Fontaine writes *sachant*, not *croyant*. But he skilfully puts his own commonplace to ironic use by concluding these vigorous lines with the statement that the lady besieged by such infallible assaults, 'tint bon'.

To concentrate on the ironic twist in the tale, La Fontaine seems to have felt it necessary to reduce or eliminate all pathos. Giannina's love for her ailing child and Federigo's for his falcon are essential to Boccaccio's story; La Fontaine curiously attenuates them. In the first case, Clitie's sorrow becomes the excessive emotion of a doting and over-solicitous mother:

> On sait que d'ordinaire
> A ses enfants mère ne sait que faire
> Pour leur montrer l'amour qu'elle a pour eux;
> Zèle souvent aux enfants dangereux.

The sick child appears as merely a cranky nuisance:

> Il dit qu'il veut seulement le faucon
> De Fédéric; pleure, et mène une vie
> A faire gens de bon coeur détester:
> Ce qu'un enfant a dans la fantaisie
> Incontinent il faut l'exécuter,
> Si l'on ne veut l'ouïr toujours crier.

La Fontaine's skepticism even affects the key role of the falcon, which, amusingly enough, although it made a delicious meal in the original, now furnishes tough and tasteless fare: 'La dame en mange et feint d'y prendre goût.' Surprisingly, too, La Fontaine's Fédéric hunts partridges, which naturally enough makes us wonder, why not have served some of these rather than his prize bird of prey? Further attenuating his falcon's importance, Fédéric tells Clitie that good ones may still be found:

> Ce que je puis pour vous est de chercher
> Un bon faucon; ce n'est chose si rare
> Que dès demain nous n'en puissions trouver.

Indeed, one cannot help discerning a basic uneasiness in La Fontaine's part, a revolt against even those rare pathetic moments he preserves from the original. Thus, in the conclusion he hastily returns to firmer ground by explaining that the widow's grief was shortlived:

> Deux médecins la traitèrent de sorte
> Que sa douleur eut un terme assez court:
> L'un fut le Temps, et l'autre fut l'Amour.

Again, almost as if he deplores his own choice, he emphasizes the rarity of such a case: 'Il ne faut qu'on se trompe/A cet exemple.' Quite clearly the kind of devotion that Federigo displayed has no place in the skeptical universe of the *contes*.

I have ventured to call the most pervasive type of irony in the *contes* the 'irony of female insatiability'. This irony depends on the two basic concepts of womanhood, the courtly concept, which sees her as essentially pure and lofty, and the Gallic tradition, according to which she is lust personified. Although this type of irony occurs in almost all of the Boccaccian *contes*, perhaps the best example may be found in 'La Fiancée du roi de Garbe', the story of a beautiful Saracen, Alatiel, who in four years of adventure passes through the hands of eight lovers before finally marrying her betrothed. La Fontaine creates ironic humor by assigning various lofty motives to his heroine's sexual complaisance, such as pity, charity or gratitude. Thus, when she succumbs to a lover who had threatened to kill himself, the way in which she yields 'Gaîment, de bonne grâce, et sans montrer de peine', while it actually describes her true feelings, manages to suggest self-constraint and a generous overriding of reluctance.

This ironic tone depends in large measure on a major change in La Fontaine's version of the story; the omission of violence. The original is full of blood and slaughter, with the heroine a tearful victim in fear for her life. Each of her first four lovers is murdered by his successor. In the case of the first, it is fratricide, and the fifth, after murdering his rival and a servant enjoys the princess his hands still covered with blood. La Fontaine's heroine emerges instead as a languorous and sensual beauty whose resistance is rarely more than token. In Boccaccio, Marate, after murdering his brother, threatens Alathiel with death if she makes a sound. In La Fontaine, the pirate who takes the castle of one of her lovers also makes threats, but only to deprive her of food until she yields, which she loses little time in doing. 'S'accommoder à tout est chose nécessaire', explains La Fontaine.

Boccaccio's heroine is first seduced while under the influence of wine, of whose power, as a Mohammedan, she was unaware. But La Fontaine's Alaciel was already in love with Hispal, who escorts her on the ill-fated journey to Garb, and they had exchanged letters during the voyage, long before consummating their passion in a friendly grotto after reaching shore.

Not only does violence disappear, but passion itself is replaced by a kind of sunny sensuality that at times can even be cloying.[1] The youthful pair finally tire of so much love, and Alaciel sends Hispal back to the court; a subsequent lover grows weary too, and asks a friend to take his place. Alaciel never fails to acquiesce gently, unlike her Italian counterpart who after each abrupt change of bedfellows is 'grandement et amerement dolente' (I, 173). Whatever tinge of violence remains exists on a broad, mock-heroic scale, exemplified by the attack of the pirates, whose leader the giant Grifonio carries Alaciel off 'comme un moineau', only to be sliced in two by Hispal's sword, or the two assaults on one of the lovers' castles. The first of these, launched by Grifonio's 'lieutenant', supposedly brings about the end of the lover he replaces, but we learn only that he 'cursed his fate'. The second, after which (but only reportedly) the pirate is hanged from the battlements, includes the following almost gentle account of the killing of his sleeping crew:

> Presque tout le peuple corsaire
> Du sommeil à la mort n'ayant qu'un pas à faire,
> Fut assommé sans le sentir (455).

One incident, original with La Fontaine, does include at least incipient sexual violence, although it is not directed at Alaciel but at one of her ladies-in-waiting. A gentleman of the court, known for his impetuousness, manages to lure the girl into a pavilion, locks the door, and is about to rape her when the princess appears. (La Fontaine explains that Alaciel had the key.) The desperate seducer then

---

[1] See Renée Kohn's interesting discussion of amorous satiety in *Le Goût de La Fontaine*, p. 227.

threatens both women with violence unless one yields; they must draw lots to decide which will do his bidding. Alaciel, however, always nobly motivated, offers herself immediately:

> Il ne sera pas dit que l'on ait, moi présente,
> Violenté cette innocente.

But the brute insists on the draw; she wins (La Fontaine adds ironically that Fortune favors her), and the girl escapes.

Yet even in this case the poet mitigates the violence, or at least the moral implications of resistance to it, by refusing to ascribe the girl's refusal to virtue. This is apparently why, alone of Alaciel's eight inamorati, the would-be rapist is possessed of a 'character'. Not only is he violent, skipping all niceties and preamble, he is a gossip, boasting of his conquests, and that is, suggests La Fontaine, the real reason why women resist him:

> Sa médisante humeur, grand obstacle aux faveurs,
> Peste d'amour et des douceurs
> Dont il tire sa subsistance,
> Avait de ce galant souvent grêlé l'espoir.
> La crainte lui nuisait autant que le devoir.

The ambiguity of feminine virtue could scarcely be more clearly stated.

But one of the principal sources of irony lies in Alaciel's independence as well as in her amorality. Part of this independence springs from a new characteristic, her articulateness. In the original she utters not a word, since she is ignorant of the language of all but one of her lovers, until she has returned to her father's court, where she delivers a lengthy and mendacious account of her activities since the shipwreck. Even in this case she has been carefully rehearsed by an old retainer. La Fontaine's Alaciel speaks frequently, and to the point, and the poet even makes us privy to her thoughts. Marooned on the reefs, she urges Hispal to express his love:

> Hispal, dit la princesse, il se faut consoler:
> Les pleurs ne peuvent rien près de la Parque dure.

She takes frequent initiatives: for example, when she and Hispal grow weary of love-making and long for the court, and she sends him there to bring back a ship that will return her to her home. She delivers herself, in the process, of some interesting comments on the nature of love:

> Mais qu'est-ce qu'un amour sans crainte et sans désir?
> Je vous le demande à vous-même.
> Ce sont des feux bientôt passés,
> Que ceux qui ne sont point dans leurs cours traversés;
> Il y faut un peu de contrainte.

As the story nears its close, far from being a mere victim, she is even offered the choice of returning home or of continuing on to Garb and her fiancé. She firmly chooses her father's kingdom.

On occasion she reflects, or weighs the pros and cons of her actions. As a lover entreats her, his loyal actions pass before her mind's eye. Another swain goes on a hunger strike, and she muses:

> Laisser mourir un homme, et pouvoir l'empêcher!
> C'est avoir l'âme un peu dure.

She can even strike bargains, like the one with the lover who promises to return her to the court, and whom she agrees to reward, but by degrees:

> Non tout à coup, mais à mesure
> Que le voyage se ferait;
> Tant chaque jour, sans nulle faute.

This autonomy of character had already been suggested in the preamble:

> Ce n'était après tout que bonne intention,
> Gratitude, ou compassion,
> Crainte de pis, honnête excuse.

Indeed, the word *excuse* occurs frequently, serving as an ironic leit-motiv which in general follows this pattern: 'After all, what else could she do in the circumstances?' Thus, when she yields to Hispal, La Fontaine presents her action as merely a rather common failing:

> Que l'on la blâme ou non, je sais plus d'une belle
> A qui ce fait est arrivé
> Sans en avoir moitié autant d'excuse qu'elle.

We recall that one reason for her lack of reluctance and even her enthusiasm in preventing one lover from starving himself to death was that otherwise the remedy would have been lacking in effect. When in turn the pirate threatens to starve *her*, the poet links her compliance with the previous incident, drawing his ironic effect chiefly from the word *force*:

Si par pitié d'autrui la belle se força,
Que ne point essayer par pitié de soi-même?
Elle se force donc, et prend en gré le tout.
Il n'est affliction dont on ne vienne à bout.

Thus Alaciel's amorality appears as the triumph of generosity over adversity.

The tale in both versions concludes on a note of ironic humor. Boccaccio's Alathiel reports to her father that she has spent her exile in a convent devoted to the worship of 'Saint-Croissant en Vaucreuse, auquel les femmes de ce pays-là portent grande amitié (I, 183).

After her lengthy oration Antigone, the Sultan's old servitor, who had met her in Cyprus and escorted her to her father's court, gravely confirms the truth of her recital. In the French version the tutor of her last lover had accompanied her to Alexandria, and it is he who tells her father of her exemplary conduct while in exile. Alaciel remains silent during his dithyramb, but La Fontaine adds that as she listens she 'riait sans doute dans l'âme'. The tutor's speech affords a superb example of La Fontaine's ironic treatment of love. Rejecting the rather obvious pun of 'St Crescent', as well as *Vaucreuse* (hollow vale),[1] La Fontaine nevertheless expands Boccaccio's suggestion of the religion of love, in a tone of wonderment at strange customs reminiscent of *Les Provinciales* or *Les Lettres persanes*:

Je ne vous aurais jamais dit
Tout ses temples et ses chapelles,
Nommés pour la plupart alcôves et ruelles.

The reader may recognize in the god worshipped in these strange temples,
un certain oiseau
Qui dans ses portraits est fort beau
Quoiqu'il n'ait des plumes qu'aux ailes,

either as Cupid or a veiled allusion to the phallus. Alaciel, the tutor goes on, has served this god well, and had her father known, he would have thanked Heaven for a 'fille tant accomplie'.

For La Fontaine only the young can really love, and this opinion appears again with regard to their exotic god:

[1] He uses it, however, in 'Le Roi Candaule', where he repeats an error in Le Maçon's translation, *Vavoureuse*, suggesting he may have missed the pun.

Au contraire des autres dieux,
Qu'on ne sert que quand on est vieux,
La jeunesse lui sacrifie.

The customs of the Muslims are skillfully evoked to suggest through contrast the true nature of Alaciel's activities:

Au reste en ces pays on vit d'autre façon
Que parmi vous; les belles vont et viennent;
Point d'eunuques qui les retiennent;
Les hommes en ces lieux ont tous barbe au menton.

The conclusion contains the same ambivalence as the ironic counterpointing of the heroine's character and actions. The story, says La Fontaine, proves that husbands seldom know the truth about their wives' adventures, yet as if fearful that the reader might take this as an invitation to license, he brings himself up short: 'Filles, maintenez-vous'. It proves as well that loss of virginity and a series of amorous adventures need not produce tragic consequences; the remedy restates the ironic paradox: like Alaciel, one should 'rire en son malheur'.

In 'La Fiancée', as we have seen, the poet attenuates or transforms the violence of the original so that the heroine's plight becomes ironic. The chief interest of 'Le Faiseur d'oreilles et le raccommodeur de moules' derives from the way the violence inherent in this story of wife-trading is first suspended, then transformed by the trick of sexual vengeance. This incipient violence is nowhere in Boccaccio or in the corollary source, *Les Cent Nouvelles nouvelles*. In the former's version, Seppe sees his wife and his friend embracing and going into the bedroom, and immediately reflects on how he can take vengeance without making his reasons public, yet satisfying his self-respect. The theme of the fear of scandal or humiliation so frequent in Boccaccio recurs here: Seppe says nothing because he realizes that 'shouting can in no way lessen his injury'.

Guillaume, La Fontaine's cuckold, on his return home learns of his disgrace from the gullible Alix herself, and in his fury actually grabs a weapon to kill her. Somewhat appeased by her pleas of innocence, he nevertheless threatens her if she fails to carry out his order to entice her seducer to the house: 'Soyez secrète, ou bien vous êtes morte.' When she does his bidding to the letter, La Fontaine emphasizes her stupidity by noting, 'La crainte donne aux bêtes de l'esprit'.

It appears for a moment that Guillaume's vengeance will be drastic indeed, for he threatens castration,

> Ne le voulant sans doute assassiner;
> Mais quelque oreille au pauvre homme couper:
> Peut-être pis, ce qu'on coupe en Turquie (392).

He sends Alix to fetch André's wife, and to tell her that if she fails to comply her husband will suffer

> Chose terrible et dont le seul penser
> Vous fait dresser les cheveux à la tête.

Meanwhile, however, Guillaume has changed his mind; his vengeance will be to enjoy André's wife before his eyes; violence has become sexual. In Boccaccio this vengeful intercourse takes place on a chest in which the seducer is hiding; La Fontaine's brutal Guillaume throws his friend's wife down upon the bed beside which André crouches in fear,

> Sire Guillaume était de son côté
> Si fort ému, tellement irrité,
> Qu'à la pauvrette il ne fit nulle grâce.

In the last line we recognize an ironic pattern similar to that of 'La Fiancée du roi de Garbe'. André's wife heroically submits to the assault, blessing Heaven

> que la vengeance
> Tombait sur elle, et non sur sire André,
> Tant elle avait pour lui de charité.

Although in Alix' case violence is not involved, hers is also a command performance, for André, before spinning his yarn about the need to forge an ear for her unborn child, indulges in no formalities:

> André survient, qui sans long compliment
> La considère, et lui dit froidement...

Alix is one of a long line of women seduced because of their ignorance, but this does not prevent her from enjoying her task:

> Tant ne fut nice (encor que nice fût)
> Madame Alix, que ce jeu ne lui plût.
> Philosopher ne faut pour cette affaire.

Secondary ironies derive from André's and Alix' intercourse viewed as a *task*. André sets to work *diligently* and *efficiently*; one notes the play on the word *affection*:

> André vaquait de grande affection
> A son travail; faisant ore un tendon,
> Ore un repli, puis quelque cartilage;
> Et n'y plaignant l'étoffe et la façon.

When he returns the next day he tells Alix he has dropped everything to finish the job, and she replies that she had been on the point of sending him a message that the work must be dispatched as soon as possible.

By thus transforming physical into sexual violence, La Fontaine not only creates an irony similar to that of 'La Fiancée' but suggests, through the two women who enjoy their experience, a sense of discovery, even joy. Revenge in this case may be really sweet – 'Qu'on dit bien vrai que se venger est doux' – and the old saw about the futility of jealousy takes on new meaning:

> Puisqu'il voulait son honneur réparer,
> Il ne pouvait mieux que par cette porte
> D'un tel affront, à mon sens, se tirer.

Similar irony derives from the discovery of the flesh in 'Le Diable en enfer'. An innocent girl decides to emulate the saints about whom she has read by forsaking home and parents and wandering alone into the wilderness. She falls in with a youngish hermit who takes her in so as to test his powers of resistance to temptation. These fail, however, in the face of her beauty, as do finally his sexual powers, and the girl returns home, to find a husband who will not tire of 'putting the devil into hell'.

The irony of innocence permeates the story. In a few lines La Fontaine evokes the dreamy idealism of the adolescent:

> Oh! Quel plaisir j'aurais, si tous les ans,
> La palme en main, les rayons sur la tête,
> Je recevais des fleurs et des présents! (585)

Yet even this naïve girl incarnates temptation, as we can see from the near panic of the old man at whose door she knocks when in her wanderings she seeks shelter. His comic haste to be rid of her suggests the secondary theme: that love triumphs over fasting, mortification of the flesh, even decrepitude:

> Allez le voir, ne tardez davantage:
> Je ne retiens tels oiseaux dans ma cage.
> Disant ces mots, le vieillard la quitta,
> Fermant sa porte, et se barricada.

The seduction itself is a process of resistance and compliance, in a skillful blend of participles and the adverb *moitié*, leading to the consummation of the last lines:

> Moitié forcée et moitié consentante,
> Moitié voulant combattre ce désir,
> Moitié n'osant, moitié peine et plaisir,
> Elle crut faire acte de repentante;
> Bien humblement rendit grâce au frater;
> Sut ce que c'est que le diable en enfer.

From the equivalence *diable* = male member; *enfer* = female member, the poet draws an abundance of ironic wit. *Enfer* also becomes a prison, so that the girl may say wistfully when her lover tires,

> Qu'il n'est prison si douce que son hôte
> En peu de temps ne s'y lasse sans faute.

When she returns to her family, somewhat like Alaciel, the metaphor expands to include her whole demeanour, the prison becoming a *chartre* which reveals nothing of her past:

> Mais cette chartre est faite de façon
> Qu'on n'y voit goutte, et maint geôlier s'y trompe.

In the end Alibech, like Alaciel, marries an unsuspecting husband, who is happy for being none the wiser.

Insatiability is not so much the subject of 'Le Calendrier des vieillards' as unjust starvation, and the butt of the irony is Richard, the generous but aged and impotent husband of the beautiful Bartholomée, who in order to excuse his sexual inadequacy claims that the act is impious on saint's or holy days, and creates a calendar which prohibits almost every day in the year. La Fontaine elaborates on Richard's ingenuity, showing us how he manages, if saint's days are lacking to invoke,

> les jours malencontreux,
> Puis les brouillards, et puis la canicule (432),

or assigning to each day of the week particular attributes, unsuited to husbandly duties. Finally four days remain, and thus,

> Quatre fois l'an, de grâce spéciale,
> Notre docteur régalait sa moitié.

When Bartholomée is captured by a handsome pirate, her resistance, as we may expect from the tradition, is perfunctory: 'La belle fit son devoir de pleurer'. When Richard traces her to the pirate's ship, her captor offers to let her go if she so choses, and in a remarkable confrontation scene with her husband she first pretends not to recognize him, and later, when they are alone together, tells him frankly why she prefers to remain with the lusty corsair:

> Je suis de chair, les habits rien n'y font:
> Vous savez bien, Monsieur, qu'entre la tête
> Et le talon d'autres affaires sont.

In most of these *contes*, behind the suggestion of feminine insatiability lurks the hint of male impotency. In the case of Bartholomée and Richard, La Fontaine transforms the Gallic tradition into a plea for the rights of nature.

No single character better illustrates the power of the sexual drive in woman than the nun, a favorite subject of the *contes*. Salacious monks are legendary; they hold the power of religion over their female parishioners, and their libidinous acts interest but scarcely surprise us. Furthermore, the nun's dalliance illustrates a favorite theme of the Boccaccian *contes*, that 'Desire is the daughter of constraint', so that paradoxically, like the story of the old man's calendar, prohibition militates in favor of following nature.

'Mazet de Lamporechio' tells of a country bumpkin who pretends to be a deaf-mute in order to be engaged as a gardener in a convent; who lets himself be seduced by the nuns, and finally, at the end of his strength, has to speak up in order to obtain respite. Irony results from both imagery and symbolism in this *conte*. The whiteness of the nuns' wimples and of their skin provides an ironic play on the purity traditionally associated with that color. The author warns:

> ne faut qu'on s'imagine
> Que d'être pure et nette de péché
> Soit privilège à la guimpe attaché (469).

Again he associates the whiteness of this ecclesiastical garment with the nun's worldly concern for their appearance:

Tant ne songeaient au service divin,
Qu'à soi montrer ès parloirs aguimpées
Bien blanchement, comme droites poupées.

At high noon, he tells us, the garden is almost deserted because the nuns are afraid of sunburn.

Another symbol stresses their earthiness, their natural urges, despite their solitude and regimentation. The age-old correspondence between tilling the earth and the sexual act had already been suggested by Boccaccio, whose Mazet mentally promises the abbess, 'je laboureray tellement vostre jardin qu'il ne fust jamais si bien labouré' (250). La Fontaine develops this into a series of *quiproquos* in the aged retiring gardener's warnings to his young successor. Thus, the nuns are 'un étrange bétail', and the old man, in order to say that whoever does not know their whims should beware, uses the suggestive expression 'tâter de cette marchandise', and to explain that they were forever asking him to do contrary things, tells Mazet, 'l'un voudra du mou/L'autre du dur'. Again, the equivocal nature of the verb *planter* in this context is clear:

L'une voudra que tu plantes des choux,
L'autre voudra que ce soit des carottes.

One finds a similar play on words *jeûne* or *jeûner*; fasting is of course a religious penance, but when Mazet spends all his time with the abbess, 'les soeurs jeûnèrent très longtemps'. In the next line we learn that she fed him well: 'Mazet n'avait faute de restaurants', but that this was not enough to maintain his vigor in the situation. Finally, when in desperation he speaks, the abbess cries Miracle, summons the sisters and announces that their fasting has restored to Mazet the power of speech.

To this type of irony one might add that of the lively dialogue between the two nuns who first discover Mazet, the first of whom immediately makes plans, choosing the place, rejecting her companion's half-hearted scruples and proposing that one of them act as a guard while the other is with the gardener. The more timid sister repeatedly offers to be obliging in exactly the same manner as Alaciel:

Je passerai, si tu veux, la première
Pour t'obliger: au moins à ton loisir
Tu t'ébattras puis après de manière
Qu'il ne sera besoin d'y retourner:
Ce que j'en dis n'est que pour t'obliger.

La Fontaine apologized humorously for the fact that nuns figure prominently in his *contes*; they appear in five, to be exact, only two of which are imitated from Boccaccio. 'Le Psautier', the story of a nun who is scolded before the assembled sisters for entertaining a lover by the abbess who herself has just left the arms of the local priest, and in her haste has put his breeches on her head instead of the 'psalter', contains a brief prologue in which the author jocularly explains why nuns play such an important role. In the long run it's your own fault, he tells them,

> – Que voulez-vous? Je n'y saurais que faire;
> Si vous teniez toujours votre bréviaire,
> Vous n'auriez rien à démêler ici.

'*Proprement une nouvelle nouvelle*'

In the preamble to the fourth day Boccaccio speaks bitterly of his critics, who accuse him of being too eager to please the ladies by his stories, or of wasting his time when he should be pursuing a loftier muse. In order to illustrate how natural it is that one should admire the fair sex, he tells the story of Filippo Balducci, the hermit and son. The worthy anchorite, who had taken his infant son with him into the woods after his wife's death, some twenty years later realizes that his life is nearing its end and that he must show his son how to collect alms in the city. When his son sees its palaces, its statuary, its parks, he is full of wonder. But when some young girls pass by he is overcome with admiration and urges his father to take one back with them to the forest.

This particular story may serve to illustrate how La Fontaine could make of his source 'proprement une nouvelle nouvelle'. While retaining the skeleton of the tale, he puts it to an entirely different purpose. Its goal is now to illustrate, not how natural it is to admire womankind, but his own good will toward the fair sex in general, and to silence those who charge him with slanderously suggesting that 'les faveurs sont chez vous familières'.

One is first of all struck by the extent of La Fontaine's amplification. A fifty-five line preamble sets forth his position in a manner reminiscent of the preface to the second part. His tales are humorous, not serious, we hear again; there is much greater danger in idle flirting than in reading them, since they can amuse us even as we condemn their frivolity. He identifies himself with his literary creation, asking, how could I, who have served women in so many ways, suddenly wish to make them do ill? He then turns to the 'censors'. No moral is intended: 'Contons, mais contons bien; c'est le point principal.' You may attack my verse, even my style, he goes on, but when I tell a good story, desist!

A glance at La Fontaine's method of amplifying and reconstructing his model shows how he built, from Boccaccio's brief prologue, one of the finest of the *contes*. He first of all organizes the story in a series of reprises, summarizing the whole tale in ten lines as if to present it as a total gift to women. In the process he unerringly hits on a structure that will renovate Boccaccio's story, that of the contrast of beauties. The fact that the hermit brings his son up in the forest suggests readily the beauty of nature so that the ten-line presentation first of all compares feminine charms to the splendor of spring and the dawn:

> Vous auriez surpassé le printemps et l'aurore
> Dans l'esprit d'un garçon, si dès ses jeunes ans,
> Outre l'éclat des cieux, et les beautés des champs,
> Il eût vu les vôtres encore (478).

He completely reverses the chronological order of the story, using key phrases like the following to indicate the essential facts: 'On l'avait dès l'enfance élevé dans un bois.' – 'Son père l'amena dès ses plus tendres ans.' – 'Sa femme disparut s'envolant dans les cieux.' – 'Il voulut être hermite et destina son fils.' – 'Au fond d'une forêt il arrête ses pas.' – 'Cet homme s'appelait Philippe, dit l'histoire.'

This reversal of Boccaccio's and indeed the natural order, which begins with the identification of the main protagonist, has the immediate effect of concentrating our attention on child rather than parent. The first ten lines, in which feminine beauty is opposed to 'l'éclat des cieux, et les beautés des champs', creates a certain suspense, for one wonders how the boy 'laissa les palais' for the sake of 'vos beautés', or in what context he found 'votre personne' more attractive than 'tous les joyaux de la couronne'.

From this point on, La Fontaine progressively reveals the situation of the child. First of all, his solitude and his ignorance of human beings:

> On l'avait dès l'enfance élevé dans un bois.
> Là son unique compagnie
> Consistait aux oiseaux; leur aimable harmonie
> Le désennuyait quelquefois.

Into this atmosphere of solitude and ennui, the poet introduces the idea of schooling: 'En une école si sauvage/Son père l'amena dès ses plus tendres ans', thus preparing us for the austere discipline to which the father subjects his son:

> Au progrès de ses ans réglant en ce séjour
> La nourriture de son âme.

This idea of a gradual education, developing and expanding as the boy grows, is La Fontaine's, and lends depth and duration to the story. Thus, at intervals of five years, new elements are introduced: at five he learns the names of flowers, animals and birds, and, curiously, is warned of the Devil. It is here we encounter the strange line, 'La crainte est aux enfants la première leçon'. At ten, the boy learns something about Heaven, and finally, at fifteen, his Father tells him of the Deity. At each step La Fontaine reminds us that the boy is taught nothing about women.

As a result, when the time comes for him to accompany his father to the city, the expedition appears as a further step in the boy's education, and the stress on his ignorance of 'la créature' in the preliminary stages also deftly prepares the scenes of his visual wonderment. Just before these scenes occur, La Fontaine inserts a brief sketch that attenuates our impression of the hermit's cold austerity, for he is beloved by the city-dwellers and especially by the children:

> Tous les petits enfants
> Le connaissaient, et, du haut de leur tête,
> Ils criaient: Apprêtez la quête!
> Voilà frère Philippe.

La Fontaine further humanizes the character by showing his fear at exposing his son to the temptations of the city: 'ce ne fut qu'en pleurant qu'il exposa ce fils'.

The poet also succeeds remarkably in conveying the delighted amazement of the boy whose eyes take him from one wonder to the next. The laconic replies of the hermit reveal his reluctance to expatiate on the nature of such marvels:

> Le jeune homme, tombé des nues,
> Demandait: Qu'est-ce là? – Ce sont gens de cour.
> – Et là? – Ce sont palais. – Ici? – Ce sont statues.

But these aspects of the 'cité superbe, bien bâtie' fade before the most exquisite of apparitions: a group of girls. The lines that record the youth's delight are linked to those of the preamble: 'il n'eut d'yeux que pour vous;/il laissa les palais':

> Dès lors nulle autre chose
> Ne put ses regards attirer.
> Adieu palais; adieu ce qu'il vient d'admirer.

The questions begin again and follow fast: 'Qu'est-ce là...Comment l'appelle-t-on?' To which the hermit makes the grumpy reply: 'C'est un oiseau qui s'appelle oie.' One should note in passing that where Boccaccio has the hermit say merely, 'Elles se nomment oyes', La Fontaine specifically links them to birds, the very birds that had been the youth's companions in solitude:

> Là son unique compagnie
> Consistait aux oiseaux...
> ....
> Tout son plaisir était cet innocent ramage.

The repetition of *oiseau* somewhat obscures the usual connotation of stupidity associated with geese, but more than that, it emphasizes the naiveté of the youth's request that they bring one back to the forest with them.

The last lines are the youth's entreaty to the girls and to his father:

> Oie, hélas, chante un peu, que j'entende ta voix.
> Peut-on point un peu te connaître?
> Mon père, je vous prie et mille et mille fois,
> Menons-en une en notre bois;
> J'aurai soin de la faire paître.

Boccaccio's hermit offers a gloss on the word *paître* – 'tu ne sçaiz point par où elles se paissent' – which La Fontaine wisely omits, justifying Mme de Sévigné's praise of the *conte's* ending. Readers of Lucretius and Ronsard, among other poets, will recall that *paître*, from *pascere*, conveys the poetic sense of 'graze amorously' so that the equivocation is somewhat more delicate here than in the original.[1]

In fact this type of refinement pervades the entire poem. The message is obvious enough and merely reiterates a favorite theme, that nature will have her way over constraint and concealment. But to convey the glory of woman, brilliance and splendor are predominant. The only season is spring, the only hour is dawn; skies and fields shine with similar beauty. On the worldly scale the sole worthy terms

[1] See above, p. 28.

in the comparison with woman's fairness are crown jewels, or sumptuous palaces and sculptures. As to the hermit's isolation even loneliness is tinged with a delicate languor:

> Il ne s'en figura, pendant un fort long temps,
>   Point d'autres que les habitants
>   De cette forêt; c'est-à-dire
> Que des loups, des oiseaux, enfin ce qui respire
> Pour respirer sans plus, et ne songer à rien.

The merest suggestion of terror is exorcized by litotes: 'Les loups n'étaient pas gens qui donnassent l'aumône.'

'Les Oies de Frère Philippe', as well as 'La Fiancée du roi de Garbe', provide two of the richest examples of La Fontaine's inventive technique, each, although using Boccaccio as a starting point, becoming 'proprement une nouvelle nouvelle'. However, the complexity of almost all the other Boccaccian tales appears to have required of their adapter such a close concentration on the actual matter of the narrative as to leave little room for improvisation. Despite this, La Fontaine manages frequently to assert the presence of the narrator. One of his more frequent ways of doing so is to show his commitment to the main subject, the pursuit of love, by referring to his own amours, or by identifying himself with a particular amorous character. Thus, he can conclude a *conte* by wishing that in a similar circumstance he had used the same trick, or, comparing himself to a lecherous abbé who takes drastic action to have his way, demur:

> Ce n'est mon goût; je ne veux de plein saut
> Prendre la ville, aimant mieux l'escalade (569).

Elsewhere, his own experience has taught him to fear the effects of love and to resolve never to become its slave: 'Plus ne m'irai brûler à la chandelle.' Or he can appear actually to share the passion of his protagonist, exclaiming:

> A cet objet qui n'eût eu l'âme émue!
>   Qui n'eût eu des désirs!
> Un philosophe, un marbre, une statue,
> Auraient senti comme nous ces plaisirs.

The 'comme nous' in the last line evidently suggests his identity not only with the character but with his reader as well. He directly addresses reader or critic, anticipating objections and answering them, as in 'La Fiancée', when he makes sure that the lovers salvage a casket of jewels:

> Pourquoi, me dira-t-on, nous ramener toujours
> Cette cassette? est-ce une circonstance
> Qui soit de si grande importance?
> Oui, selon mon avis…(448).

On occasion he will even rebut his readers' imagined arguments: 'Ne m'allez point conter: c'est le droit des garçons' (463); or justify a seeming inconsistency by a vague reference to an overheard remark, as when one of Alaciel's lovers comes to her bedroom after she has been drugged with wine:

> Quoi trouver? dira-t-on, d'immobiles appas?
> – Si j'en trouvais autant, je saurais bien qu'en faire,
> Disait l'autre jour un certain:
> Qu'il me vienne une même affaire,
> On verra si j'aurai recours à mon voisin.

This argumentative pose emphasizes the author's concern with his esthetic as well as his freedom; in the same vein, somewhat resembling what we shall call in discussing Ariosto[1] 'the subservient narrator', he will strike a pose of voluntary ignorance or incapacity, for example, ascribing certain actions to hearsay, a method which may produce irony, as in the case of Alaciel:

> On dit même qu'en peu de temps
> Elle perdit la mémoire
> De ses deux derniers galants:
> Je n'ai pas de peine à le croire.

This suggestion of rumor softens the impression of Alaciel's looseness and permits the author to avoid indicting her; he merely believes, without difficulty, a vague allegation. He may also disclaim the ability to do justice to a scene or an action. Thus, to express Zaïr's delight at the return of his daughter, he tells us, is beyond his power,

> je n'en puis plus faire: il est bon que j'imite
> Phébus, qui sur la fin du jour
> Tombe d'ordinaire si court
> Qu'on dirait qu'il se précipite.

The mythological image diverts our attention from the rather banal scene of a father welcoming his long-lost daughter; in choosing this

---

[1] p. 96, below.

way of saying nothing, La Fontaine achieves what one might call perspective through incongruity, emphasizing his point by the very inappropriateness of the comparison to Apollo. Moreover, the disclaimer of percipience, through a skillful use of *soit que*, can maintain the aura of female mystery. The beauteous widow desires Renaud d'Ast, but her reasons remain imprecise:

> Soit que déjà l'attente du plaisir
> L'eût disposée, ou soit par sympathie,
> Ou que la mine, ou bien le procédé
> De Renaud d'Ast eussent son coeur touché.

Just as, in these examples, the narrator shuns responsibility, in others he appears to hold forthright opinions. One concept to which he adheres most consistently urges that man should 'follow Nature' – that love will have its way, that the young should marry the young, that beauty is more important than class. Others are more cynical, such as the oft-reiterated suggestion that money buys love.

Thus, love actually thrives on obstacles: 'C'est là ou l'amour fait le mieux ses affaires', and this forms the burden of his counsel to parents and husbands alike:

> Ne gênez point, je vous en donne avis,
> Tant vos enfants, ô vous, pères et mères;
> Tant vos moitiés, vous époux et maris (401).

Here, and frequently elsewhere, La Fontaine speaks as a moralist. Nature is the norm, and again, parents are at fault who, in marrying off their children, think only of the dowry and never of physical compatibility – 'ce qui fait la paix du marriage'. Yet the same parents take care to see that even their beasts of burden are suitably matched: horses, oxen, even dogs, 'de force pareille/Sont toujours pris' (430). How then, he asks, can a marriage succeed, 'étant un attelage/Qui bien souvent ne se rapporte en rien?'

But love triumphs over such difficulties, without which its delights are even diminished. Class barriers themselves, although for La Fontaine they must have been immutable, prove no obstacle; in fact the simplicity of the lower classes permits a 'natural' love that dispenses with ceremony, 'ces longs soupirs, et tout ce vain martyre'. Pinuccio's mistress, despite her origins, possesses aristocratic taste,

> Le coeur trop haut, le goût trop délicat,
> Pour s'en tenir aux amours de village (401).

Of course, for all her discrimination the girl would never dream of changing her class – 'Non qu'elle crût pouvoir changer d'état' – no doubt an attribute in La Fontaine's eyes, although the narrator can express a certain contempt for rank, declaring forthrightly, 'Prenez le titre et laissez-moi la rente' (508).

Thus the declared belief in the power of love itself, followed by an emphasis on the essential role of money, are not necessarily discordant. Frequently the idea is nuanced; it may take the guise of praise of generosity which, joined with wit and good looks, ensures success,

> Qu'on soit bien fait, qu'on ait quelque talent,
> Que les cordons de la bourse ne tiennent;
> Je vous le dis, la place est au galant (607).

Even when he announces forthrightly 'l'argent fait tout', this unpleasant truth is blunted by portraying the venality of Italy as greater than that of France through a striking pictorial image, reminiscent of emblem literature:

> Pour tout carquois, d'une large escarcelle
> En ce pays le dieu d'amour se sert (366).

Or an attenuating statement will follow. He declares:

> Gratis est mort; plus d'amour sans payer:
> En beaux louis se content les fleurettes (436).

But he hastens to add: 'Ce que je dis, des coquettes s'entend.'

The comparison between France and Italy recalls, in a general way, the duality of narrator and source, to which La Fontaine almost never fails to allude. He not only adds to the title of most of the *contes* inspired by Boccaccio (and even to some that are not!) a notation to that effect, but he will on occasion refer, in the course of the story itself, to 'Maître Boccace, auteur de cette histoire' (405). But rather than playing the 'subservient narrator', and excusing or explaining away questionable elements by referring to the need for following the source, as he does with Ariosto, he can forthrightly declare that he is adding or changing the 'plaisant cas' of 'Maître François':

> Ami lecteur, ne te déplaira pas
> Si, sursoyant ma principale histoire,
> Je te remets cette chose en mémoire (551).

This easy insouciance can even suggest he is modifying his source because he disapproves its choice of words, when actually the vocabulary is his own, in order to provide an excellent 'negligent' transition:

> Aldobrandin était de cette dame
> Bail et mari: pourquoi bail? Ce mot-là
> Ne me plaît point; c'est mal dit que cela;
> Car un mari ne baille point sa femme.
> Aldobrandin la sienne ne baillait (608).

We recall that in the second preface La Fontaine vigorously claimed the right to change his sources in this manner, whether by expanding or reducing them. As we have seen, except for major instances like 'La Fiancée du roi de Garbe' or 'Les Oies de Frère Philippe', he makes only minor alterations in the Boccaccian *contes*. The bulk of these, aside from the various types of author's interventions discussed above, appear to group themselves under two headings: (1) verisimilitude or consistency, and (2) dramatization.

Thus, it may have appeared more logical in 'Le Faiseur d'oreilles' to La Fontaine for André to hide in the *ruelle* beside the bed in which Guillaume wreaks his vengeance on André's wife, rather than in the chest on top of which the exploit takes place in Boccaccio's version. But the substitution may also have been made to increase the tension through making the husband the witness of his own betrayal, for as we shall see elsewhere, La Fontaine frequently indulges in a kind of voyeurism. The original Pinuccio replies arrogantly when challenged by the innkeeper, 'Que me sçaurois-tu faire?', while it seems more in keeping with the tone of 'Le Berceau', which involves the fear of discovery, that he should be petrified with fright. And we recall that as we saw in another tale, 'Le Muletier', the hero's fast-beating pulse appears more explicable if he does not know, as does his counterpart in the Italian version, that the king is unarmed. In the same tale, the king's easy equanimity is reinforced by his final jest, which is La Fontaine's invention.

Such an addition reinforces the lightness of tone. Similarly, expansion can heighten credibility, in particular where supplementary detail contributes to character delineation. Thus La Fontaine expands upon Fédéric's profligacy, which emphasizes both the depth of his love and his subsequent poverty. We witness the full panoply of courtly entertainment: balls, the theatre, even tournaments in the lady's honor. The favorite of Fouquet also recalls the merchants and artists that benefit from the rich man's generosity:

> marchands de toutes guises,
> Faiseurs d'habits, et faiseurs de devises,
> Musiciens, gens du sacré vallon...

Such a display of riches attracts other women, who use all their wiles to no avail,

> l'une un mot suborneur,
> L'autre un coup d'oeil, l'autre quelque autre avance.

On occasion the development of a detail can provide a thematic harmony lacking in the original. In 'Féronde' the point of departure is the sleeping powder with which the lecherous abbot drugs his mistress' husband. Boccaccio tells us merely that this was 'une pouldre de merveilleuse vertu ès parties du Levant, d'un grand prince, lequel affermoit qu'on en souloit user pour la vigille de la montaigne, quand aucun vouloit envoyer en dormant quelqu'un en son paradis ou l'en faire sortir' (I, 326). A phrase in this sentence, in Italian, 'per lo Veglio de la Montana', may have suggested to La Fontaine the 49-line passage on the false paradise. As Régnier points out, the story of the Old Man of the Mountain and his fanatical followers enjoyed considerable currency at the time, and the association of ideas must have come readily to our poet's pen.[1]

As usual La Fontaine attenuates the violence in the legend: there is no mention either of hashish or its role as an incitement to murder. The pleasures of this paradise are sylvan and sensual, a harmony of natural and human delights in which brooks warble like birds and lutes accompany the song of nightingales:[2]

> Au gazouillis des ruisseaux de ces bois,
> Au son de luths accompagnant les voix
> Des rossignols (567).

He concludes his addition by explaining it as a 'confirmation' of Féronde's story. The only obvious link between the rite of the mountain and the main body of the *conte* is the magic powder that induces a death-like trance, yet the new passage does bear a thematic resemblance to Féronde's adventure. The linking of the false Mohammedan paradise to the unscrupulous ruse of the abbot, the gullibility of

---

[1] *Œuvres*, ed. Régnier, v, 381–2.
[2] These lines are in the tradition of the *locus amoenus*. See E. R. Curtius, *European Literature and the Latin Middle Ages*, tr. W. E. Trask, (New York: Harper, 1953), pp. 183 ff.

the heathen to that of Christians, also intensifies the mockingly anti-religious tone of the *conte*, despite the care with which La Fontaine calls the prophet 'le faux Mahom' or 'ce prophète menteur'. The sensuous cleric lives only for pleasure,

> Fuyant la peine, aimant le plaisir pur,
> Ainsi que fait tout bon suppôt de Rome (569).

His delights resemble those of the Mohammedans, his languorous sloth that of the false paradise,

> N'ayant autre oeuvre, autre emploi, penser autre,
> Que de chercher où gisaient les bons vins,
> Les bons morceaux, et les bonnes commères,
> Sans oublier les gaillardes nonnains (568).

The false purgatory lends itself to amusing plays on this aspect of Christian belief. Féronde's guards are 'anges' – in reality novices hired by the abbot – who console and cleanse their charge with blows of their whips. The poet calls the gullible Féronde 'l'âme', since his captors feed him far too little for a body. When the abbot – whose 'oeuvres de charité' with the wife have borne unexpected fruit – decides to resuscitate him,

> on vit du purgatoire
> L'âme sortir, légère, et n'ayant pas
> Une once de chair.

It would probably be incorrect to assume from these thrusts any anti-clericalism on La Fontaine's part, but rather the assertion of his own skeptical and mocking personality. The addition itself serves to provide depth, to reinforce and universalize the rather slight adventure of Féronde. Like the summary of Panurge's joust with the sheep merchant in 'L'Abbesse', like the story of Gygès in 'Le Roi Candaule et le maître en droit', and the diatribe on cuckoldry in 'Le Petit Chien qui secoue de l'argent et des pierreries', the oriental paradise provides an analogical function, underlining the exemplary quality of the tale. But it also constitutes a declaration of independence, the creation of a perspective slightly different from that of the source, which the author may conclude at will, always reminding the reader of his control: 'Or ai-je été prolixe...', or 'Mon dessein n'était pas d'étendre cette histoire...'

Another aspect of the author's recreation of his material is the dramatic quality La Fontaine imparts to certain of his Boccaccian *contes.* The convention Boccaccio chose for his tales, that of a group whose members take turns telling stories, so that the audience is itself composed of narrators, may explain in part La Fontaine's continual presence in his tales, but the dramatic tone that results may also have inspired the poet to seek a similar quality through accentuating dialogue and by increasing on occasion the number of interlocutors. In some instances he will even identify the speakers as in the text of a play.

One has only to glance at the dialogue between Richard and Catelle after the success of his ruse to realize the remarkable range and movement, wholly dramatic in form, into which La Fontaine has transformed Catelle's diatribe in Boccaccio's version. Now her speech is clearly addressed to an interlocutor, upon whom she heaps imprecations; 'C'est trop souffrir, traître, ce lui dit-elle'; 'Parle, méchant'; whom she bombards with orders, 'Laisse-moi-là', and rhetorical questions:

> suis-je pourvue
> De moins d'appas? Ai-je moins d'agrément,
> Moins de beauté, que ta dame Simone?

When Richard, who has kept silent with difficulty, bursts out laughing, after she tearfully wonders why she doesn't summon the adoring Minutolo:

> Tu ris, dit-elle, ô dieux! quelle insolence!

Thus, even when for comic effect one protagonist must remain silent during the tirade, Catelle's imprecations and exclamations, and finally Richard's guffaw, maintain the illusion of a dialogue.

Lively exchanges between two or more characters are frequent. The rapid discussion, just before they rob him, between Renaud D'Ast and the highwaymen masquerading as simple wayfarers, replaces the lengthy talk in Boccaccio. La Fontaine succeeds admirably in conveying the casual, bantering tone of the thieves as they ask Renaud if he believes in prayers:

> Mais vous, ce lui dit-on,
> Savez-vous point aussi quelque oraison?
> De tels secrets, dit-il, je ne me pique (80).

Renaud goes on simply and slightly sententiously, to explain how each morning he addresses a brief prayer to Saint Julian. His companion continues the game:

Et ce matin, Monsieur, l'avez-vous dite?
Lui repartit l'un des trois en riant.

This swift repartee has all the elements of drama and in addition it produces dramatic irony. We are aware of the fate that awaits Renaud, as the bandit seems almost to wink at us, while the victim carefully propounds the conditions of a wager already lost.

Similar dramatic irony occurs in 'La Gageure des trois commères', where the chief interest of the first ruse consists almost entirely of the wife's tirade, which illustrates once again how well La Fontaine's decasyllabic line lends itself to an easy flow of words, sarcastic, denunciatory, triumphant, creating a remarkable effect of spontaneity. The irony arises out of the double meaning, both for the reader and for the disguised lover, of the wife's words. When she exclaims:

Un peu plus tôt vous me le deviez dire:
J'aurais chez moi toujours eu des tendrons.
De celui-ci, pour certaines raisons,
Vous faut passer (423),

we do not miss the irony of the phrase 'pour certaines raisons', as well as her concluding remark to the 'chambermaid':

A l'avenir, je vous jure ma foi
Que nuit et jour vous serez près de moi.

Another dramatic characteristic of the same tirade is the way the wife implicates, by directly addressing them, the two other protagonists:

Et vous, la belle au dessein si gaillard,
Merci de moi, chambrière d'un liard...

Then she swings around, as if addressing an audience, and one almost sees her gesture: 'voyez un peu, dirait-on qu'elle y touche?', before she marches 'her' off in seeming disgrace to her own bedroom.

The first wife's victory seems the greater because only she speaks, but the second episode, involving the false hallucination of the husband in the pear tree as the lovers sport below, includes a portion of dialogue between the three characters which has the effect of putting all three on an equal footing and at the same time placing them in the foreground once one or the other has climbed down from his observation-point. The dramatic disposition of this exchange also permits one of the three to address either of the other two, or both, as in the following example:

GUILLOT: Oui, monsieur, je veux être
  Écorché vif, si tout incontinent
  Vous ne baisiez Madame sur l'herbette.
LA FEMME: Mieux te vaudrait laisser cette sornette,
  Je te le dis, car elle sent les coups.
LE MARI: Non, non, m'amie, il faut qu'avec les fous
  Tout de ce pas par mon ordre on le mette.

This device, which consists of writing the dialogue as if it belongs to a play, occurs occasionally in the non-Boccaccian *contes*, for a brief moment in 'La Courtisane amoureuse', at some length in 'La Servante justifiée' and in the first edition of 'La Coupe enchantée'. It not only helps to create a close-up but permits the omnipresent author to eclipse himself voluntarily.

Such close-ups, bringing the characters momentarily into the foreground, are one aspect of the visual quality of these *contes* which produces dramatic effects. In confrontation scenes the actual presence of two or more characters creates a strong impact. Bartholomée's aged husband asks her pirate captor to let him see her, declaring he fears only 'qu'à me voir de joie elle ne meure'. On the contrary, the young wife gives no sign of recognition:

  Devant ses yeux voit son mari paraître
  Sans témoigner seulement le connaître (434).

But the husband, far from being discouraged, tells Pergamin her indifference is the result of nervousness; leave me alone with her, he urges, and she'll fall into my arms. When they are alone, Richard begins by urging her to look at him:

  Regarde-moi. Trouves-tu, ma chère âme,
  En mon visage un si grand changement!

Bartholomée coldly answers his plea with a devastating attack on marriage between persons of different ages, including a magnificent dramatic gesture as she indicates the discrepancy between them: 'Vous, vieux penard, moi, fille jeune et drue'. Visual impact is similarly stressed at the beginning of the moving encounter between Fédéric and Clitie in 'Le Faucon':

  Fédéric prend pour un ange des cieux
  Celle qui vient d'apparaître à ses yeux.

But Clitie's supplication is remarkable chiefly for its pathos and her dignified persistence despite a feeling of hopelessness, as in the course of her plea she halts abruptly, aware of the impossibility of her request, yet resumes because of her maternal duty. The decasyllabics take on the nobility of alexandrines, and the speech as a whole almost belongs in the company of Phèdre's confession to Hippolyte or Jocaste's plea to her sons:

> je m'en viens, pour comble d'injustice,
> Vous demander...Et quoi? c'est temps perdu;
> Votre faucon. Mais non, plutôt périsse
> L'enfant, la mère, avec le demeurant,
> Que de vous faire un déplaisir si grand.
> Souffrez sans plus que cette triste mère,
> Aimant d'amour la chose la plus chère
> Que jamais femme au monde puisse avoir,
> Un fils unique, une unique espérance,
> S'en vienne au moins s'acquitter du devoir
> De la nature; et pour toute allégeance
> En votre sein décharge sa douleur.
> Vous savez bien par votre expérience
> Que c'est d'aimer, vous le savez, Seigneur,
> Ainsi je crois trouver chez vous excuse.

By Clitie's constant allusions implicating her interlocutor (Vous demander...Vous savez bien...vous le savez, Seigneur) La Fontaine maintains in the reader's eye the presence of Fédéric, in a method reminiscent of Racine.

The eavesdropping scene is essentially a dramatic device, intensifying our vision of an action, through a hidden listener or observer on stage. In a sense, we see or listen through his eyes and ears as well as our own. When this device appears in the *contes* it may approach voyeurism, even sadism, for example when a husband must watch his wife being seduced before his eyes. Such a situation need not, however, involve violence. The gullible Pierre fully consents to the strange ceremony that Frère Jean performs with his wife, although he finally interrupts at a crucial moment. Even the shivering André, crouching beside the bed and witnessing his friend's novel vengeance, is thankful the punishment is no greater:

> André vit tout et n'osa murmurer;
> Jugea des coups; mais ce fut sans rien dire,
> Et loua Dieu que le mal n'était pire (393–4).

The credulous husband of 'La Gageure des trois commères' from his perch in the pear-tree watches his manservant dallying with his wife, the first time in unbelieving rage, the second without protest:

> Pour cette fois le mari voit la danse
> Sans se fâcher et descend doucement.

Similar visualizations, adding dramatic dimension, occur in two *contes*, not inspired by Boccaccio but of Boccaccian flavor, 'La Servante justifiée' and 'Les Rémois'. In the first, a gossip sees her neighbor sporting in his garden with a chambermaid. Aware that he has been spied upon, he conducts his wife to the same place and repeats his actions, so that when the spy denounces him to his wife and continues her denunciations, she keeps replying, in a refrain suggestive of comedy, 'C'était moi'. In the second, a wife connives with her husband so that he will return unexpected when two of her suitors are about to dine with her. They hide in a closet from which they watch the husband seduce in turn each of their wives, whom the hostess has invited in their place. These two 'regardants', like their fellow-dupes in the Boccaccian *contes*, are constrained by the situation to watch their own humiliation; as one says to the other, 'en vos lacs/Vous êtes pris'.

Although he witnesses not his betrayal, but all unwittingly, its preparation, the husband in 'Le Magnifique' is the audience of the dramatic scene played by the hero and the wife. The latter replies only by dumb show to the Magnifico's passionate declarations, but by scrutinizing her face he can tell his suit is well received, and since the husband remains out of earshot, he can formulate her replies aloud. The first time she makes no audible answer he understands from her expression her husband's command:

> Je vois, je vois, c'est une tricherie
> De votre époux (610).

As he voices her imagined responses, her glance confirms them:

> ce coin d'oeil, par son langage doux,
> Rompt à mon sens quelque peu le silence.

To involve facial expression in language in this way is to bring the dialogue close to that of the drama itself.

Like the Magnifico composing aloud his mistress' speech, La Fontaine thus attempts to lend a new voice to the old Boccaccian tales that could no longer speak to the seventeenth century. At the same time he remained fully conscious of his predecessor's great art, on occasion questioning the value of his changes and emendations:

> ma main pleine d'audace
> En mille endroits a peut-être gâté
> Ce que la sienne a bien exécuté (650–1).

Certainly this inherent respect of his source insured, with one or two notable exceptions, that the essential themes of certain Boccaccian tales were preserved, although La Fontaine's particular vision and subtle reworking make of them 'proprement des nouvelles nouvelles'.

3

Ariosto and La Fontaine: a literary affinity

Orlando Furioso ranks without doubt among the most fertile of the many books, ancient and foreign, that nurtured French Renaissance and classical literature, not merely enriching it with specific source materials but, like some wondrous *terra infinita*, even overshadowing the real world or coexisting with it. Its influence ranged through every genre, beyond poetry and beyond the boundaries of centuries.[1]

What was it that drew such disparate writers to the *Furioso*, for that lengthy epic is by far the most popular of Ariosto's works? What maintained Ariosto's popularity in France throughout the sixteenth and seventeenth centuries, despite the fact that he served both Montaigne and Boileau as an illustration of how *not* to write? The primary appeal lay in his infinite variety, his power of invention. As C. S. Lewis, who does not hesitate to rank him with Homer, admirably puts it,

His actors range from archangels to horses, his scene from Cathay to the Hebrides. In every stanza there is something new: battles in all their detail, strange lands with their laws, customs, history, and geography, storm and sunshine, mountains, islands, rivers, monsters, anecdotes, conversations – there seems no end to it. He tells us what his people ate, he describes the architecture of their palaces; when you tire of one adventure he plunges you into another with something so ludicrous or questionable in its exordium you feel you must read just one more.[2]

Such diversity had its critics, of course. Montaigne complained of him that 'on le voit...voleter et sauteler de conte en conte comme de

---

[1] Cf. Alice Cameron, *The Influence of Ariosto's Epic and Lyric Poetry on Ronsard and his Group* (Baltimore: Johns Hopkins Press, 1930); Alexandre Cioranescu, *L'Arioste en France* (Paris: Les Presses Modernes, 1939).
[2] C. S. Lewis, *The Allegory of Love* (Oxford: Clarendon Press, 1936), pp. 301–33.

branche en branche, ne se fiant à ses aisles que pour une bien courte traverse, et prendre pied à chaque bout de champ, de peur que l'haleine et la force luy faille'.[1] But the poet who boasted 'diversité c'est ma devise' could scarcely have failed to be won by Ariosto. Indeed two other self-descriptive phrases of La Fontaine's sound like a poetic paraphrase of Montaigne's characterization of the Italian poet:

> Je suis chose légère, et vole à tout sujet
> Je vais de fleur en fleur et d'objet en objet (OD, 643).[2]

These lines suggest at the very least that he must have felt a strong affinity for a writer whose variety was almost infinite. He declared outright his feeling in the 'Epître à Huet': 'Je chéris l'Arioste et j'estime Le Tasse' (OD, 647). He could not have failed to make Ariosto's acquaintance early for his vogue was widespread. The *Furioso* inspired poems, plays, operas, and that most spectacular offspring of all, the royal divertissement *Les Plaisirs de l'île enchantée*, in which Louis XIV played the amorous Ruggiero and Louise de La Vallière the enchantress Alcina – perhaps unaware or unconcerned that in the poem Alcina is actually a withered hag whose beauty is the product of magic. Among the Italian poet's admirers was Racine, who praised him frequently in his letters, on one occasion comparing him to Homer, thus anticipating Mr Lewis.[3] La Fontaine obviously agreed, since in the opera *Daphné* he placed the bust of Ariosto in the palace of Apollo alongside those of Homer, Anacreon, Pindar, Virgil, Horace, Ovid, Tasso and Malherbe.

References to the *Furioso* sprang readily to our poet's mind. For the opera *Roland* by Lully and Quinault he turned a gracious dedicatory ode, comparing Angelica to Helen of Troy and urging the king,

> Plaignez le paladin que mon art vous présente
> Son malheur fut d'aimer; quelle âme en est exempte? (OD, 622).

In the amusing *ballade* 'Je me plais aux livres d'amour', he seems to be speaking through the lips of the prude who inadvertently admits her pleasure in love stories and, in particular, those of Ariosto:

---

[1] Montaigne, *Œuvres*, ed. Thibaudet and Rat, II, x, 392.

[2] Page references in the text to miscellaneous works (preceded by OD) are to the Clarac edition.

[3] Cf. Georges May, *D'Ovide à Racine* (Paris: Presses Universitaires de France, 1949), pp. 98–100; Vittorio Lugli, *Il Prodigio di La Fontaine*, pp. 121–31; Philip Wadsworth, *Young La Fontaine: A Study of his Artistic Growth in his Early Poetry and First Fables* (Evanston, Ill.: Northwestern University Press, 1952), pp. 145–51.

J'ai lu maître Louis mille fois en ma vie;
Et même quelquefois j'entre en tentation
Lorsque l'Ermite trouve Angélique endormie (OD, 586).

This reference to the amusing passage about an old hermit who tries
in vain to rape the sleeping heroine recalls the plaintive 'O che
sciagura' voiced in a similar situation in *Candide*.[1]

We encounter in the *contes* a number of such incidental allusions
to the *Furioso*, but these have nothing extraneous about them; they
invariably fulfill a function. In 'Les Aveux indiscrets', for example,
it is rather startling that this prosy, matter-of-fact tale of a husband
who symbolized his cuckoldry by wearing a saddle should contain a
reference to Orlando:

Quand Roland sut les plaisirs et la gloire
Que dans la grotte avait eus son rival,
D'un coup de poing il tua son cheval (636).[2]

The episode La Fontaine recalls so exactly is Orlando's discovery of
the triumphant message his rival Medoro inscribed above the entrance to the cave and on the surrounding trees after making love to
Angelica. Mad with grief, the paladin kills Medoro's horse with one
blow and drags Angelica's mare away by the tail. At this point La
Fontaine innocently asks, concerning Orlando,

Pouvait-il pas, traînant la pauvre bête,
Mettre de plus la selle sur son dos;
Puis s'en aller, tout du haut de sa tête,
Faire crier et redire aux échos:
Je suis bâté … ?

Here he treats his source in much the same way as Ariosto approached
the romances of chivalry and the hero of the *Furioso* appears as
ludicrous as the talkative Damon of the *conte*.

The incongruity of Orlando's appearance in such a context would
have been typical of Ariosto. For his variety did not consist merely of
multiplying scenes, incidents and characters; it frequently produced
an intentionally ironic counterpoint. He achieved this in a number of
ways, all of them pertinent to our study of La Fontaine. First of all,
he deliberately stresses his position as an omnipresent author. He is

---

[1] Other incidental references: in *Psyché*, Angelica has her place in the palace of Cupid
alongside Armida, Cleopatra and Helen of Troy (OD, 143), and Chancellor Séguier's
finery is compared to that of Medoro (OD, 510).

[2] Page references in the text to *contes* and *fables* are to the Groos and Schiffrin edition.

forever commenting on his narrative, his characters, his art; pluck-
ing the reader by the sleeve, often in the midst of the most tumultu-
ous action. He will pause to declare variety one of his chief methods
of creating interest:

> Cosi mi par, che la mia istoria, quanto
> Or qui or là piú variata sia
> Meno a chi l'udirá noiosa fia (XIII, 80).[1]

In this particular instance he is justifying the way he abruptly
changes scenes or interrupts one action to describe another. Such
asides may be addressed to various persons: his patron, Ippolito
d'Este, to whom he is presenting his story; the reader; his 'lady';
or one of his own characters, both fictional and real. The levels of
action and of setting are legion, but there are also different levels of
time: the present, the historic past of Italy, the legendary past of the
epic itself. Nor does the poem progress in an orderly chronological
fashion: it frequently interrupts its flow like an old-time serial
movie, halting one action just before its climax to take up another.
And Ariosto constantly reaches back into his story, reminding his
reader of earlier events and the characters' roles in them.

To intervene in this way is to produce various effects of suspension
and distance. The reader is invited to take a detached viewpoint, to
inspect and judge for himself. When Ariosto comments, in a variety
of tones, upon his characters, he produces a precariously balanced
relationship between author, characters and reader which he delights
in tipping this way and that. One of the best examples is his remark
when his heroine, the pure Angelica, has declared

> che'l fior virginal cosí avea salvo,
> Como se lo portó del materna alvo (I. 55).[2]

The author gently intrudes:

> Forse era ver, ma non peró credible
> A chi del senso suo fosse signore;
> Ma parve facilmente a lui possibile,
> Ch'era perduto in via più grave errore (I, 56).[3]

---

[1] 'So it seems to me that my story, when it is more varied now in this way and now in
that, will be less wearisome to him who listens to it.' The text is that of L. Casetti's
edition (Milan–Naples: Ricciardi, n.d.); references are to canto and stanza. The
translations are from Allen Gilbert's version (New York: S. F. Vanni, 1954).

[2] 'that thus she had her virginal flower as safe as when she brought it from her mother's
womb'.

[3] 'Perhaps it was true, but all the same not credible to one in command of his senses;
but it seemed easily possible to him who was lost in a much more serious error.'

Remember that this is the heroine, who for the story's basic interest must remain virginal until she yields to Medoro!

Yet Ariosto is far from espousing the misogynist's cause. For example, when Rodomonte denounces the female sex, the author tells us he must have lost his mind:

> E certo da ragion si dispartiva;
> Che per uno o per due che trovi ree,
> Che cento buone sien creder si dee (XXVII, 122).[1]

In these lines Ariosto seems to be fulfilling an earlier promise that for every woman denounced he would praise a hundred. Yet this fulfillment becomes almost ludicrous when we hear him regret, a moment later, that personally he has never found a woman faithful to him, although he announces that he will continue to seek one before his hair gets any whiter, a hint that he has already spent the better part of a lifetime in a fruitless search.

These startling contrasts in Ariosto's attitude toward women have been seen as one evidence of the deliberate parallelism between his own and his characters' experience, and as a way of dramatizing the infinite variety of human experience.[2] Ariosto's oscillation between attacks on fickle women and belief in female virtue runs through the whole poem. We are concerned here, however, with the three insertions that La Fontaine chose to imitate, all of which deal specifically with feminine unchastity: the story of Giocondo (XXVIII, 1–74), and two tales illustrating the triumph of cupidity over virtue (XLII, 70–XLIII, 143). The author prepares us for the first of these through the mood of Rodomonte, who is furious at having been rejected by Doralice. His blanket denunciation of woman swiftly narrows to the single theme of infidelity. On arriving at an inn, he asks the guests if any of them believe their wives faithful. All assure him that they do. But the innkeeper offers to tell tales that prove no chaste woman ever existed. Whereupon the Saracen demands to hear one that 'will fit his opinion'. Not content with showing the bias of both narrator and listener, when the story ends Ariosto brings forward an old man who defends womankind, thus effectively countering, by its framing, the antifeminist content of the tale.

---

[1] 'and certainly he departed from reason, because for one or two bad ones you find, it must be believed a hundred are good'.

[2] Cf. Robert Durling, *The Figure of the Poet in Renaissance Epic* (Cambridge, Mass.: Harvard University Press, 1965), p. 150.

Further ironic contrasts develop from shifts between fantasy and realism. This interplay occurs in both the structure and the descriptive technique of the *Furioso*. The 'realistic' story of Giocondo, for example, follows upon the intervention of archangels and the Goddess of Discord in the Saracen camp. In describing the Hippogriff, the magician's winged horse, Ariosto takes pains to tell us that this new Pegasus is not a magical but a real creature, borne by an ass to a griffin. Though rare, he adds, such beasts may be found on the other side of the frozen seas. Thus he seasons the magical element by the witty intrusion of pseudozoology.

There is no dearth of such examples – for instance, the contrast between realistic and magic hindrances to love when Ruggiero, in his amorous haste, tries to remove his armor and knots up two laces for every one he unties. When he is finally ready to embrace Angelica, however, she pops the magic ring into her mouth and disappears into thin air (x, 114–xi, 9).

A final device which produces an effect of ironic detachment is the pose of the subservient narrator. Thus Turpin, the feigned chronicler of the *Furioso*, serves to justify certain of Ariosto's more ludicrous flights:

> Il buon Turpin, che sa che dice il vero
> E lascia creder poi quel ch'a l'uom piace (xxvi, 23).[1]

Ariosto also shelters behind Turpin to excuse the antifeminism of the story of Giocondo by urging women not to read it. He had only set it down because Turpin did so and not through any ill will toward them:

> Ch'io v'ami, oltre mia lingua che l'ha espresso
> Che mai non fu di celebrarvi avara,
> N'ho fatto mille prove; e v'ho dimostro
> Ch'io son né potrei esser se non vostro (xxviii, 2).[2]

But all the protests in the world could not disguise the burden of the Giocondo tale, woman's weakness and sensuality, and it was probably inevitable that La Fontaine should adapt precisely the three novellas on that theme, which was central to the *contes*. The first, 'Joconde', had previously been translated into French by a certain Bouillon; of the other two, 'La Coupe enchantée' had been adapted

---

[1] 'The good Turpin, who knows he speaks the truth and lets men believe what they please.'

[2] 'That I love you, besides my tongue that has set it forth – which has never been stingy in praising you – I have given a thousand proofs, and I have shown you I am and I cannot be other than yours.'

once by Deimier, but 'Le Petit Chien qui secoue de l'argent et des pierreries' had never appeared in a French version.[1] In the Italian original all three stories are complete insertions; that is, they do not, as Ariosto's other tales do, include characters who participate in the main action of the epic. Each is told to a paladin who has, at that particular moment at least, cause to despair of woman's fidelity. In the case of 'Giocondo', this was the fiery Rodomonte, king of Algiers, who was furious with all women because he had been forsaken by Doralice for Mandricardo. The other two tales are heard by the despondent Rinaldo, after he has learned of Angelica's infidelity.

'Joconde'

Here is a summary of the story as Ariosto tells it, the main lines of which La Fontaine follows. Giocondo, renowned for his good looks, is summoned to the court of Astolfo, king of Lombardy, a famous *coureur* who is curious to see whether he might prove a worthy rival. The hero, shortly after setting out, realizes he has forgotten his wife's parting gift and when he returns to get it, finds her in the arms of another man. He takes no action, however, but departs, disconsolate, for Astolfo's court. There he languishes, pale and sickly, until by chance he discovers the queen herself in dalliance with an ugly dwarf, a discovery which quite restores his humor and good looks. When he tells the king, the two husbands decide to set out on a journey of seduction in order to avenge themselves on the female sex. In the final episode they share the favors of an innkeeper's daughter, who manages to entertain them and a third lover all in the same bed. Upon discovering this crowning example of feminine infidelity, they good-humoredly resign themselves to the fact that women are all alike and return, full of tolerance, to their wives.

In discussing La Fontaine's version of this story, Alexandre Cioranescu errs, I believe, in finding the chief difference between the two writers to be the Italian's realism and the Frenchman's fantasy. Superficially defining realism as mere attention to detail in such matters as the careful identification of characters, the use of proper names, or exact physical and topographical description, he claims that the French version lacks realism, explaining, somewhat tautologically, that La Fontaine 'aime mieux l'indécis, l'atmosphère de pure fantaisie qui caractérise les contes'.[2] I would reproach him not so much

---

[1] Cf. *Œuvres*, ed. Régnier, IV, 18.   [2] Cioranescu, *L'Arioste en France*, p. 63.

for such a gross misstatement concerning the *contes*, but for failing to see that each author could command both realism and fantasy at will.

Actually, La Fontaine employs or suppresses detail in his own way, and to a special purpose. In his version he establishes the contrast, familiar in French classical literature from Guez de Balzac to Mme de La Fayette, between court and countryside. Thus, when he tells us, not that Joconde lives in Rome, as Ariosto notes in the original, but simply in the country 'loin du commerce et du monde', he is not shirking a detail but suggesting an opposition between court and country life. This contrast appears in the farewell speech of Joconde's wife, a lyrical passage which replaces a few lines of indirect discourse in the original:

> As-tu bien l'âme assez cruelle
> Pour préférer à ma constante amour
> Les faveurs de la cour?
> Tu sais qu'à peine elles durent un jour;
> Qu'on les conserve avec inquiétude,
> Pour les perdre avec désespoir.
> Si tu te lasses de me voir,
> Songe au moins qu'en ta solitude
> Le repos règne jour et nuit;
> Que les ruisseaux n'y font du bruit
> Qu'afin de t'inviter à fermer la paupière.
> Crois-moi, ne quitte point les hôtes de tes bois,
> Ces fertiles vallons, ces ombrages si cois (352).

Such reflective moments help to provide, in the brief framework of the *conte*, some of the depth and variety Ariosto achieved through the scope and movement of the entire epic.

Further details not present in the Italian stress aristocratic values. In the French version Joconde smarts at his disgrace because his betrayer is not of his class:

> Encore si c'était un blondin
> Je me consolerais d'un si sensible outrage;
> Mais un gros lourdaud de valet!
> C'est à quoi j'ai le plus de regret,

where Ariosto merely notes that Giocondo recognized in his wife's arms his servant whom he had befriended as a youth.

In the *Furioso*, Giocondo's failure to take vengeance on the lovers is an effect of his deep love. Boileau, in his 'Dissertation sur "Joconde"', berated the Italian poet for intruding such a serious note in a comic tale, and concluded in favor of La Fontaine: 'Un mari qui se résout à souffrir discrètement les plaisirs de sa femme, comme l'a dépeint M. de La Fontaine, n'a rien que de plaisant et d'agréable, et c'est le sujet ordinaire de nos comédies.'[1] Thus, it is not the complaisant but the jealous husband that La Fontaine finds ridiculous, in accord with the aristocratic morality which considered marital jealousy or proprietariness essentially a bourgeois trait, a manifestation of middle-class rapacity and acquisitiveness. Molière shared La Fontaine's attitude. From La Jalousie du barbouillé on down through L'Ecole des femmes and Amphitryon, not only cuckoldry but the fear of it evoked hearty laughter; such a fear revealed the bourgeois's basic sense of inferiority, his fundamental fear of woman.[2] In the Italian poem, before telling the king his shocking news, Giocondo makes Astolfo swear a sacred oath not to take vengeance (XXVIII, 40). Despite this, when the king witnesses his own betrayal he reacts so violently that only the thought of the oath restrains him. La Fontaine's Astolphe, on the other hand, shows the blasé detachment of the aristocrat:

> Il fut comme accablé de ce cruel outrage.
> Mais bientôt il le prit en homme de courage
> En galant homme, et, pour le faire court,
> En véritable homme de cour.

By other realistic details, absent in Ariosto, La Fontaine emphasizes rank and hierarchy. In the French version the king and Joconde decide to list their conquests *according to rank*. By this innovation La Fontaine heightens the movement of the story since the willing victims' haste to be inscribed in the register resembles a contest in which wives of high and low degree take part with alacrity:

> Heureuses les beautés qui s'offrent à leurs yeux!
> Et plus heureuse encor celle qui peut leur plaire!
> Il n'est en la plupart des lieux
> Femme d'échevin, ni de maire,
> De podestat, de gouverneur,
> Qui ne tienne à fort grand honneur
> D'avoir en leur registre place.

---

[1] Boileau, *Œuvres complètes*, ed. Charles H. Boudhors (Paris: Belles Lettres, 1934–43), IV, 15.
[2] Cf. Paul Bénichou, *Morales du grand siècle* (Paris: Gallimard, 1948), pp. 178–95, for a thorough study of Molière's attitude.

After these conquests, the wanderers' eyes fall upon the innkeeper's daughter, and in another departure from the original, where the two men conduct their entire campaign on a basis of perfect equality, the king demands his royal prerogative to be the first to enjoy the favors of their last bedmate.

This may be because La Fontaine presents this final and most ludicrous conquest as a result of Astolphe's disenchantment with ladies of quality, rather than his belief that a woman might prove faithful to two men if never to one alone. 'Laissons-là la qualité', proclaims the king denouncing the rigors of courtly love:

> Sous les cotillons des grisettes
> Peut loger autant de beauté
> Que sous les jupes des coquettes.
> D'ailleurs il n'y faut point faire tant de façon,
> Etre en continuel soupçon,
> Dépendre d'une humeur fière, brusque ou volage:
> Chez les dames de haut parage
> Ces choses sont à craindre et bien d'autres encor.
> Une grisette est un trésor,
> Car, sans se donner de la peine,
> Et sans qu'aux bals on la promène,
> On en vient aisément à bout;
> On lui dit ce qu'on veut, bien souvent rien du tout.[1]

Curiously, despite this clearly expressed preference, which again depends for its point on class distinction, Cioranescu tells us that in the French poem the adventures 'tirent au sort à qui aura la fortune de la *courtiser* le premier, après quoi ils commencent à lui faire la cour selon toutes les règles de la galanterie, avec des compliments, des danses et des rendez-vous'. But La Fontaine says instead that she readily yields her favors with alacrity, in exchange for a ring:

> A cet objet si précieux
> Son coeur fit peu de résistance:
> Le marché se conclut.

Nor is it correct that the Fiammetta of the French version is 'une jeune vierge qu'il faut conquérir à force d'assiduités et de promesses'. La Fontaine, on the contrary, derives one of his most original effects from the two friends' naive belief in the wench's virginity, producing an irony that affects the erotic element in the story. We

[1] Cf. *The Greek Anthology*, v, 18.

must also reject the suggestion that La Fontaine is more explicit than his predecessor: 'L'imitateur s'emploie autant qu'il peut à mettre les points sur les *i* avec une ironie et une sincérité toutes gauloises', although Cioranescu qualifies this statement almost to the point of self-contradiction: 'il est curieux de constater que là où le tableau du modèle devient trop osé, l'imitateur français recule'. Actually, rather than suppressing any crudity of detail, La Fontaine used the method he described in 'Le Tableau':

> Nuls traits à découvert n'auront ici de place;
> Tout y sera voilé, mais de gaze, et si bien
> Que je crois qu'on n'en perdra rien. [1]

Thus, while he preserved the erotic episode of three men in bed with one girl, La Fontaine displaces it from the position of central interest it held in the Italian version by his stress on the gallants' foolish belief in her virginity. Joconde states his opinion with almost ludicrous intensity:

> Je la tiens pucelle sans faute,
> Et si pucelle qu'il n'est rien
> De plus puceau que cette belle:
> Sa poupée en sait autant qu'elle.

When the two draw lots to determine which will teach her 'la première leçon du plaisir amoureux', La Fontaine comments dryly:

> De la chape à l'évêque, hélas, ils se battaient
> Les bonnes gens qu'ils étaient!

And to the recital of the night's event, he adds a fourteen-line comment on the naiveté of Joconde, 'qui crut avoir rompu la glace'. He further 'veils' the Ariostian coarseness with comic allegories such as 'maître Pucelage', who 'joua dex mieux son personnage'.

He achieves a further 'veiling' by heightening the effects of illusion, so prevalent throughout the *Furioso*. To the conclusion he adds a speech by Astolphe suggesting magic as a cause of infidelity and the influence of 'quelque astre malin' on errant husbands and wives:

> D'ailleurs tout l'univers est plein
> De maudits enchanteurs, qui des corps et des âmes
> Font tout ce qu'il leur plaît: savons-nous si ces gens,
> Comme ils sont traîtres et méchants,
> Et toujours ennemis soit de l'un, soit de l'autre,

[1] See above, p. 34.

101

> N'ont point ensorcelé mon épouse et la vôtre?
> Et si par quelque étrange cas
> Nous n'avons point cru voir chose qui n'était pas?

Such a universe of enchantment and illusion is also that of the *Orlando Furioso*.

But despite the indulgence of this conclusion, La Fontaine will not go as far as the Renaissance optimist in his defense of woman. He expresses his skepticism through various interventions similar to those in the *Furioso*, assuming an omniscience, an awareness surpassing those of his gullible readers:

> Vous autres, bonnes gens, eussiez cru que la dame
> Une heure après eût rendu l'âme;
> Moi, qui sais ce que c'est que l'esprit d'une femme,
> Je m'en serais à bon droit défié.

In typically Ariostian fashion he parries imagined objections at the number and rapidity of the two gallants' conquests:

> J'entends déjà maint esprit fort
> M'objecter que la vraisemblance
> N'est pas en ceci tout à fait.

But he concludes, all that matters is my adherence to Ariosto:

> Je le rends comme on me la donne;
> Et l'Arioste ne ment pas.

In this last line La Fontaine assumes the pose of the subservient narrator, pretending to efface himself before his Italian master, as Ariosto with Turpin. By this means he boldly justifies distortions which suit his particular purpose, or even omissions. In the French version, as Joconde leaves for the court of Astolphe, his wife delivers her long and tearful farewell, whereupon, writes La Fontaine:

> L'histoire ne dit point ni de quelle manière
> Joconde put partir, ni ce qu'il répondit,
> Ni ce qu'il fit, ni ce qu'il dit;
> Je m'en tais donc aussi de crainte de pis faire.

This is simply not true. Actually Giocondo's reply takes almost a whole stanza and is full of sadness at the prospect of his parting. But through the device of the subservient narrator La Fontaine has been able to voice his doubts about the durability of conjugal love: 'Marié depuis peu; Content, je n'en sais rien.'

'La Coupe enchantée'

The episode in Ariosto extends through 101 stanzas (XLII, 70–XLIII, 67). Rinaldo, crossing the Po as evening approaches, meets a courteous stranger who asks if he is married and, upon receiving an affirmative answer, invites him to spend the night in his palace. After a sumptuous meal his host urges him to drink from a gold cup that possesses magical properties. If his wife is faithful he will be able to drink all the wine, but if she is unchaste, every drop will spill. But after a moment's thought, Rinaldo refuses:

> ben sarrebbe folle
> Chi quel che non vorria trovar cercasse (XLIII, 6).[1]

Whereupon his host, in tears, begins his story. He had married the daughter of an elderly man and inherited all his possessions, including the palace, after his death. But his wedded bliss was interrupted when a sorceress fell in love with him and, on being rebuffed, dared him to try his wife's chastity. She gave him the magic goblet, he drank, and all was well. But, urged the magician, he must leave for a time and make the test again when he returned. He refused, and she next offered to change his appearance so that he might besiege his wife in the guise of one of her admirers. This he did, and when his wife was on the point of yielding, revealed the trick. Furious at his distrust, she left him for the suitor he had impersonated. Since that time he has been urging travelers to drink from the magic cup, and finding consolation in the numbers whose draft of wine is spilled.

Rather than begin with Rinaldo's story, La Fontaine elaborates, in a sprightly prologue, a new theme: the baseness of jealousy, a sentiment worthy only of the bourgeois, and one which conquers its victims by means of illusion. We recognize at once the *morale aristocratique* he had made a basic element of 'Joconde'. But he develops here to a far greater extent the role of illusion as a source of jealousy, bringing into play all manner of devices, that demonstrate how the passion enslaves human intellect, and despite abundant wit and irony, delivering what amounts to a serious plea for intellectual freedom. Illusion operates on several levels, one of them dialectical. In illustration, the prologue transforms, in skillful steps, the abhorrent concept of cuckoldry into a dream of comfort and delight. La Fontaine knew well Chapter XXVIII of Rabelais' *Tiers Livre*, a book on

---

1 'he would surely be a fool who would look for what he did not want to find'.

the perils of marriage, and one of Friar John's burlesque replies to Panurge's oft-expressed fear may have provided the basis for our poet's paradoxical argument that 'Cocuage est un bien'. 'Il n'est (respondit Frere Jan) coqu qui veult. Si tu es coqu, *ergo* ta femme sera belle, *ergo* tu seras bien traicté d'elle; *ergo* tu auras des amis beaucoup, *ergo* tu seras saulvé.' He may well have read Montaigne's remark: 'J'en sçay qui à leur escient ont tiré et proffit et avancement du cocuage, dequoy le seul nom effraye tant de gens.'[1]

The alacrity with which the poet proves first, that cuckoldry is not an evil, and then that it is actually a good, demonstrates, through the illusion of dialectic, the flimsiness of the evidence on which jealousy is based. Thus, to show that this all-consuming malady 'n'est mal qu'en votre idée, et non point dans l'effet', he invokes the stability of appearance; the horns of the cuckold exist only in his imagination:

> En mettez-vous votre bonnet
> Moins aisément que de coutume?
> Cela s'en va-t-il pas tout net? (173)

Nor does the mirror reveal any change:

> Ne retrouvez-vous pas toujours les mêmes traits?
> Vous apercevez-vous d'aucune différence?

To prove cuckoldry an advantage the poet presents two scenes: one of the husband and his wife at table, her blond admirers vying with each other to please him:

> Quand vous parlez, c'est dit notable;
> On vous met le premier à table;
> C'est pour vous la place d'honneur,
> Pour vous le morceau du seigneur:
> Heureux qui vous le sert! la blondine chiorme
> Afin de vous gagner n'épargne aucun moyen...

From this Lucullan interlude we pass to the gaming-table, where the suitors willingly relinquish their best cards so the cuckold may win. Cuckoldry will even pay his debts, for if some 'Monsieur Dimanche', some persistent creditor, should pursue him, 'mille bourses vous sont ouvertes'. The final point in what La Fontaine calls his 'discours en forme', perhaps the most audacious, is that promiscuity increases the cuckold's wife's beauty, and the poet reaches back, via Ovid, to the Trojan war for an illustration:

[1] Montaigne, *Œuvres*, ed. Thibaudet and Rat, I, xiv, 62.

Ménélas rencontra des charmes dans Hélène
Qu'avant d'être à Pâris la belle n'avait pas.[1]

The reminiscence of Molière in the reference to the Monsieur Dimanche of *Dom Juan* leads us to another probable source, Chrysalde's
speech in *L'Ecole des femmes* (IV, 8), where we find the suggestion
that the jealous husband is ridiculous because he conceives of honor
only in terms of his wife's fidelity, that to be cuckolded should be
thought of as an 'accident', a trick of fate, and that in short, as
Molière's spokesman puts it,

> le cocuage
> Sous des traits moins affreux aisément s'envisage.

But, as one would expect, he concludes by advising moderation. As
much to be deplored as Arnolphe's intransigence is the complaisance of

> ces gens un peu trop débonnaires
> Qui tirent vanité de ces sortes d'affaires.

La Fontaine, in unequivocally associating himself with this one of the
two *extrémités* against which Chrysalde cautions, seems to take a far
more uncompromising stand against bourgeois morality than Molière.

The tone is no longer that of indulgent reasonableness, nor is the
poet content with such mild statements as the following concerning
Joconde's inaction when confronted with his betrayal:

> Et mon avis est qu'il fit bien;
> Le moins de bruit que l'on peut faire
> En telle affaire
> Est le plus sûr de la moitié.

His interventions are now no longer merely tranquilly ironic
asides, for he has a thesis and on occasion leaves his story to point the
moral at some length, carefully indicating the juncture at which he
picks up the narrative again by some such phrase as 'venons à
notre histoire', or 'Vous allez entendre comment'. He preaches directly at his readers who, if they are not cuckolds themselves, appear to
take cuckoldry seriously. When halfway through the prologue, like
Diderot's anonymous interlocutor, they retort in protest: 'Oui, mais
l'honneur est une étrange affaire!' this provokes the heated rejoinder:

> Qui vous soutient que non? ai-je dit le contraire?
> Et bien, l'honneur, l'honneur? je n'entends que ce mot.

[1] Ovid, *Remedia amoris*, 11, 773–6.

Various additions to the original express that skepticism about marriage which is one ingredient of the *morale aristocratique*. Departing from his source, the author of 'La Jeune Veuve' tells us, for example, that the wife's father had adamantly forsworn marriage. When his mistress died in childbirth his grief was the more sincere because it was not that of a widower:

> Le pauvre homme en pleurs
> Se plaignit, gémit, soupira,
> Non comme qui perdrait sa femme,
> Tel deuil n'est bien souvent que changement d'habits,
> Mais comme qui perdrait tous ses meilleurs amis.

The subservient narrator reappears to comment on Damon's resistance to the sorceress' advances, artfully declaring some of the more preposterous phenomena in the *Furioso* to be more believable than a faithful husband:

> Où sont-ils ces maris? La race en est cessée,
> Et même je ne sais si jamais on en vit.
> L'histoire en cet endroit est, selon ma pensée,
>   Un peu sujette à contredit.
> L'Hippogriffe n'a rien qui me choque l'esprit,
>   Non plus que la Lance enchantée.
> Mais ceci, c'est un point qui d'abord me surprit.

Such surprise clearly relegates marital fidelity to the realm of the preposterous. At least it has no place in the aristocratic norm. The suggestion is obvious: it is a bourgeois virtue, as the sorceress argues when trying to tempt Damon:

> Je vous croyais plus fin,
> Et ne vous tenais pas homme de mariage.
> Laissez les bons bourgeois se plaire en leur ménage:
> C'est pour eux seuls qu'Hymen fit les plaisirs permis.

But the suggestion falls on deaf ears; only jealousy, through her suggestion that a friend, Eraste, has betrayed him, succeeds in transforming his trust into suspicion.

At this point La Fontaine calls upon a variety of means to illustrate the power of illusion. The jealous husband, at the merest hint, succumbs to the *songe*, that ready vision of his own discomfiture to which he is so vulnerable:

> Ses songes sont toujours que l'on le fait cocu;
> Pourvu qu'il songe, c'est l'affaire.

But because of his fears, the *songe* is a waking dream, a true illusion bordering on hallucination:

> Qu'à l'entour de sa femme une mouche bourdonne,
> C'est Cocuage qu'en personne
> Il a vu de ses propres yeux.

Such visions remain those of the imagination. Significantly, when the sorceress plies Damon with magic potions they fail to sway him. Her verbal magic has greater power, and insinuation creates illusions far more occult. By hinting at an affaire between Caliste and Eraste she produces a *songe* of remarkable vividness. A rapid line suggests the stroke of a wand: 'Ce discours porta coup, et fit songer notre homme.' The vision at once appears; there is no preparatory verb; in an instant Damon is watching the tableau of a faithless Caliste and her lover:

> Une épouse fringante, et jeune, et dans son feu
> ....
> Un personnage expert aux choses de l'amour,
> Hardi comme un homme de cour,
> ....
> ...la donzelle
> Montre à demi son sein, sort du lit un bras blanc,
> Se tourne, s'inquiète et regarde un galant
> En cent façons...

The illusion is complete:

> Damon a dans l'esprit
> Que tout cela s'est fait...
> Sur ce beau fondement le pauvre homme bâtit
> Maint ombrage et mainte chimère.

Physical metamorphoses follow these intellectual transformations. Damon rubs his wrist with the magic 'eau de la métamorphose' which in a trice transforms him into a likeness of the suitor, Eraste, so that he may put his wife to the test.

The next metamorphosis, that of Caliste's chastity, ensues when Damon, in the guise of Eraste, employs every device to break her resistance. His compliments comparing her to a spring day avail nothing, tears and sighs fail as dismally, until finally he offers money.

At this point La Fontaine recalls the central theme of Ariosto's prologue: the power of avarice, which he recasts in a few cynical lines, to declare that wealth will always win against mere youth and beauty:

> Soyez beau, bien disant, ayez perruque blonde,
> N'omettez un seul petit point;
> Un financier viendra qui sur votre moustache
> Enlèvera la belle; et dès le premier jour
> Il fera présent du panache;
> Vous languirez encore après un an d'amour.

He later returns to this theme, when after she has been imprisoned by her husband, Caliste's jailer remains adamant only because she has no money with which to bribe him:

> Comme on ne lui laissait argent ni pierrerie
> Le geôlier fut fidèle.

Caliste's willingness to yield to the bribe appears metaphorically as a magical transformation. Having compared her virtue to a rock, the poet effects an instantaneous metamorphosis: 'Le rocher disparut, un mouton succéda.' Just as she is about to succumb, her husband becomes himself again, to confound her with still another lightning change.

These transitions take place with a rapidity which characterizes La Fontaine's narrative technique in general, as he tells the story of Caliste's life, from birth to marriage, in a dazzling combination of verbs of action and descriptive images. Five remarkable lines take her from infancy to womanhood:

> La fille crût, se fit: on pouvait déjà voir
> Hausser et baisser son mouchoir.
> Le temps coule: on n'est pas sitôt à la bavette
> Qu'on trotte, qu'on raisonne: on devient grandelette,
> Puis grande tout à fait; et puis le serviteur.

With what skill La Fontaine supports the dry narrative past definites *crût* and *se fit* with the charming concrete and dynamic image of the maiden's breast swelling beneath the modest shield of her neckerchief! The impersonal pronouns suggest her flowering is a universal truth, thus preserving the *exemplary* nature of her story.

Her convent upbringing is dispatched with similar verve; she learns to ply a needle, to shun dangerous books,

> ces livres qu'une fille
> Ne lit qu'avec danger, et qui gâtent l'esprit,

and to scorn her own beauty. At this point La Fontaine inserts in the swift narrative a deftly dramatic moment, in Caliste's reaction to a nun's praise of her loveliness:

> Mon Dieu fi! disait-elle, ah ma soeur, soyez sage;
> Ne considerez point des traits qui périront.
> C'est terre que cela, les vers le mangeront.

A long passage in the edition of 1669, subsequently suppressed, openly adopts the dramatic form, when Damon, in the guise of Eraste, tempts his wife. La Fontaine uses such props as a mirror, which Damon presents to Caliste so that she may see her beauty as he describes it, and a satin coffer, containing the jewels with which he bribes her. The swift replies, the teasing badinage suggest Marivaux, rather than Molière:

> LE FEINT ERASTE: Faut-il toujours vous dire
>   Qu'on brûle, qu'on languit, qu'on meurt sous votre empire?
> CALISTE: Mon Dieu! Non, je le sais, mais après?
> LE FEINT ERASTE: Il suffit.
>   Et quand on est mort c'est tout dit.
> CALISTE: Vous n'êtes pas si mort que vos yeux ne remuent,
>   Contenez-les, de grâce...
>   ....
>   Un remerciement donc ne peut vous contenter?
> LE FEINT ERASTE: Des remerciements? Bagatelles.
> CALISTE: De l'amitié?
> LE FEINT ERASTE: Point de nouvelles.
> CALISTE: De l'amour?
> LE FEINT ERASTE: Bon cela.

Although La Fontaine finally deleted, perhaps for the sake of succinctness, this delightful exchange which ends with Eraste's opening the jewel-box, like a prestidigitator, it illustrates the far greater liberties he took with his second story from Ariosto than with 'Joconde': the convent upbringing of Caliste, the imprisonment of the errant wife by the husband, the 'armée royale' of cuckolds, each with his military designation, the final reconciliation of Damon and Caliste, all represent changes from the original. He skillfully reverses Ariosto's structure, which placed Rinaldo's refusal to test his wife before the host's narration. Renaud's rejection of the magic goblet effectively ends Damon's campaign and the story itself. Such esthetic independence is typical of Ariosto. La Fontaine was to exercise it even more freely in his third and last adaptation.

'*Le Petit Chien qui secoue de l'argent et des pierreries*'

After his night's repose Rinaldo continues on his journey down the Po, and as he rests the boatman tells him still another story, running through seventy-two *ottavi* (XLIII, 72–143), and once again demonstrating the power of gold over virtue. The tale of the magic dog might have been subtitled 'La précaution inutile', since this time the jealous husband, called away on a mission to Rome, showers his wife with riches in a vain effort to forestall the inevitable effect of lovers' bribes. As we might expect, there is a suitor, the penniless Adonio, who is befriended by the fairy Manto (the scene is in Mantua) after having saved her from being killed by a peasant as she lay helpless in the form of a snake. Manto promises Adonio to help him win the beautiful but virtuous Argia. To this end she transforms him into a pilgrim and herself into a white dog, which not only does remarkable tricks but with one shake can produce gold coins and jewels. Argia yields to the pilgrim in exchange for his dog. When the husband Anselmo returns, an astrologer tells him of Argia's fall from virtue and he dispatches a servant to kill her. The magic dog makes her disappear in the nick of time. When Anselmo goes to the spot, he finds a magnificent palace, at the door of which an ugly Moor bids him enter. All this will be his, says the Moor, if...

> E gli fa la medesima richiesta
> Ch'avea già Adonio alla sua moglie fatta (XLIII, 139).[1]

Out of cupidity Anselmo agrees to this monstrous proposal, whereupon Argia appears and demands that he grant her pardon, since his guilt is equal to hers. As in the other two *contes*, reconciliation results, 'E sempre poi fu l'uno all'altro caro'.[2]

If magic and metamorphosis add one element of interest to 'La Coupe enchantée', they form an integral part of 'Le Petit Chien', whose complex plot depends upon a series of disguises, transformations, apparitions and supernatural interventions. In adapting Ariosto La Fontaine intensifies these fantasmagoria, creating a magical world

[1] 'And he makes of him the same demand that Adonis had earlier made of his wife.'
[2] 'and ever after one was dear to the other' (142).

in which illusion and self-delusion function to the benefit of young love. Only incidentally does he follow the original theme of the power of avarice, and although he imitates his master's four stanzas on *avarizia*, he attenuates their eloquence. True, he begins by announcing outright that 'La clef du coffre-fort et des coeurs c'est la même'. But a *nuance* becomes immediately apparent; money is not so much the key as presents. And indeed the beauteous Argie, unlike Caliste, does not yield to an offer of gold but rather to the marvels of the magic dog and his miraculous tricks; she is overwhelmed by wonderment rather than avarice. After turning the tables on her husband, she presents an eloquent plea based on 'la qualité du présent', for no one, be she Highness, Majesty or Lucretia herself, could have resisted such a gift.

The creator of the dazzling metamorphoses who will, among other things, transform herself into the fabulous dog, appears suddenly before Argie's disconsolate suitor, now called Atis, beside the river Mincio. La Fontaine introduces the apparition with a solemn mythological allusion:

> à l'heure que l'Aurore
> Commence à s'éloigner du séjour de Téthys,
> Une nymphe en habit de reine,
> Belle, majestueuse, et d'un regard charmant,
> Vint s'offrir tout d'un coup aux yeux du pauvre amant (533).

The fairy, Manto, appears 'tout d'un coup' with a rapidity that characterizes all the transformations she operates. When she announces that she will change Atis into a pilgrim and herself into a performing dog,

> Aussitôt fait que dit; notre amant et la fée
> Changent de forme en un instant.

When Anselme, having learned of his wife's infidelity, hires an assassin who waylays her, the benevolent fairy envelops her in a cloud, and when the disgruntled husband hurries to the spot another miracle has taken place:

> Il y trouve un palais de beauté sans pareille:
> Une heure auparavant c'était un champ tout nu.

So the fairy Manto builds and creates magically; had she not constructed by her charms the very walls of Mantua?[1] The metamorphosis

---

[1] Many of these effects recall the machine-plays, in particular Torelli, whom La Fontaine praised (OD, 524). See my article 'Metamorphosis in Corneille's *Andromède*', *UTQ*, XXXIX (1970), 164–80.

111

of the characters themselves lends itself to a delightful interplay between appearance and reality. When she finally agrees to receive the 'pilgrim', Argie expresses pleased surprise at his grace:

> Vous n'avez pas, ce lui dit-elle,
> La mine de vous en aller
> A Saint-Jacques de Compostelle.

Another lightning transformation follows upon the first kiss:

> Aussitôt que le drôle tint
> Entre ses bras madame Argie,
> Il redevint Atis.

After the venerable judge has accepted the Moor's conditions for giving him the palace, in a trice he appears in the costume of a page boy, retaining only his beard, and at this point the poet stresses the powers of the magician who can transform herself and others as well as create fantastic structures with the same rapidity:

> Par son art métamorphosée,
> Et par son art ayant bâti
> Ce Louvre en un moment; par son art fait un page
> Sexagénaire et grave.

The thrice-reiterated *par son art* emphasizes the range of Manto's magic, which La Fontaine has increased considerably over that of his original. Yet like the Italian poet, who as we saw earlier in mingling realism and fantasy frequently dwelt on the realistic qualities of strange or magical phenomena, La Fontaine will counterbalance the magical effects of the story. He rounds out Ariosto's explanation of Adonio's intercession in favor of the snake by the odd coincidence that he was a descendant of Cadmus, whose arms he bore, and adds that Cadmus became a serpent in his old age.[1] He then goes on to 'naturalize' the hero's action by an aside reminiscent of the *Fables*:

> Il est à remarquer que notre paladin
> N'avait pas cette horreur commune au genre humain
> Contre la gent reptile et toute son espèce.

He gives the magic dog a rather ordinary name, Favori, and at the point in the story where it must warn Argie of her danger, addresses the reader:

[1] Ovid, *Metamorphoses*, IV, 563–603.

Si vous me demandez comme un chien avertit,
    Je crois que par la jupe il tire;
    Il se plaint, il jappe, il soupire,
Il en veut à chacun: pour peu qu'on ait d'esprit,
    On entend bien ce qu'il veut dire.

After this brief description of a real dog warning his mistress, the magical tale begins again with the phrase, 'Favori fit bien plus...'

The preoccupation with illusion, with dizzily rapid transitions shows in some of his stylistic devices. He accentuates the swift rhythm of the show Atis and his dog put on for the astonished Argie by a dazzling succession of verbal infinitives; when the spaniel shakes himself,

    Aussitôt perles de tomber,
    Nourrice de les ramasser,
    Soubrettes de les enfiler,
    Pèlerin de les attacher
    A de certains bras, dont il loue
La blancheur et le reste.

Illusion presupposes this element of display, of performance before an appreciative audience of characters, 'Valets et gens du lieu s'assemblèrent autour d'eux'. The dramatic tone of 'Le Petit Chien' also derives from an increased emphasis on dialogue; of the 525 lines in the poem, 222 are in direct quotation. The characters admonish, cajole, instruct or berate one another. The venerable Anselme, before leaving for Rome, warns his wife against the blandishments of her admirers and their gifts, sounding, with his sententious tags, a little like Polonius:

    Fuyez la ville et les amants,
        Et leurs présents;
    L'invention en est damnable,
Des machines d'amour c'est la plus redoutable:
    De tout temps le monde a vu Don
    Etre le père d'Abandon.

His wife, having eavesdropped on his conversation with the Moor, confronts her ludicrously attired husband with a series of ironic exclamations:

    Est-ce Anselme, dit-elle,
  Que je vois ainsi déguisé?
Anselme! Il ne se peut; mon oeil s'est abusé.
....

> ...Oh, oh, Monsieur notre barbon,
> Notre législateur, notre homme d'ambassade,
> Vous êtes à cet âge homme de mascarade?

The fairy Manto's first words to Atis have some of the solemnity of an expositional *récit*, as she identifies herself and expounds upon her power and the desire to help her benefactor:

> Je veux, dit-elle, Atis, que vous soyez heureux:
> Je le veux, je le puis, étant Manto la fée,
>   Votre amie et votre obligée.
>   Vous connaissez ce nom fameux;
> Mantoue en tient le sien: jadis en cette terre
>   J'ai posé la première pierre
> De ces murs en durée égaux aux bâtiments
> Dont Memphis voit le Nil laver les fondements.

In contrast to these rather ponderous lines, Atis' lyric monologue recalls the *stances* of earlier tragedy:

> Atis, il t'est plus doux encor
> De la voir ingrate et cruelle
> Que d'être privé de ses traits,
> Adieu, ruisseaux, ombrages frais,
> Chants amoureux de Philomèle;
> Mon inhumaine seule attire à soi mes sens.

From monologue to *style indirect libre* is a mere degree; and in 'Le Petit Chien' this device, in which the *fables* abound, serves to create effects both comic and dramatic. Some of the characters even acquire thereby a certain 'interiority'. La Fontaine first suggests their state of mind. In Anselme's case, the mission to Rome is not entirely to his liking:

> Ce ne fut pas sans résister
> Qu'au choix qu'on fit de lui consentit le bon homme.

Once his attitude is established, his thoughts, always related in the Imperfect tense, tumble forth:

> Il devait demeurer dans Rome
> Six mois et plus encor; que savait-il combien?
> Tant d'honneur pouvait nuire au conjugal lien:
>   Longue ambassade et long voyage
>   Aboutissent à cocuage.

In the case of Argie's woman servant, on hearing Atis' bold offer, 'La proposition surprit fort la nourrice', yet her exclamations of dismay are in *style indirect libre*:

> Quoi! Madame l'ambassadrice!
> Un simple pèlerin! Madame à son chevet
> Pourrait voir un bourdon! Et si l'on le savait!

Occasionally as in the above and in Argie's own reaction to the proposal, we have a shift from the indirect to the direct style:

> Il ne s'en fallut rien qu'Argie
> Ne battît sa nourrice: Avoir l'effronterie
> De lui mettre en l'esprit une telle infamie!
> Avec qui? Si c'était encor le pauvre Atis!
> Hélas! mes cruautés sont cause de sa perte.

Such oscillations suggest the author's impulsion toward the dramatic form. In the final version of 'La Coupe enchantée', as we have seen, he suppressed a passage of pure dramatic dialogue, but in the present story he inserts a similar exchange at the point where the Moor makes his indecent proposal to Anselme:

LE MORE: Tu connais l'échanson du monarque des dieux?
ANSELME: Ganymède?
LE MORE: Celui-là même.
> Prends que je sois Jupin.

To present the offer in this way completely effaces the author and brings the speakers into the foreground, yet the poet 'veils' the scabrous both through their hesitant replies and through the distance created by the mythological allusion.

We hear another dramatic echo as the nurse – resembling the go-between of Roman comedy – expostulates with her reluctant mistress. Here, as in Molière, it is the servant who bluntly asserts woman's right to sexual independence.

> Pour qui ménagez-vous les trésors de l'amour?
> Pour celui qui, je crois, ne s'en servira guère.

In her hour of triumph over the *barbon* Anselme, Argie exclaims:

> Ne le soyez donc point; plus on veut nous contraindre,
> Moins on doit s'assurer de nous.

115

These lines echo those of Léonor's servant Lisette, in *L'Ecole des maris*:

> Et si par un mari je me voyais contrainte,
> J'aurais fort grande pente à confirmer sa crainte (I, 2).

In handling the cuckoldry theme, however, La Fontaine adopts in 'Le Petit Chien' a less frenetic tone. Just as he tempers in the following way his cynical declarations of 'La Coupe enchantée' concerning the power of money to buy love,

> La clef du coffre-fort et des coeurs, c'est la même.
> Que si ce n'est celle des coeurs,
> C'est du moins celle des faveurs,

so, in 'Le Petit Chien', although the nurse repeats La Fontaine's well-worn point that amorous dalliance never shows outwardly – 'Cela nous fait-il empirer/D'une ongle ou d'un cheveu!' he contradicts himself in his gently indulgent comment on the love affair:

> Chacun s'en aperçut; car d'enfermer sous l'ombre
> Une telle aise, le moyen?
> Jeunes gens font-ils jamais rien
> Que le plus aveugle ne voie?

Although the *conte* ends, as had the other two, on a note of reconciliation, each partner agreeing to keep his share of the bargain, the wife to remain faithful and the husband to resist suspicion henceforth, La Fontaine refuses to follow Ariosto in making Anselmo more blameworthy than his spouse. He seems rather to tend towards Montaigne's conclusion in 'Sur des vers de Virgile': 'Le fourgon se moque de la poele.'

4

The Gallic Tradition

'Les Cent Nouvelles nouvelles'

La Fontaine tells us, in a *conte* imitated from Marguerite de Navarre, that despite the preeminence of Boccaccio, he had dipped into another stock of stories,

> Vieux des plus vieux, où Nouvelles nouvelles
> Sont jusqu'à cent, bien déduites et belles
> Pour la plupart, et de très bonne main (418).[1]

Actually of the nine tales he borrows from the fifteenth-century *Cent Nouvelles nouvelles* that Pierre Jourda considers to be the first collection of modern short stories in French Literature,[2] less than half seem sufficiently 'bien déduites et belles' to warrant our attention here. La Fontaine's tendency to prune and summarize serves him ill in 'Le Mari confesseur' (287–90), in which a cuckold suspicious on his return home from a voyage puts on a priest's habit and hears his wife confess to having given herself to a gentleman, a knight and a priest. The original tells the pithy tale of how the jolly wife receives in succession a gentle squire, 'frisque, frez and friant en bon point', a knight and a priest, from each of whom she managed to obtain many gifts. La Fontaine completely ignores the wife's cupidity, as well as the fact that it was the sight of the riches – what the storyteller calls the 'butin qu'elle avoit a la force de ses reins conquesté' – that made the husband suspicious. Our poet ignores another point in the story: the wife's presence of mind when, after her confession, the husband can no longer contain himself, and she pretends she has known of his trick all along. In La Fontaine's version, there is no reason for her to confess to the relationship with 'un gentilhomme,

---

[1] Page references in the text are to the Groos and Schiffrin edition of La Fontaine's works.

[2] *Conteurs français du XVIᵉ siècle*, ed. Pierre Jourda (Paris: Bibliothèque de la Pléiade, 1965), p. xix. Page references in the text for the conteurs will be to this edition.

un chevalier, un prêtre', except to illustrate the husband's gullibility.

This Boccaccian feminine ruse reappears in 'On ne s'avise jamais de tout', in which a typically suspicious husband constantly consults a volume containing all the tricks of female ingenuity, with La Fontaine exclaiming:

> Pauvre ignorant! Comme si cette affaire
> N'était une hydre, à parler franchement!

To show how hydra-headed is feminine ingenuity, the *conteur* of the *Cent Nouvelles* (164-7) has told how the errant wife arranges to have a pail of water dropped on her as she is returning from Mass, from a window in her lover's house, so that she may go in there to change her clothes. La Fontaine's staccato version omits all preliminaries: the wife's encounter with the gallant, the exchange of letters, the various details of the stratagem. But the adaptation reveals considerable vigor; the obsession with betrayal appears as a religion with the husband bearing his book of female guile like a psalter. (In his jealous curiosity, he even keeps track of the hairs on her head for fear she may have offered a bracelet of her hair to a lover!) The duenna, in the original simply 'une vieille serpente', takes on the attributes of Argus: 'une vieille au corps tout rempli d'yeux'.

The hand of the master also shows in the episode of the bucket thrown from above: curiously, he makes its contents more disgusting. What had been carefully described in the source as 'un grand seau d'eau et de cendres entremeslées' becomes 'un panier d'ordure', 'cette immondice', offering a rapid glimpse of the degrading aspects of love. In the alacrity with which the adventure takes place, we recognize the dexterity of 'L'Oraison de Saint Julien'; almost two full pages in the Pléiade edition are skillfully condensed as follows:

> Un jour de fête, arrive que la dame
> En revenant de l'église passa
> Près d'un logis, d'où quelqu'un lui jeta
> Fort à propos plein un panier d'ordure.
> On s'excusa: la pauvre créature
> Toute vilaine entra dans le logis.
> Il lui fallut dépouiller ses habits (438).

La Fontaine does not reveal the ruse until the end; the only hint of previous arrangement is in the phrase 'fort à propos'; amorous fatality is thus man- or rather woman-made.

The role of chance in love is stressed by La Fontaine in 'Les Quiproquo', based both on the ninth tale of the *Cent Nouvelles nouvelles* and the eighth story in the *Heptaméron*. The main lines are the same; when a husband lays siege to his wife's chambermaid, the two women concoct a ruse whereby the wife takes her servant's place. The husband's discomfiture is increased by the fact that he allows a friend to enjoy the supposed chambermaid's favors the same night; he is thus a cuckold by his own devices, and Dame Fortune has permitted his wife to partake without guilt of the joys of adultery.

La Fontaine's *conte* expands rather than reduces the two sources. He intervenes frequently; first of all to establish a personal identity in a chatty prologue, placing the events squarely under the aegis of Dame Fortune who has a habit of confounding our amorous hopes by her tricks:

> Au lieu des biens où notre coeur aspire,
> D'un quiproquo se plaît à nous payer (650).

Of these 'biens', Chloris had given him some hope, but when he paid her a visit at an opportune time, she was absent;

> Je vais un soir chez cet objet charmant,
> L'époux était aux champs heureusement,
> Mais il revint la nuit à peine close.
> Point de Chloris...
> ....
> le sort en sa place suppose
> Une soubrette à mon commandement.
> Elle paya cette fois pour la Dame.

This rather vague 'personal' memory provides an excellent transition, for the story at hand tells of the reverse situation; a lady substituting for her maid.[1]

Once the *persona* of the poet is established, esthetic considerations present themselves. He is aware that such substitutions are staple diet: 'De pareils traits tous les livres sont pleins'. The *Decameron* in particular favors them, and as we recall, our poet has adapted, in addition to 'Le Berceau' which he mentions here as the best example, three stories involving confusion of identity. It is in this context that La Fontaine praises Boccaccio once again, effacing himself before his master with the rueful admission that his overbold hand

[1] A similar story of frustration occurs in the *Elégie première*, OD, p. 600.

> En mille endroits a peut-être gâté
> Ce que la sienne a bien exécuté.

Such praise serves to remind the reader of the poet's task to treat an improbable situation convincingly,

> Sans rien forcer et sans qu'on violente
> Un incident qui ne s'attendait pas.

Despite the banality of the subject, La Fontaine presents his *conte* as a real-life illustration of the theme – he will show us still another example of Dame Fortune's tricks and thus prove her whimsy by 'quelque nouveau tour'. The incident took place in Marseille, he adds, and it is true: 'Tout en est vrai, rien n'en est controuvé', and he calls his hero Clidamant because respect prevents him from revealing his real name.

This appeal to the reality of the *fait divers* precludes mention of his sources. He remains closest to Marguerite de Navarre and appears to owe nothing to the *Cent Nouvelles nouvelles*. As in the *Heptaméron*, the wife is beautiful and the husband's infidelity due to the search for variety. As Marguerite charmingly, but a tinge indignantly, puts it, 'auquel change il ne gaignoit que le plaisir qu'apporte quelquefois la diversité des viandes' (742). In both authors the wife marvels at her supposed husband's new vigor, a commonplace in these situations. But two prevalent attitudes supersede the early versions: first, the venality of love, and second, despite the essential innocence of both women, the female cynicism and licentiousness of the Gallic tradition.

Clidamant, a 'Provençal un peu chaud', urges his suit to the extent of offering the chambermaid, Alix, 100 crowns (the sources contain no hint of a bribe). Unlike his earlier counterparts, he does not share the 'chambermaid's' favors out of friendship but because his friend offers to pay half her fee: 'Cinquante écus à sauver étaient bons'. Once the theme of venality has entered the tale, doubts arise even concerning the virtuous wife as the poet provides a subtle counterpoint to the qualities she duly inherits from the earlier stories,

> L'honnêteté, la vertu de la dame,
> Sa gentillesse et même sa beauté.

La Fontaine intervenes to comment that 100 crowns was a good price, and suddenly, almost automatically, asks, 'sur ce pied-là qu'eût coûté la maîtresse?' answering in the same breath, 'Peut-être moins; car le hasard y fait', then suddenly catching himself up, to declare, 'Mais je me trompe.' Then, in a remarkable example of his genius with transitions, he seizes on a word in one of the lines reasserting the lady's honor: 'Ni dons, ni soins, rien n'aurait réussi', to ask himself why he has added the theme of venality in love: 'Devrais-je y faire entrer les dons aussi?' This permits a diatribe of the *o tempora, o mores* variety:

> Las! ce n'est plus le siècle de nos pères.
> Amour vend tout, et nymphes et bergères;
> Il met le taux à maint objet divin:
> C'était un dieu, ce n'est qu'un échevin.
> O temps! ô moeurs! ô coutume perverse!

This digression helps to cast doubt upon the other female participant in the ruse. Unlike the timid, frightened girls in the sources, she plans a rendezvous before consulting her mistress. Her self-possession, and the fact she takes the bribe after merely pretending anger, suggests a certain ambivalence, as does the insinuation, after the trick has been played, that she regretted her passive role:

> Aucuns ont dit qu'Alix fit conscience
> De n'avoir pas mieux gagné son argent:
> Plaignant l'époux, et le dédommageant.

Her mistress' reactions are also curious; in the earlier versions the wife, the picture of injured innocence, berates her husband, who begs forgiveness. In particular, the *Heptaméron* succeeds in portraying his remorse, mingled with tenderness: 'Qui fut bien désespéré, ce fut ce pauvre mary, voyant sa femme tant sage, belle et chaste, avoir esté delaissée de luy pour une qui ne l'aymoit pas' (745). La Fontaine's ending sidesteps the confrontation between husband and wife. Although she attributes her spouse's unusual ardor to his belief that he is holding the maid in his arms and resolves to confront him with this, she says nothing. Contrary to the sources, immediately after the trick she sees the friend with her husband and suspects the truth, as do the two men. *She almost* fails to maintain her composure, thereby evoking the poet's sly comment:

> J'en suis surpris: femmes savent mentir;
> La moins habile en connaît la science.

And so the tale ends without a final resolution, suspicions and scruple in both minds, and the wife 'toujours inconsolable', her virtue counterpointed by the poet's skepticism about women in general:

> Dieu gard de mal celles qu'en cas semblable
> Il ne faudrait nullement consoler.
> J'en connais bien qui n'en feraient que rire.

In these closing lines, the word *consoler* should be read with its secondary meaning of *seduce*. La Fontaine has just introduced two questions: was the husband really a cuckold, and did not the lady have the right to seek genuine revenge, i.e. take a lover? To the first he answers no, to the second, yes, and the suggestion that she will go on to seek further 'consolation' has been subtly planted.

The encounter between the wife and two men who have shared her favors takes place because of a significant alteration: the amorous rendezvous occurs not in the chambermaid's bedroom but in the cellar, from which Clidamant, to his surprise, sees his wife emerge. La Fontaine is quite specific about the spatial details:

> La fête étant de la sorte passée
> Du noir séjour ils n'eurent qu'à sortir.
> L'associé des frais et du plaisir
> S'en court en haut en certain vestibule:
> Mais quand l'époux vit sa femme monter...

As in the Boccaccian tales the element of darkness is accentuated, although fear and violence are absent.[1] The silence necessary for the success of the ruse, combined with the 'noir séjour' as the scene of the sexual activity, correspond to the repression of the truth with which the open ending of the *conte* leaves the participants, suggesting further ruse and betrayal.

Dame Fortune played her tricks in 'Les Quiproquo' because of what Marguerite de Navarre called 'le plaisir qu'apporte la diversité des viandes', and in 'Pâté d'anguille' La Fontaine both uses a similar metaphor and claims diversity as his watchword, repeating the refrain 'Diversité c'est ma devise' five times throughout the *conte*. The tale proves the power of diversity by demonstrating that even the tastiest dish can cloy; a nobleman, chided by a faithful servant for infidelity to his beautiful wife, serves his critic a favorite delicacy, eel pâté, every day until he protests 'mon estomac en est si travaillé

---

[1] See above, p. 51.

que, tantost qu'il les sent, il a assez disné'. (57). Whereupon the master agrees to suspend the monotonous food if the servant, as before, provides him with other delectable fare.

As in 'Les Quiproquo', the author's *persona* begins the tale by introducing the basic metaphor: sex = food:

> Même beauté, tant soit exquise,
> Rassasie et soûle à la fin.
> Il me faut d'un et d'autre pain;
> Diversité, c'est ma devise (594).

His principal change is to make the servant a valet cuckolded by his master; thus permitting the introduction of a familiar theme: the unimportance of cuckoldry:

> Bien sot de faire un bruit si grand
> Pour une chose si commune.

The servant, who is foolish enough to entreat his master not to seduce his wife, receives neither yes or no for an answer; a hint at the 'droit du seigneur' that is original with La Fontaine. The lesson of the eel loaf results in the valet's emulating his master, and his success is due to an old recipe: 'mots dorés', the venality in love that, as he admits,

> J'ai rebattu cent et cent fois
> Ceci dans cent et cent endroits.

In addition to these favorite saws, La Fontaine succeeds in artfully fusing his own *persona*'s amoral tastes with those of the licentious nobleman, and eventually of the valet. The refrain, applied three times to himself, then to the master, then finally to the manservant, skilfully suggests the latter's transformation. The last third of the *conte* so closely mingles the author's view with that to which the valet comes that the reader is at first in doubt as to who declares in line 108 'J'aime le change'. I believe it should be read 'To whomever says, like the valet, I like variety...' The answer, 'gagnez...les intéressés' meaning 'bribe all those involved', should apply to the reader, the master, the valet and the poet himself. For the valet had had second thoughts, wondering

> doit-il suffire
> D'alléguer son plaisir sans plus?

The master pays up, and the line 'notre jaloux devint commode' completes the fusion of the tale at hand with the twenty-one lines of amorous philosophy that precede it.

In 'Pâté d'anguille' the servant emulates the master, his success with his 'gilded words' suggesting that we are all cast in the same mold:

> Mots dorés font tout en amours,
> ....
> Ils persuadent la donzelle,
> Son petit chien, sa demoiselle...
> ....
> Il en croqua, femmes et filles,
> Nymphes, grisettes, ce qu'il put.

A similar concept of emulation serves to transform 'L'Abbesse', the story of an abbess cured of a mysterious malady by sexual intercourse. Doctors unanimously prescribe this remedy, but her qualms are allayed only when all the nuns heroically offer to emulate her, 'affin que vous n'ayez pensée ny ymaginacion qu'en temps advenir vous en sourdist reprouche de nulle de nous' (94). In La Fontaine's version it is the nuns' example, not their promise that encourages the abbess to submit. The theme of emulation suggests the most famous of illustrative passages: Rabelais' story of Panurge and the sheep of which the poet makes his prologue. In order to introduce his summary of Rabelais, La Fontaine uses the image of men as sheep: 'ouailles sont la plupart des personnes.' The example of a sheep throwing itself into the river, and the use of Rabelais' phrase:

> Vous ne verrez nulle âme moutonnière
> Rester au bord

permits him to beg our indulgence:

> Ami lecteur, ne te déplaira pas
> Si sursoyant ma principale histoire,
> Je te remets cette chose en mémoire.

But far from superseding the main story, La Fontaine's remarkably deft résumé of Panurge's vengeance on the sheep merchant sets the stage for the nuns' orgy, underlying which is the familiar irony of female insatiability, since the nuns' alacrity is solemnly attributed solely to their devotion to the abbess:

> Nulle ne veut demeurer en arrière.
> Presse se met pour n'être la dernière
> Qui ferait voir son zèle et sa ferveur
> A mère abbesse.

The same irony is evident in the abbess' reaction to the proposed remedy. In the source, she resigns herself to death rather than submit. Her reply in La Fontaine's version strikes the reader by its vigor, but there is no hint of dying:

> Jésus! reprit toute scandalisée
> Madame abbesse: hé! que dites-vous là?
> Fi!

The poet reveals her inmost thoughts; her refusal is based only on her fear of her sisters' opinion:

> Non pas que dans son âme
> Ce bon ne fût par elle souhaité;
> Mais le moyen que sa communauté
> Lui vît sans peine approuver telle chose!

The image of the 'franche moutonnaille' is maintained throughout. The nun who attempts to convince her superior is called 'Soeur Agnès', and in their eagerness to try the remedy the sisters resemble the sheep jumping overboard:

> De ses brebis à peine la première
> A fait le saut, qu'il suit une autre soeur.

(In the preceding line, *faire le saut* has an additional meaning that is made clear in 'Les Troqueurs' when Etienne seduces Tiennette: 'Bref, ils firent le saut').

Were one to attempt to characterize the tone of this story one might call it simply joyous. In their bustle and haste to provide sufficient examples to allay their superior's scruples the nuns may resemble Dindenaut's sheep, but they are warm, sentient beings as well, saddened by the abbess' illness and enthusiastic at the possibility of curing her. When Sister Agnès makes her suggestion,

> Cet avis fut approuvé de chacune;
> On l'applaudit.

When the cure is finally administered, the poet expresses the result in joyous rather than sensual terms:

> Elle redevient rose,
> Oeillet, aurore, et si quelque autre chose
> De plus riant se peut imaginer.

The enthusiasm that pervades the *conte* spills over into La Fontaine's conclusion, which consists of a paean to the 'remède' of sexual intercourse, and concludes with a hostile glance at the restraints imposed by 'le point d'honneur' – jealousy, prudery, marital proprietariness and all the hindrances society imposes upon the most marvelous cure of all:

> O doux remède! ô remède à donner!
> Remède ami de mainte créature,
> Ami des gens, ami de la nature,
> Ami de tout, point d'honneur excepté.
> Point d'honneur est une autre maladie:
> Dans ses écrits Madame Faculté
> N'en parle point. Que de maux en la vie!

La Fontaine's smiling approval of sensual nuns carries over to their male counterparts at least in the Boccaccian tales, in which the libidinous monk frequently earns our sympathy as he triumphs by ruse over credulous or selfish husbands. But the tales from the *Cent Nouvelles nouvelles* take on a sterner tone. The monk now appears as a conniving lecher, deserving only the contempt and merciless punishment of his victims. 'Les Cordeliers de Catalogne' tells how Franciscan monks persuade all the women of a town to share their favors with them as a kind of tithe or *dîme*. When the husbands discover this unusual tribute, they burn down the monastery together with its lusty occupants.

La Fontaine's chief addition is once again the 'irony of female insatiability' that we have already noted in the Boccaccian tales. In the original, the wives appear as innocent victims – 'les pauvres simples femmes, qui mieulx cuidoient ces bons frères estre anges que hommes terriens' (140) – whereas in La Fontaine's version they comply with all the alacrity of an Alaciel: they actually quarrel over who is to make the first payment, and so enthusiastic are they at fulfilling their obligation that the monastery protests

> De par Dieu, souffrez qu'on respire;
> C'en est assez pour le présent;
> On ne peut faire qu'en faisant (396).

Several of the ladies have acquired considerable credit, and the monks begin to weary of their debt-collecting.

Our poet increases the violence of the husbands' revenge. In the *Cent Nouvelles nouvelles*, the first to learn of the tithe entices his wife's friar to his home and threatens him with an axe until he reveals the nature of his brethren's exactions. La Fontaine's hero puts a dagger to the monk's throat and upon his confession ties both him and his wife hand and foot and locks them up. But our poet is more delicate than his source concerning church property: 'Par respect de la demeure' the monks are herded into a barn which is then burned, while in the older *conte*, 'Dieu mesmes…eut sa maison brullée' (146). But the relish at the friars' fate is all La Fontaine's; the vengeful husbands dance around the burning barn to the beating of drums and while the early *conteur* merely shows all the property being consumed by flames, La Fontaine details each part of the monks' clothing as they burn:

> Robes, manteaux et cocluchons
> Tout fut brûlé comme cochons
> Tous périrent dans les flammes.

In the second tale, 'L'Ermite', a lustful hermit achieves his goal with impunity as La Fontaine warns us in Rabelaisian accents:

> Avez-vous soeur, fille, ou femme jolie
> Gardez le froc! (464)

The lecherous cleric, an 'imposteur' who recalls Tartuffe, tricks an innocent female by the ancient ruse of feigning divinity of which La Fontaine gave another, pastoral version in 'Le Fleuve Scamandre'. The cognate story in Boccaccio tells of a monk who seduces a Venetian lady by pretending to be the angel Gabriel, but the actual model is the fourteenth-century tale in the *Cent Nouvelles nouvelles* which our poet follows quite closely. A hermit lusts after an innocent girl, and in order to seduce her, inserts in the wall of the house where she lives with her widowed mother a horn through which in sepulchral tones he bids the mother take her daughter to his cell. From the union of the girl and the hermit, promises the voice, will be born a future Pope. The story of the God-priest seducing the virgin is as old as the Vestals and as modern as the Italian film of the forties, 'The Miracle'.

Hitherto as in 'Féronde' La Fontaine had merely suggested the hypocrisy of clerics; now he clearly makes it his theme, choosing as his protagnost the most unworldly, but potentially, as Rabelais had pointed out, the most sexually formidable of all, the hermit. The story he tells us, will relate an exploit in which 'Dame Vénus' and 'Dame

Hypocrisie'join forces. The contrast between appearance and reality, essential to the hypocrisy theme, expresses itself in a number of ways. First, the hermit's saintly garb conceals a lecher:

> sous la houppelande
> Logeait le coeur d'un dangereux paillard.

In describing his clerical garb, La Fontaine employs obvious sexual symbolism to suggest his potency:

> Un chapelet pendait à sa ceinture
> Long d'une brasse, et gros outre mesure.

Using Rabelais' term, the poet exclaims 'O papelards! Qu'on se trompe à vos mines!' and proceeds to show the hypocrite in action in gesture and expression:

> il faisait le cafard,
> Se renfermant voyant une femelle,
> Dedans sa coque, et baissant la prunelle.

When the mother and daughter pay him the visit ordered by the mysterious voice, he prepares a scene of penitence as he sees them approaching, pretending to flog himself as they enter his cell. He feigns dismay at the supernatural command and at first refuses to obey on the pretext that he suspects the Devil's hand in the matter. When he finally yields, he undresses the girl as if he were about to baptize her. Later, when she is pregnant and leaves his cell for home, he piously offers thanks to Heaven 'qui soulageait son pauvre serviteur'.

The use of antonomasia aids in depicting La Fontaine's Tartuffe. The poet calls him first 'l'homme de Dieu' or 'l'anachorète', but as the ruse develops, he becomes 'le corneur', 'notre cagot', 'le papelard', 'l'hypocrite', and finally le 'forge-pape'. When he pretends to lash himself, La Fontaine depicts him ironically as a soldier of the Lord,

> comme un brave soldat,
> Le fouet en main, toujours en un état
> De pénitence, et de tirer des flammes
> Quelque défunt puni pour ses méfaits.

The violence inherent in such a tableau is new to the story. In the *Cent Nouvelles nouvelles*, the hermit merely kneels in prayer and leaves his door ajar so as to be seen. Indeed violence underlies the ruse throughout. The first hermit speaks softly through his wooden tube, and returns only once to the widow's house. But howling winds accompany Friar Luce's stentorian cries and even, the poet adds, 'favorisaient le dessein', which suggests that fear is a necessary ingredient of the ruse. The thunderous voice fills both women with terror – in the original only the mother hears it – 'La peur les tint un quart d'heure en silence.' And when the mother decides to ignore the supernatural command, the second time the voice threatens her with death.

The hermit's actions, before he seduces the girl, involve piercing apertures in walls, and the 'long cornet' he inserts, like the enormous rosary hanging from his waist, is clearly an erotic symbol. When the girl conceals her pregnancy for fear of being sent home because 'le jeu d'amour commençait à lui plaire', the reader is made to ask 'D'où lui vient tant d'esprit?' and receives the reply that the game of love is 'l'arbre de science', recalling the basic play on words of 'Comment l'esprit vint aux filles'.

This sexual imagery in addition to the violence that underlies the hermit's desire, intensifies the menace of the hypocritical cleric. In addition to the monks' lechery, the poet evokes their love of luxury and acquisitiveness in the hermit's wily promises that the miraculous offspring will bring wealth to his whole family:

> Ferez monter aux grandeurs tous les vôtres,
> Princes les uns et grands seigneurs les autres,
> Vos cousins ducs, cardinaux vos neveux;
> Places, châteaux, tant pour vous que pour eux,
> Ne manqueront en aucune manière...

La Fontaine, like Molière, sees the religious hypocrite as an abuser of families, grossly sensual and capable of invoking the Deity to his own ends, and like the playwright he satirizes the clergy's interest in worldly goods. It is not without interest that 'L'Ermite' was published in 1667, the year in which *L'Imposteur* first reached the stage.

Bonaventure des Périers

The *Nouvelles Récréations et joyeux devis* attributed to Bonaventure des Périers, author of the gravely satirical, anti-Christian *Cymbalum mundi*, provided three Gallic *contes*, 'Le Faiseur d'oreilles', already studied in Chapter 2; 'Les Lunettes' and 'Le Gascon puni'. In the second the spectacles of the title are worn by a mother superior in whose convent a lusty youth, disguised as a nun, has been sporting with the inmates. When she learns of these illicit pursuits, she calls all the sisters together and bids them undress. The culprit, fore-warned, has tied himself so as to pass inspection, but the beauteous nudity confronting him proves too much and his rebellious member, bursting its bonds, knocks the short-sighted abbess' glasses from her inquisitive nose.

Such a story interested our poet not only because, as his slyly rueful prologue tells us, he never tired, despite good resolutions, of recounting the amorous adventures of nuns, but because the main point provides a challenge to a poet who would 'conter d'une manière honnête'. The problem inspires a 22-line digression consisting of a witty circumlocution that permits him to avoid naming outright the male member. The 'difficulty' arises when he must describe the nature of the impostor's precaution:

> Nécessité, mère de stratagème
> Lui fit…eh bien? Lui fit en ce moment
> Lier…et quoi? Foin, je suis court moi-même (599).

There follows the 'détour', a story reminiscent of Diotima's tale of the Androgyne. Men and women had once a window in their bodies, convenient to doctors, but inconvenient when located near the heart, especially to women who must conceal their feelings. Nature decided to tie up the aperture, but in women's case used too short a lace, in man's one too long, and so, says La Fontaine, a trifle out of breath,

> Il est facile à présent qu'on devine
> Ce que lia notre jeune imprudent…

It is instructive to compare the prose recital of the comic episode with La Fontaine's version. As the *Nouvelles récréations* tell it,

Les nonnes comparurent toutes. L'abbesse leur feit sa remonstrance et leur dit pourquoy elle les avoit assemblées, et leur commanda qu'elles eussent à se dépouiller toutes nues. Elle prend ses lunettes pour faire sa reveue, et, en les visitant les unes apres les aultres, il vint au reng de soeur Thoinette, laquelle, voyant ces nonnes toutes nues, fraisches, blan-ches, refaictes, rebondies, elle ne peust estre maistresse de ceste cheville qu'il ne se fist mauvais jeu. Car, sur le poinct que l'abbesse avoit les yeux le plus près, la corde vint rompre, et, en desbandant tout à un coup, la cheville vint repousser contre les lunettes de l'abbesse et les fit sauter à deux grandz pas loing (495).

La Fontaine stresses two elements in the passage; the power of the
young women's nudity and its dynamic, almost explosive effect on the
imprisoned sex of the youth. Such beauty would have tempted a
saint, the very angels:

> amenez-moi des saints;
> Amenez-moi si vous voulez des anges;
> Je les tiendrai créatures étranges.
> Si vingt nonnains telles qu'on les vit lors
> Ne font trouver à leur esprit un corps.

Their beauty is such that it can transform the spirit into flesh; it is
worthy of the three Graces; charms such as have never before been
revealed, save in the New World where nudity is the rule. The effect
of these lines is to idealize the nuns' beauty; La Fontaine brings into
play the celestial, the mythological, the exotic in order to emphasize
its force, but without details. Their charms are *trésors, fiers appas*,
their nudity described in circumlocution:

> un habit que vraisemblablement
> N'avaient pas fait les tailleurs du couvent.

Thus we are brought back to the earthly scene, and the torture ('la
question') the sight inflicts on the fettered youth. The poet becomes
more specific as the zero hour approaches:

> Touffes de lis, proportion du corps,
> Secrets appas, embonpoint et peau fine,
> Fermes tetons, et semblables ressorts
> Eurent bientôt fait jouer la machine.

The explosion is far more violent in the poetic version; the 'machine'
bursts forth 'Comme un coursier qui romprait son licou', sending the
abbess' spectacles flying up to the ceiling (rather than Des Périers'
paltry two paces), and almost knocking her to the ground. This is
not only the force of the sexual urge but the dynamism of nature itself, in which the poet sees an essential rightness to which all must
yield. In the prose version the youth is merely sent away, but La
Fontaine adds a lengthy passage that shows his hero in dire straits.
The spiteful old nuns who could not enjoy his favors are charged
with his punishment. They tie him up to a tree, and while they go in
search of whips to scourge him a passing miller stops. When the
youth tells him he is being punished for refusing to yield to the

nuns' amorous entreaties, the lusty miller offers to take his place, and suffers the whipping instead of the delights he had expected.

The whipping scene takes place with something of the same frenzy and violence that we noted in 'Les Cordeliers de Catalogne'. The vengeful crones refuse to release the duped miller:

> – Tant pis pour toi, tu payras pour le sire.
> Nous n'avons pas telles armes en main,
> Pour demeurer en un si beau chemin
> Tiens, tiens, voilà l'abat que l'on désire.

As they beat the unfortunate substitute, one has the impression of an erotic impulsion, with the victim's supplications only increasing the nuns' furor; 'points de suspension' actually suggesting the breath literally beaten from his body:

> A ce discours fouets de rentrer en jeu,
> Verges d'aller, et non pas pour un peu;
> Meunier de dire en langue intelligible,
> Crainte de n'être assez bien entendu:
> Mesdames, je...ferai tout mon possible
> Pour m'acquitter de ce qui vous est dû.
> Plus il leur tient des discours de la sorte,
> Plus la fureur de l'antique cohorte
> Se fait sentir.

La Fontaine achieves an ironic counterpointing as he shows the miller's mule gambolling in the grass nearby while the blows fall upon his master's back. The concluding lines afford an example of the particular kind of nonchalance we have seen in 'Le Tableau' and 'La Coupe enchantée', the poet refusing to provide a tidy ending:

> Ce qu'à la fin l'un et l'autre devint,
> Je ne le sais, ni ne m'en mets en peine.

What matters only is that the youth escaped his fate, an escape which underlines La Fontaine's approval of his actions. In his final aside to the reader, he makes it clear that his addition of the punishment to the original tale is intended to create suspense, even fear in the mind of the reader; it was very likely for this reason he rejected Des Périers' facile ending:

> Suffit d'avoir sauvé le jouvenceau.
> Pendant un temps les lecteurs, pour douzaine
> De ces nonnains au corps gent et si beau,
> N'auraient voulu, je gage, être en sa peau.

La Fontaine also considerably increases the element of fear in the third story imitated from Des Périers, 'Le Gascon puni'. As in 'Le Berceau', 'Richard Minutolo' and other stories, the main point involves one person taking another's place in bed. In this case, however, the substitute is forced to remain silent and motionless for fear of discovery. Two young Italians, in Spain on business, fall in love with two Spanish beauties. One of them promises to entertain her lover if his friend will take her place in her bed simply to ensure her husband's awareness of a presence there, since he usually does nothing but sleep soundly. The lovers have their way, and the following morning awaken the shivering substitute who has all along been lying beside the lady he loves.

La Fontaine uses the trick as the punishment of a boastful Gascon, whereas in Des Périers' version the lovers receive high praise, the man for having risked danger to help his friend, the woman for remaining continent while lying beside him. La Fontaine saw at once that the story had little point; why, he must have asked, as we do, did she restrain herself?

La Fontaine's delightful widow, on the other hand, is determined to take revenge for the Gascon Dorilas' boasting that he has already enjoyed her favors, and it is she who spends the night by his side. The braggart shows his fear of the supposed husband by shrinking to the edge of the bed:

> Se fait petit, se serre, au bord se va nicher,
> Et ne tient que moitié de la rive occupée (443).

To increase the suspense, the Gascon's bedmate is extremely restless; thereby heightening the illusion:

> Son coucheur cette nuit se retourna cent fois;
> Et jusque sur le nez lui porta certains doigts
> Que la peur lui fit trouver rudes.
> ....
> L'on étendait un pied; l'on approchait un bras:
> Il crut même sentir la barbe d'Eurilas.

In the original story, to Alessio's amazement, at dawn the lovers enter the bedchamber after banging the door; La Fontaine transfers this 'tintamarre' to the pseudo-Eurilas, who noisily rings a bell next to the bed as the trembling Gascon awaits discovery. His punishment is made even more exquisite when Philis, after answering in dulcet

133

tones his frightened pleas for pardon, reveals in part what he had missed:

> En lui montrant ce qu'il avait perdu
> Laissait son sein à demi-nu.

These concluding lines remarkably portray Philis' gesture as she leaves the room, and one imagines the Gascon's expression as it changes from 'peine et frayeur extrême' to incredulity and discomfiture.

La Fontaine here indulges in interventions more frequently than in the other *contes* from Des Périers almost seeming unable to conceal his relish at the predicament of the boastful Gascon. A few deft lines paint the comely and carefree Philis, from whom love exacts no pain:

> son humeur libre, gaie, et sincère
> Montrait qu'elle était sans affaire,
> Sans secret, sans passion...

The poet subtly indicates her virginal quality (she had been married to a 'vieux barbon'):

> La belle avait de quoi mettre un Gascon aux cieux,
> Des attraits par-dessus les yeux,
> Je ne sais quel air de pucelle...

This is the prize that the Gascon, unlike his counterpart in the earlier story, must forego as a reward for his braggadocio. His origins characterize him sufficiently: 'il était Gascon, c'est tout dire.' His declarations of love should be taken strictly for what they are worth:

> Ceux des Gascons et des Normands
> Passent peu pour mots d'Evangile.

A wry comment stresses La Fontaine's scorn for slander; for which the Gascon is all the more blameable because of its power:

> tout médisant est prophète en ce monde:
> On croit le mal d'abord...

The narrator's presence also shows in his remarks on Dorilas' state of mind; his fear that the 'husband' by his side will awaken and be stirred by a 'caprice amoureux'; his generalizations concerning such cases show indirectly the Gascon's disquiet:

> tels cas sont dangereux,
> Lorsque l'un des conjoints se sent privé du somme.

Point of view and indirect monologue intensify the impression of uneasiness; when the two lovers appear with torches, this is the 'comble de tous maux', and we watch Dorilas' consternation as the poet assures us,

> Le Gascon, après ces travaux,
> Se fût bien levé sans chandelle.
> Sa perte était alors un point tout assuré.

As the only one of the Des Périers stories to be told in *vers libres*, 'Le Gascon puni' succeeds by means of a rhythm and grace that counterpoint its rather malicious tone. Here is Philis giving her instructions to the Gascon:

> – Notre but est qu'Eurilas pense,
> Vous sentant près de lui, que ce soit sa moitié.
> Il ne lui touche point, vit dedans l'abstinence,
> Et, soit par jalousie ou bien par impuissance,
> A retranché d'hymen certains droits d'amitié;
> Ronfle toujours, fait la nuit d'une traite:
> C'est assez qu'en son lit il trouve une cornette.

One could hardly describe better the gap that can arise between husband and wife; she has become simply a presence that one merely feels and the reasons for the estrangement are not even clear. The final line succeeds by the image of the *cornette* or woman's nightcap, that demonstrates depersonalization; Dorilas will need only this headgear to pass for Eurilas' wife.

Rabelais

The spirit of Rabelais pervades both the *Fables* and the *Contes*, and La Fontaine declared openly that he was his disciple.[1] One fable, 'Le Bûcheron et Mercure', was directly inspired by the prologue of Book IV, and a reference to Picrochole suggests that 'La Laitière et le pot au lait' owes its inspiration to Chapter 33 in Pantagruel, where the agressor king listens eagerly to his counsellors' promises of conquest but fails to head a prudent adviser who cautions, 'J'ay grand peur que toute ceste entreprise sera semblable à la farce du pot au laict'.

One constantly hears the ring of Rabelais' voice in such proper names as Rodilardus, Thibault l'Agnelet, Robin Mouton, Martin Bâton, Messer Gaster, Maistre Jean Chouart and Frère Frappart.

1 'Maître François, dont je me dis encore le disciple' (OD, 672).

Although he owes him only two *contes*. 'L'Anneau de Hans Carvel' and 'Le Diable de Papefiguière', Rabelaisian allusions and turns of speech abound.

We have admired the dexterous summary of Panurge's adventure with the sheep merchant so skilfully integrated into 'L'Abbesse' and heard the spectacle-wearing superior of 'Les Lunettes' described by the epithet 'lunetière' that Dindenaut applied to Panurge. Other echoes are heard: in 'Joconde' the jealous queen accuses her dwarf-lover of preferring to play 'au lansquenet', one of the young Gargantua's favorite games, and followed in Rabelais' list, curiously enough, by 'Au cocu'; the warning 'Gardez le froc' in 'L'Ermite' has a Rabelaisian resonance, as has the 'c'est basme' of Jeanne's husband in 'Les Troqueurs' and the designation of a comely servant girl as 'bonne robe'.[1] In 'La Jument du compère Pierre', the monk's concupiscent stare reminds La Fontaine of the dog eyeing his bone in the prologue to *Gargantua*: 'Si veu l'avez, vous avez peu noter de quelle devotion il le guette, de quel soing il le guarde, de quel ferveur il le tient, de quelle prudence il l'entomme, de quelle affection il le brise, et de quelle diligence il le sugce'. With similar 'devotion' La Fontaine's monk watches the succulent Magdeleine,

> comme un chien qui fait fête
> Aux os qu'il voit n'être par trop chétifs;
> Que s'il en voit un de belle apparence,
> Non décharné, plein encore de substance,
> Il tient dessus ses regards attentifs;
> Il s'inquiète, il trépigne, il remue
> Oreille et queue; il a toujours la vue
> Dessus cet os, et le ronge des yeux
> Vingt fois devant que son palais s'en sente.

A similarly appetizing young wife torments old Hans Carvel in a story Frère Jean tells Panurge to show how 'jamais ta femme ne te fera coqu sans ton sceu et ton consentement'. The Devil appears in a dream to the worried husband, offering him a ring which, if worn constantly, will keep his wife from straying. When Hans awakes, he finds his finger, as La Fontaine puts it, 'où vous savez'. He strays from his source to echo Villon in describing the wife Babeau's beauty:

---

[1] Rabelais, *Œuvres*, ed. Jourda, IV, 9: 'elle estoit bonne robe, en bon poinct'; 'si m'avez trouvé bonne robe et vous plaist encore en me battant vous esbatre'; II, 9: 'Ce sera basme de me voir briber.'

du bon poil, ardente et belle,
Et propre à l'amoureux combat (440).

Such dancing octosyllabics constitute about the only merit of this rather unrewarding anecdote, in which the husband, like Molière's Arnolphe reading to Agnès, offers moral lessons:

Blâmait ces visites secrètes,
Frondait l'attirail des coquettes;
Et contre un monde de recettes,
Et de moyens de plaire aux yeux,
Invectivait de son mieux.

The Devil also plays a role in the second story imitated from Rabelais, although in 'Le Diable de Papefiguière', Lucifer in the person of one of his 'diabletaux' is the dupe. One of the strange lands visited by Pantagruel and his friends, as they search for the 'Oracle of the Divine Bottle' is Papefiguière, whose inhabitants had mocked the Pope with an obscene gesture, 'making a fig' at his portrait, and are henceforth punished by pestilence and forfeiture of their crops to devils. The inhabitants of a second island, Papimanie, so idolize the Pope, they worship even his picture, and when they land there, they venerate Pantagruel and his followers as well because they have actually laid eyes on the Vicar of Christ. Rabelais devotes nine chapters to the two islands and their inhabitants, three to Papefiguière and six to Papimanie.[1] The story of the peasant of Papefiguière who tricks a little devil out of his crops has clear social overtones, suggesting the struggle between the Seigneur and the crafty peasant who succeeds, despite his bondage under the feudal system, in keeping a goodly portion of his gains for himself. Rabelais' devil is 'extraict de noble et antique race' and he tells the farmer, 'tu n'es qu'un villain'. The peasant outsmarts his master, who agrees first to taking as his share whatever grows beneath the ground, leaving the rest to his vassal. The peasant thereupon plants wheat. When the *diablotin* angrily demands, of the next crop, whatever grows above ground, the *villain* promptly plants turnips. Having lost on both scores the devil challenges his adversary to a scratching match, but the peasant's wife frightens him away by claiming that her husband's powerful scratching has produced the enormous scar she shows him by raising her skirts.

Aside from its coarse humor, Rabelais' story of the peasant and the devil illustrates the naive cunning of the people, their ability to

[1] *Ibid.* xlv--liv.

survive despite onerous feudal burdens, pestilence, inclement weather and even the condemnation of Rome. The chapters on the Pope-mad people satirize ridiculous idolatry, with their long-winded spokesman, Homenaz, easily refuted and mocked by Panurge and Pantagruel, as he praises the Papal Decretals which 'subtly draw gold from France to Rome'.

La Fontaine's adaptation sacrifices much of Rabelais' richness and variety, and retains almost nothing of the religious satire. Indeed he greatly simplifies the distinction between the two islands, making of Papimanie a land of Cockayne, 'un pays où les gens sont heureux', and curiously, the only land where true sleep exists. The Papimanes are rubicund folk, but the Papefiguières are recognized by their scrawny faces, and as to their island, 'le long dormir est exclu de ce lieu'. For the rest, the poet summarizes faithfully, adding here and there an interesting descriptive detail. He suggests the devil's prowess in scratching by a reference to contemporary engravings:

> Peuple ayant queue, ayant cornes et griffes,
> Si maints tableaux ne sont point apocryphes.

Rabelais' peasant plants *touzelle*, a dialectal word for wheat that is immediately understood by the devil; La Fontaine makes of the incomprehensible word a partial explanation for the dupe's gullibility, as he replies,

> comment dis-tu? Touselle?
> Mémoire n'ai d'aucun grain qui s'appelle
> De cette sorte: Or emplis-en ce lieu:
> Touselle soit, touselle, de par Dieu.

When harvest-time arrives Rabelais' peasant tranquilly threshes his grain, but La Fontaine suggests his haste by having him sell it 'Pour le plus sûr, en gerbe, et non battue'.

The most striking change concerns the social satire. From Rabelais La Fontaine took the noble devil's command, 'Travaille, villain, travaille'. But where the original has him say merely 'Bled semer, toutesfoys, n'est mon estat', La Fontaine's devil, characterized twice as a 'gentilhomme', offers us a foretaste of Beaumarchais:

> Manant, travaille; et travaille, vilain:
> Travailler est le fait de la canaille:
> Ne t'attends pas que je t'aide un seul brin,
> Ni que par moi ton labeur se consomme:
> Je t'ai jà dit que j'étais gentilhomme
> Né pour chommer, et pour ne rien savoir.

If La Fontaine scarcely commiserates with the peasant, he obviously satirizes the arrogance and self-sufficiency of the Seigneur. Not only this adaptation of Rabelais but the 'Conte d'un paysan qui avait offensé son seigneur' reveals, if little pity for the peasant who is tortured and beaten for a minor offense, a clear condemnation of the master who laughs at his victim's suffering.

Marguerite de Navarre

The amorous ruse involving confusion of identities, so frequent a subject in the Boccaccian tales, caught La Fontaine's attention in *L'Heptaméron* because of a simple wife's obstinate refrain, 'C'étoit moi' in answer to her neighbor's insistence that she had seen her husband making love to the maidservant in the garden. As we saw earlier, 'La Servante justifiée', is one of the few *contes* to use dramatic dialogue, by means of which La Fontaine stresses the comic reply of the gullible wife, as well as highlighting the confrontation of the two women.

Marguerite de Navarre's tale of an upholsterer who seduces his chambermaid when he pretends to give her a beating for laziness, first in her room and then outside in the snow (!), undergoes considerable emendation; first of all, La Fontaine's servant-girl accepts her master's advances with only token resistance, whereas in the original she tells her mistress he had done her 'Le plus grand tort que jamais on feit à chamberiere' (996), which of course the wife assumes to mean the whipping. La Fontaine emphasizes the garden as setting. The errant husband finds the girl picking a bouquet of flowers for her mistress; her only defense is to throw the flowers at her seducer. 'Faire un bouquet' henceforth signifies dalliance in the garden. So when the husband realizes they have been spied upon he repeats the scene with his wife, and 'Fleurs de voler; tétons d'entrer en danse'. In the dramatic dialogue the flowers permit the use of innuendo leading to the climax of the neighbor's denunciation. First of all,

> tous deux se sont mis
> A se jeter quelques fleurs à la tête.

The wife's answer, 'c'étoit moi', goads the gossip to further specificity:

> Les bonnes gens se sont pris à cueillir
> Certaines fleurs que baisers on appelle.

The successive revelations, less and less veiled, and the symbolism of flowers and greenery are La Fontaine's fortunate invention; the lovers pass 'Du jeu des fleurs à celui des tétons', the maid falls 'sur l'herbe tendre', her skirt 'a paré la verdure'. As La Fontaine puts it in the introductory lines, repeating his statement in the prologue to the *Contes*, 'J'y mets du mien selon les occurrences.' His 'licences' in the case of Marguerite's story consisted of replacing tears and the threat of brutality with joyful gamboling on the green.

Tales without sources

Four *contes* that appear to have no readily discernible sources partake strongly of the Gallic tradition. The first of these, 'Les Troqueurs', treats a familiar subject: man's quest for sexual variety, as the opening lines repeat, through a similar metaphor, the paradox of 'Pâté d'anguille': 'Le changement de mets réjouit l'homme.' In the course of the story the image of sexual intercourse as a meal is wittily developed from a proverb-like couplet that makes the same point that Montaigne had expressed in the phrase 'La cherté donne goust à la viande':

> Pain qu'on dérobe et qu'on mange en cachette,
> Vaut mieux que pain qu'on cuit, ou qu'on achète (554).

The poet imagines the Gods of Marriage and Love as cooks, whose menus differ:

> Hyménée et l'Amour
> Ne soient pas gens à cuire en même four.

The unexpected encounter between Etienne and Tiennette, ending in their love-making, is presented as a banquet:

> On y fit chère; il ne s'y servit plat
> Où maître Amour cuisinier délicat
> Et plus friand que n'est maître Hyménée
> N'eût mis la main.

The protagonists in this culinary love-scene are man and wife; the paradox (for such it is in La Fontaine's canon) of their enthusiasm stems from an agreement between two villagers who decide to exchange wives; they are 'Les Troqueurs'. Etienne's new delight in his spouse after the trade has been in effect for some time provides

further illustration of Ovid's comment, already translated by La
Fontaine in 'La Coupe enchantée':

> Ménélas rencontra des charmes dans Hélène,
> Qu'avant qu'être à Pâris la belle n'avait pas.

La Fontaine espouses the various themes of the *esprit gaulois* despite
the fact that he has no source to blame, thus apparently identifying
himself more fully with them than in the Boccaccian tales. First of all,
like Rabelais and the *Cent Nouvelles nouvelles*, he clearly associates the
clergy with licentiousness. Thus, when the two countrymen arrange
to trade wives through a notary, the association with a priest immediately springs to his pen, first in a comparison between a wife and a
parish:

> Notre pasteur a bien changé de cure:
> La femme est-elle un cas si différent?

Father Grégoire had also said, one of the husbands remembers, 'Mes
brebis sont ma femme. Cependant/Il a changé.' The old double-
entendre about the payment of tithes reappears when Jeanne and
Tiennette reward the clergy for its silence concerning the trade:

> Mais il en vint au curé quelque vent.
> Il prit aussi son droit...
> ...curés y manquent peu souvent.

The comparison between wives and the pastor's flock leads to another
aspect of the *esprit gaulois*: the description of human sensuality in
terms of animality. Their husbands portray the two women as horse-
traders discuss the qualities of their beasts; one of them asks the
crafty lawyer, Oudinet, if one cannot trade 'de femme ainsi que de
monture?' and the same Oudinet, arguing that female attributes are
not always immediately visible, calls their hidden charms 'le meilleur
de la bête'. Vaunting his wife's health, Etienne declares her free of
equine maladies: 'Tiennette n'a ni suros ni malandre.' Finally, La
Fontaine almost certainly has Dindenault's sheep in mind when he
has Gille say of his wife's attractiveness, 'C'est basme'.[1]

This and other Rabelaisian echoes contribute an archaic flavor.
The two husbands use such expletives as *pargué* and *parguenne*, the
familiar Rabelaisian exclamations *or ça* and *or sus*; *jamais* is replaced
by *onc*, and Oudinet is called 'un bon apôtre'. But these are externals;

---

[1] *Ibid.* IV, 7: 'La chair en est tant delicate, tant savoureuse et tant friande que c'est
basme.'

the story's charm derives chiefly from the dexterity of the dialogue, and from the smiling presence of the poet, as evidenced in his eleven-line prologue and various interventions. His own *persona* as that of the errant husband is underlined by his feigned jealousy of the two *troqueurs*; there is a sigh of exasperation that two country bumpkins could manage such a delightful trick. The immediacy of the story appears in its open ending, since the case of Gille against Etienne remains pending in Rouen, which permits an indirect gibe at the ponderousness of the law.

The scene of 'Les Rémois', like that of 'Les Troqueurs', is a French city, Rheims, that La Fontaine admires not only for its wines but for its 'charmants objets'. The anecdote involves once again a complaisant married couple, a painter on whose philandering his wife, far from being jealous, looks not only with a tolerant but an amused eye. She herself, despite her coquetry, remains virtuous, a kind of Célimène who takes malign pleasure in the calf-eyes and windy sighs of two neighbors. They visit her in her husband's absence and when by prearrangement he appears unexpectedly, hide in a closet from which they are forced to watch the gallant painter fondle and perhaps seduce their own wives, whom the Célimène had invited to dinner upon her husband's return.

The voyeurism, which recalls similar examples in the earlier *contes*, has nothing brutal or violent about it as in Boccaccio. The comedy is one of *desengaño*, in which would-be seducers must witness their own betrayal. The tone throughout is one of playful glee at their discomfiture, with the poet intervening to urge women to punish those who pursue them in search of pleasure alone:

> Femmes, voilà souvent comme on vous traite.
> Le seul plaisir est ce que l'on souhaite (490).

In a mock-melancholy reference to the ethereal love stories of *L'Astrée*, the poet deplores the fact that only sensual appetites remain:

> Amour est mort: le pauvre compagnon
> Fut enterré sur les bords du Lignon.

Thus La Fontaine identifies himself with the trick his Célimène will play on her two swains; she is to snare them and pluck them clean:

> Le beau premier qui sera dans vos lacs
> Plumez-le-moi, je vous le recommande.

By the following line, 'La dame *donc*, pour tromper ses voisins' makes it appear that the lady's prank follows La Fontaine's own recommendation; that he is, in a sense, a co-conspirator. Later one husband tells the other, 'en vos lacs/Vous êtes pris'.

Other interventions stress the poet's involvement in the story in different ways. At the beginning he hints that he knows the beauty of the women of Rheims through personal experience. We hear an echo of his 'praise of cuckoldry' as he notes, concerning the painter's kissing one of the wives:

> époux, quand ils sont sages,
> Ne prennent garde à ces menus suffrages
> Et d'en tenir registre c'est abus.

We find a brief example of what I have called the irony of female insatiability when the poet explains that the second wife to be fondled by the painter would have left, but for the fact that he was pulling her dress and that she was too thrifty to let him tear it.

The dramatic staging of the *conte* deserves notice. As in 'Les Quiproquo', La Fontaine makes use of the wine-cellar to which the hostess leads each of the wives in turn as the dinner progresses, thus leaving the painter alone with one of the charming guests. Surprise is created by the various exits and entrances, as the frustrated audience watches. The skill with which La Fontaine adapts the rhythm of the *conte* to these departures and arrivals is excellently illustrated in the lines following the first return from the wine-cellar, in which the festivities recommence, until the wine runs out again, necessitating a second departure:

> On se remit en train;
> On releva grillades et festin:
> On but encore à la santé de l'hôte,
> Et de l'hôtesse, et de celle des trois
> Qui la première aurait quelque aventure.
> Le vin manqua pour la seconde fois.

The successive 'on's re-establish the collectivity, but the rapidity of the toasts returns the actors to the situation requiring their separation.

Except for their immobility the predicament of the errant husbands resembles that of Orgon, and they are doubly frustrated, for when the painter retires they cannot take their vengeance because of his wife's virtue.

'La Chose impossible' again celebrates female ingenuity in a sexual context. Once again, as in 'Le Diable de Papefiguière', a demon is bested by his would-be victim. The Devil promises to make a lady amenable to her lover's desires if he undertakes, on pain of losing life and soul, to issue rather than obey continuous commands to a demon who will serve him constantly. Eventually the lover runs out of orders to give and turns in desperation to his mistress. She immediately plucks a hair from her pubis, which the devil is ordered to straighten and flatten. After a valiant but vain struggle he surrenders, and releases the fortunate bondsman.

What a flimsy basis for a verse tale of eighty-five lines! Yet through the vivacity of the narrative, and in particular the artistry of the *vers libre*, the poet succeeds in maintaining the reader's interest to the end. The reward for compliance is described in two brisk lines:

> Ce fut que le premier jouirait à souhait
> De sa charmante inexorable (605).

When the inexorable charmer yields, an amusing tableau shows the lovers embracing with the devil flitting about his victim's ears:

> notre amant
> S'en va trouver la belle; en a contentement,
> Goûte des voluptés qui n'ont point de pareilles;
> Se trouve très heureux; hormis qu'incessamment
> Le diable était à ses oreilles.

The rapidity of the conquest appears in the succession of verbs without repetition of pronouns, a sequence of pleasure that comes to an abrupt halt as the devil appears. After this momentary pause the race is on again as the devil fulfils the lover's orders as fast as he can conceive them. Among these tasks one notes that of 'bâtir des palais', an exploit reminiscent of Ariosto, at least when it is done 'en moins d'un tour de main'. La Fontaine's description of the recalcitrant hair reminds one, in its circumlocutory effects, of 'Le Tableau'. He never uses the word *cheveu* or *poil*, but informs us that the lady takes it from the 'verger de Cypris'. Another allusion to a duke who honored it by creating an order of knights in its name suggests without difficulty the *Toison d'or* (the 'Golden Fleece'), and fourteen lines later we find the word itself applied to the resilient capillary:

> Quelque secret qu'il eût, quelque charme qu'il fît,
> C'était temps et peine perdue:

> Il ne put mettre à la raison
> La toison.

In this *conte*, certainly, La Fontaine succeeds remarkably in that classical goal of 'making something out of nothing'. But in the lover's parting remarks to the devil that had he mastered the one hair there were more where that one came from, we hear a hint of that joy in the multiplicity and perpetuity of the sexual act that frequently permeates the *contes*, in particular 'L'Abbesse'.

The same joy in this 'jeu dont l'ardeur souvent se renouvelle' pervades 'Comment l'esprit vient aux filles', which begins with a gay poem in its praise, three regular five-line stanzas with a refrain: 'Or, devinez comment ce jeu s'appelle.' The narrative begins with the poet's entry into the poem, and the carefree question, 'Qu'importe-t-il?' Rather than guess further, he implies, this game brings 'wit and reason' to its players. The story of how simple Lise sought and obtained wit from Father Bonaventure is perhaps the most transparent of all the tales of sexual adventure. Unlike 'L'Ermite', which it recalls, there is no violence, and almost no symbolism. The priest's prompt tumbling of the girl is portrayed as the acquisition of 'esprit', and the explicitness of the act is scarcely veiled by equivalating the 'esprit' and the male member:

> Il suit sa pointe, et d'encor en encor
> Toujours l'esprit s'insinue et s'avance.

When Lise tells her story to a friend, it includes 'Dimensions de l'esprit du beau père'.

These four tales confirm, if there was any doubt, that La Fontaine's genius was infused with the Gallic spirit. Yet in his vision, *l'esprit gaulois* had nothing of the veiled contempt of some earlier writers. The suggestion that women's wit is merely the result of sexual intercourse is countered by his smiling approval of his sensual wives and maidens. The 'Gallic' *contes* contain nothing that would belie his protestations of fidelity to the fair sex in 'Les Oies de Frère Philippe'.

5

The Esthetic of Beauty

Feminine beauty

When La Fontaine protested his innocence in reply to accusations of misogyny, he was far from making a conventional disclaimer. Even when he admitted, in the first preface, that his book might have wronged womenkind if he had been speaking seriously, the reader would have felt doubt, for nothing in the *contes*, serious or humorous, maligns woman. On the contrary, there arises from these pages an almost continuous hymn in her praise.

This eulogy bears as its chief element the physical beauty of woman. With the exception of one or two lusty goodwives who are not described at all, the young girls, the widows, the nuns, who frolic throughout these tales, whose function is to love and be loved, entrance and entice us by their pulchritude. In most cases La Fontaine sketches his heroines in a few lines, but with a warmth and deftness of touch that suffuses not only the stories in which they figure but their dialogue, their glances and their movements with a special grace.

And indeed, one of the commoner characteristics of woman in the *contes* is her grace of bearing, 'la grâce, plus belle encor que la beauté', accompanied often by a gentleness of glance or character, as well as youthfulness. The rhythm of a single verse can portray her tripping gait: 'leste, pimpante et d'un page suivie' (369).[1] Far from being antipathetic, the wife who tricks her elderly spouse in 'Le Cocu battu et content' is of 'gracieux maintien/De doux regard, jeune, fringante et belle' (370), the innkeeper's daughter in 'Le Berceau' 'gracieuse et gentille,/D'esprit si doux et d'air tant attrayant' (400), and the toothsome widow of 'L'Oraison de Saint Julien' 'pleine d'appas, jeune et de bonne grâce' (412). Throughout, grace is coupled with beauty. The female figure itself, in addition to a graceful bearing or gait must possess a delectable roundness, a nice balance between

---

[1] Page references in the text to *contes* and *fables* are to the Groos and Schiffrin edition.

plumpness and slenderness, an 'embonpoint raisonnable', as in the case of the widow whose charms reveal 'trop ni trop peu de chair et d'embonpoint' (415). Firmness must accompany *embonpoint*, and together with their 'embonpoint et peau fine' the nuns of 'Les Lunettes' are endowed with 'fermes tétons'.

True to his principle that 'Tout y sera voilé', the poet rarely presents the female body in the nude, and even when he does, clothes it in circumlocution or allusion. In 'Les Lunettes', when the mother superior suspects that a man disguised as a nun is living in the convent she summons the members of her flock and makes them undress. The naked girls possess, writes La Fontaine,

> tous les trésors
> De ces trois soeurs dont la fille de l'onde
> Se fait servir (600).

By another device of indirection, female nudity may be described through its various effects on the male observer, as in the same story, when the masquerader, having camouflaged the clue to his identity, is overwhelmed by the spectacle of

> Secrets appas, embonpoint et peau fine
> Fermes tétons, et semblables ressorts.

Elsewhere, the sight of female nudity may appear all the more powerful because evoked solely through the wonderment of the beholder, as in the case of Gygès, whom King Candaule permits to gaze upon his naked wife as she is bathing. Before Gygès sees her, however, the king praises her hidden beauties, which far surpass that of her face:

> Vous voyez, lui dit-il, le visage charmant,
> Et les traits délicats dont la reine est pourvue;
> Je vous jure ma foi que l'accompagnement
> Est d'un tout autre prix, et passe infiniment;
> Ce n'est rien qui ne l'a vue
> Toute nue (576).

But Candaule warns Gygès to look upon the queen 'Comme un beau marbre seulement', and the impact of the vision appears the greater through his efforts to restrain his emotion. His first inclination is to be silent, but because that would arouse suspicion in the king, instead he exaggerates, praising all the queen's physical qualities since, as La Fontaine hints, the ability to enumerate in such abundant detail suggests detachment. Thus, 'Chaque point, chaque article eut son fait, fut loué'. Yet we have only the poet's word for this, since Gygès' actual exclamations remain extremely vague: 'Le beau corps! le beau cuir! ô ciel! et tout le reste!' Of the lasting impression the queen's nudity makes on the observer, we learn only that 'chaque endroit' obsessed him, and even later, when the couple have become lovers, their amours are presented as visual rather than physical:

> Tandis qu'aux yeux de Gygès
> S'étalaient de blancs objets.

Such terms as *étaler, admirer, ce doux objet*, suggest the pleasure of the *voyeur*, and even hint at its superiority over other joys.

On an earthier level, Friar Jean, savoring plump Magdeleine's beauty before he succeeds, by his ruse, in making her strip, reminds the poet of a dog eyeing a meaty bone:

> Il tient dessus ses regards attentifs,
> Il s'inquiète, il trépigne, il remue
> Oreille et queue; il a toujours la vue
> Dessus cet os, et le ronge des yeux
> Vingt fois devant que son palais s'en sente (590).

The eroticism is here at a more obvious level, if only because in the *conte* in question the identification of *queue* and the male member is quite specific.

With an intensity somewhere between that of Gygès and Friar Jean, Cimon in 'Le Fleuve Scamandre' watches a girl bathing:

> il contemple, il admire;
> Il me sait quels charmes élire;
> Il dévore des yeux et du coeur cent beautés (624).

In two of these cases whiteness is an important quality of female flesh, and in describing the peasant girl in 'La Jument du compère Pierre', La Fontaine makes clear this preference as he writes of Magdeleine:

> le hâle avait fait tort
> A son visage, et non à sa personne.

He adds a personal aside, 'Ce rustic ne m'eût plu.' Thus gleaming whiteness is an attribute of female flesh in La Fontaine's esthetic, and it is no accident that the beauteous nuns of 'Mazet de Lamporecchio' seldom ventured into the garden in the afternoon, 'crainte du hâle' (148). Indeed the whiteness of their habit reflects the hidden beauty of their flesh; in the *parloir* they sit 'blanchement, comme droites poupées', and their sisters in 'Le Tableau' combine 'Blancheur, délicatesse, embonpoint raisonnable'.

La Fontaine furnishes a brief detail on the nature of this *embonpoint*, confessing in a 'Conte tiré d'Athénée' that he worships at the altar of Callipygean Venus. For the rest, one seeks in vain in the *contes* for such other feminine attributes as those he admired in the Duchesse de Bouillon, who possessed in addition to a shapely white foot,

> brune et longue tresse,
> Nez troussé, c'est un charme encor selon mon sens;
> C'en est même un des plus puissants (OD, 577).

Of the female anatomy, most important in La Fontaine's esthetic are the breasts, characterized not only by the requisite whiteness but by a provocative dynamism. Both their shapeliness and hue are praised; they are 'fait(s) au tour' or 'Un sein/Pour qui l'ivoire aurait eu de l'envie' (519). A *conte* in archaic style praises their texture: 'De blanc satin...mollette' (OD, 607).[1]

But La Fontaine is at his most original as he portrays them not in statuesque immobility but pulsating with life. We have seen how in 'La Coupe enchantée' their heaving illustrates the rapid onset of puberty:

> on pouvait déjà voir
> Hausser et baisser le mouchoir (497).

In 'Le Diable en enfer' their movement torments the hermit in his dreams:

> certain sein ne se reposant point;
> Allant, venant; sein qui pousse et repousse
> Certain corset... (587)

In the first example, the handkerchief, artfully tucked into the bodice, both masks and reveals the bust. It was such a handkerchief that Tartuffe handed to Dorine, with averted eyes, begging her, 'Couvrez ce sein que je ne saurais voir'. In the fable 'Le Jardinier et son seigneur', the noble intruder, flirting with the luckless gardener's daughter, 'lève un coin du mouchoir'. The widow of 'L'Oraison de Saint Julien' wears a black handkerchief 'de deux grands doigts trop court', that hints at, 'sous ce mouchoir, ne sais quoi fait au tour'. But whether it be a handkerchief or, as in the case of Alibech, a corset, what we have already seen as a veil, esthetic as well as material, can

---

[1] Page references in the text to miscellaneous works (preceded by OD) are to the Clarac edition.

on occasion serve to present fleshly beauty more excitingly than nudity, as in 'Le Tableau', when the poet urges us to imagine the nuns' bodies 'sous ceci, sous cela, que voit peu l'oeil du jour' (615).

On a less sensual level than opulent flesh, the eyes traditionally speak the silent language of love, and although expectedly enough La Fontaine rarely alludes to them, he does devote one *conte* to an amusing debate won by the mouth personifying physical love (OD, 593–5). The eyes, however, make a valiant effort to prove their worth. As we saw earlier, the veil or, in this case, the mask, heightens their power: 'Sous un masque trompeur leur éclat fit si bien...' (594).[1] In the same *conte*, the eyes claim superiority over their rival, not on the grounds of beauty, but of eloquence, which the mouth has claimed for its prerogative as the channel of the voice:

> Belle Bouche dit: 'J'aime,' et le disons-nous pas?
> Sans aucun bruit: notre langage
> Muet qu'il est, plaît davantage...

Thereupon the poet imagines that the eyes' lawyer produces a witness certain to impress the judges by the impact of her glances. The concept of the eye as a powerful vehicle of love is age-old, and belonged to the *précieux* esthetic. But La Fontaine, although presenting strong arguments for each of the contestants, chooses the sensual over the ideal. Despite a persuasive case for the mouth, Philis' eyes sway the judges:

> Philis eut quelque honte; et puis sur l'assistance
> Répandit des regards si pleins d'éloquence
> Que les papiers tombaient des mains.

To support her plea, she might also have instanced the case in 'La Courtisane amoureuse' of the uncouth Chimon, transformed and refined by a glance from beauteous eyes, again, we may note in passing, eyes that are veiled:

> Qui fit cela? deux beaux yeux seulement.
> Pour les avoir aperçus un moment,
> Encore à peine, et voilés par le somme (513).

The eyes' mettle has wide ramifications, effective at court or in the city; they also provide the subject for love poetry:

> La Cour, le Parnasse et la Ville
> Ne retentissent tout le jour
> Que du mot de Beaux Yeux et de celui d'Amour.

[1] Cf. p. 34, above.

But despite their fame and their wide-ranging powers, Belle Bouche, who knows a hundred ways to please a lover, wins on the grounds that she remains active during the night:

> La nuit mon emploi dure encore:
> Beaux Yeux sont lors de peu d'usage:
> On les laisse en repos; et leur muet langage
> Fait un assez froid personnage.

Obviously Belle Bouche's force lies not merely in her visual attributes, those Petrarchan qualities mentioned in her brief: 'Le nacre est en dedans, le corail en dehors', nor in her facility of speech, but in her secret ability to make love, as La Fontaine adds in a characteristic evasion, even when shrouded in darkness: 'vous me dispenserez de vous dire comment'.

In the course of the debate, Beaux Yeux' advocate had sturdily refused to accept her adversary's denunciation of tears as a defect: 'Il est des larmes de transport.' But not only can tears speak the language of love, they may actually enhance beauty in accordance with esthetics of negligence. In 'Richard Minutolo' the weeping Catelle appears all the more attractive:

> En cet état elle parut si belle,
> Que Minutol de nouveau s'enflammant,
> Lui prit la main.

Similarly, the bereaved matron of Ephesus is well served by her tears:

> Jeune et belle, elle avait sous ses pleurs de l'éclat;
> ....
> Tout y fit: une belle, alors qu'elle est en larmes,
> En est plus belle de moitié (640).

Tears of distress, humiliation and unrequited love plead successfully for the most beautiful of all women in the *contes*, the courtesan Constance, whose beauty is such that La Fontaine in order to evoke it must needs have recourse to his pose of inarticulateness:

> Une beauté si superbe et si fière!
> Une beauté!...je ne la décris point;
> Il me faudrait une semaine entière (518).

'La Courtisane amoureuse', imitated from a prose tale by Brusoni,[1]

---

[1] As V. Lugli has pointed out in 'La Courtisane amoureuse', *Studi in onore di Italo Siciliano* (Firenze: Leo S. Olschki, 1966), pp. 711–20. As Lugli points out, however, French critics as recently as 1962 have continued to claim that no known literary source exists, although La Fontaine's imitation of Brusoni was revealed by Gaston Paris in 1901.

tells of a prostitute who falls madly in love with a young man who not only refuses her advances but humiliates her, forcing her to remove his clothing and boots like a lackey, making her lie not by his side but at the foot of his bed, and callously placing his feet upon her breast, before her sobs finally force him to confess his love. To understand the importance of La Fontaine's treatment of the theme, one should recall the persistent denunciation of the courtesan in Renaissance literature, a censure which derives in part not merely from the Christian tradition but from masculine resentment of the freedom and independence of the wealthy prostitute in a society where frequently young girls were prisoners and married women chattels. In the poetry that treats this theme one encounters no happy prostitutes, but usually aged women bitterly regretting their past, as in Yeats' poem, 'Too old for a man's love...imagining men'. Du Bellay's *Vieille courtisane*[1] portrays a withered harlot who has reaped only misery and who laments the tortures of true love, which, like La Fontaine in his *conte*, he presents as Vénus' punishment for the indignities she has heaped upon her lovers:

> Me contraignant d'aymer plus que mes yeux,
> Plus que mon coeur, un jeune audacieux,
> Qui d'autant plus que d'une humble caresse
> Je m'efforçois d'amollir sa rudesse,
> Plus me fuyoit, et se paissoit, cruel,
> De mon tourment et pleur continuel.

And her lamentations conclude with a longing for death, if need be by suicide.

But unlike the traditional courtesan, La Fontaine's Constance triumphs despite her humiliation and temporary loss of beauty. To show her powers set at naught by a disdainful male partakes of the tradition, but to present her as finally victorious, and happily in love for the first time, reverses it to the greater glory of womanhood.

Constance's great powers appear first of all in her sway over Roman potentates: that she numbers bishops, cardinals, even a Pope among her lovers incidentally suggests the corruption of the Church and attenuates in comparison her own wrong-doing. Her suffering is reflected in her loss of beauty through unrequited love, a loss which La Fontaine however portrays as temporary, and even possessed of redeeming features. As with Joconde, pallor replaces the flush of her

[1] Du Bellay, *Divers jeux rustiques* (Paris: Didier, 1947), pp. 148–80.

cheeks – 'bientôt le lis l'emporta sur la rose' – yet this blemish in a sense restores her innocence, permitting her to blush, unlike hardened prostitutes whose faces glow with rouge:

> Elle rougit; chose que ne font guère
> Celles qui sont prêtresses de Vénus:
> Le vermillon leur vient d'autre manière.

Her fading complexion, far from being a defect makes her all the more admirable because of its cause:

> Pâleur encore dont la cause était telle
> Qu'elle donnait du lustre à notre belle.

La Fontaine shows his strong *parti-pris* in favor of his heroine by his interventions, which ensure that her self-abasement has nothing degrading about it. When Constance offers to perform Camille's servant's duties in order to remain in the bedroom, and takes off his clothes and finally his boots and socks, the poet seems to hear his reader's shocked exclamation, 'Quoi, de sa main! quoi! Constance elle-même!' to which he stoutly replies,

> Qui fut-ce donc? Est-ce trop que cela?
> Je voudrais bien déchausser ce que j'aime.

When Camille finally agrees that she may share his bed, but refuses to unlace her dress, in her haste she seizes his dagger and slashes her fine garments without regret. Thereupon La Fontaine turns to his reader and asks,

> Femmes de France, en feriez-vous autant?
> Je crois que non.

Constance's violent destruction of her finery in her frenzied haste to make love suggests, at a higher level of intensity, the complex relationships between nudity and dress. As we have seen, La Fontaine rarely displays the female body completely naked, for clothing acts as the veil which stimulates both desire and the imagination. The abandonment or destruction of clothing, or simply its disarray, adds another dimension of sensuality, representing a stage in the progress toward the sexual act itself. When in 'Le Calendrier des vieillards' Bartolomée's husband pleads in his own favor that he has bought her fine clothes, she can retort bluntly:

> Je suis de chair, les habits rien n'y font:
> Vous savez bien, Monsieur, qu'entre la tête
> Et le talon d'autres affaires sont.

As we saw earlier, dishevelment or actual undress indicate disdain for discipline or convention and approach sexual abandonment; simplicity or carelessness in clothing can be attractive as the prelude to the act of love. Such simplicity, artful or not, characterizes the more approachable woman of humble station, such as the heroine of 'Le Fleuve Scamandre':

> Sa beauté est sans art; elle a l'air de bergère,
> Une beauté naïve...

We recall that in 'Joconde' King Astolphe had sung the praises of country wenches who may equal in beauty the finest ladies of his court, yet dispense with fastidious preliminaries.[1]

Masculine beauty

In praising such simple charms the king addresses his comrade-in-amours, Joconde, the first exemplar of masculine beauty in the *contes*. But feminine beauty far outdistances that of the male, and La Fontaine measures the latter almost solely in terms of its power over women. Interestingly enough, he frequently suggests that men's beauty depends chiefly on its resemblance to that of women. Of his Astolphe, 'aussi beau que le jour', he tells us half of the court beauties adored him and the other half envied him. A further hint of the femininity in masculine good looks arises from the ladies' disappointment in Joconde's appearance, which the reader knows has suffered from his wife's infidelity: 'Est-ce là ce Narcisse?' they ask,

> Qui prétendait tous nos coeurs enchaîner?
> Quoi! le pauvre homme a la jaunisse! (354)

Despite the need for a rime with *jaunisse*, permitting an allusion to the color of cuckoldry, Narcisse seems an unusual model of masculine beauty, recalling the ambiguity of Cupid's good looks in Psyche.

The remaining heroes of the *contes*, with one exception, receive only the briefest of descriptions. As in the case of Renaud in 'L'Oraison de Saint Julien', we seldom hear more than that they are 'grand, bien fait, beau personnage'. On only one occasion do we witness the spectacle of nude masculine beauty and that is in 'Le Cas de conscience', in which a village girl surprises her sweetheart, the handsome Guillot, bathing nude in a river. The 'case of conscience' in the

[1] Cf. p. 100, above.

title is the sin of concupiscence, of which, as a result of her confession that she has watched the naked boy, the parish priest accuses the girl. As a penance she offers Father Thomas a fine pike Guillot has caught; he is delighted and asks her to prepare it for him and return it for a supper he is giving his fellow-priests. But the youth changes his mind, and the banqueters must do without their *pièce de résistance*. When the furious curé scolds Anne, she promptly retorts with a variant on the phrase in which he had accused her of sinning: 'Autant vaut l'avoir vu que de l'avoir mangé.'

But far more important than hoisting the friar with his own petard is the sheer delight in physical beauty as Anne's glances rove over the youth's body:

> Çà et là ses regards en liberté couraient
> > Où les portait leur fantaisie,
> Çà et là, c'est à dire aux différents attraits
> > Du garçon au corps jeune et frais,
> Blanc, poli, bien formé, de taille haute et drète...

And once again La Fontaine shows corporeal beauty through a veil. He frames the image like a painting; Anne observes the bather as from a window, the willows on the river bank shielding her like the slats of a blind. La Fontaine says only that these afford her protection from discovery – 'des saules la couvraient' – yet by thus permitting Anne to feast her eyes at leisure, the screen of willows, like the 'voile de gaze' of 'Le Tableau', lends her pleasure an esthetic quality, her eye imprinting the scene upon her mind like an artist painting a nude model:

> Quelqu'un n'a-t-il point vu
> Comme on dessine sur nature?
> On vous campe une créature,
> Une Eve, ou quelque Adam, j'entends un objet nu;
> Puis force gens, assis comme notre bergère,
> Font un crayon conforme à cet original.

The impact of the sight triumphs over the 'honte secret' instilled in Anne by her religious training:

> Elle s'assit sur l'herbe, et très fort attentive,
> > Annette la contemplative
> Regarda de son mieux.

The importance of esthetic distance is shown when, suddenly emerging from the water, the bather rudely shatters the contemplative idyll. He becomes *l'ennemi*, his proximity makes his nudity overwhelming, 'plus fort qu'à l'ordinaire', and the observer, fearful of yielding, retreats precipitately, though still savoring 'les points qui la rendaient encor toute honteuse'. Thus the tale argues once again the power of the veil, the higher delight in visualization than in the act itself, and the breaking of the willow screen stresses the gap between art and reality. That the banal theme of the story, 'autant l'avoir vu que de l'avoir touché' – the priest's definition of concupiscence – should have suggested these contrasts reveals once again their importance for La Fontaine.

The beauty of nature

Anne watched her Guillot from the river's edge and the hero of 'Le Fleuve Scamandre' observed a nymph bathing in a limpid pool; so, as in the *Fables*, the natural setting provides a pleasing background or a frame. Natural beauty can underline that of the human actors. The wind by the river Scamander plays enticingly with a maiden's veil: 'Son voile au gré des vents va flottant dans les airs.' The vast expanse of the ocean strikingly underlines the solitary predicament of the shipwrecked Alaciel and Hispal as the latter swims from reef to reef with the heroine's arms around his neck. Fearing death from starvation, the lovers probe the horizon: 'Nul vaisseau ne parut sur la liquide plaine.' When they resolve to take a chance and swim from rock to rock, their decision depends on the certainty of disaster whatever they do:

> Qu'importe que nos corps des oiseaux ravissants
> Ou des monstres marins deviennent la pâture?

Their success, however, is attributed to the intervention of a kindly nature, and they reach land:

> Avec l'aide du Ciel et de ces reposoirs,
> Et du dieu qui préside aux liquides manoirs.

Throughout this evocation of the ocean, personification remains firmly in control; and the abandoned ships 'Au gré d'Eole et de Neptune flotte'.

River or stream flowing through verdant meadows can provide the setting for love-making, with only a gentle nod in the direction of mythology, where a young lover,

> cajolait la jeune bachelette
> Aux blanches dents, aux pieds nus, au corps gent,
> Pendant qu'Io portant une clochette,
> Aux environs allait l'herbe mangeant.

But it is deep within the silent forest that the frightened Isabeau succumbs, her cries unheeded, as the *conte* concludes with these awesome lines:

> Nul n'accourut. O belles, évitez
> Le fond des bois et leur vaste silence.

As these lines imply, nature is the accomplice of love, whether by her vastness in which ravished maidens cry unheard, or by providing a *locus amoenus* such as beckons to Alaciel and Hispal after their shipwreck. Yet there is nothing primitive in their sylvan idyll, for they buy a castle with the jewels they save from the wreck. The castle has a park, and by a series of progressions, abetted by lines of decreasing length, La Fontaine suggests the lovers' stroll and their final destination:

> Ce château, dit l'histoire, avoit un parc fort grand,
> Ce parc un bois, ce bois de beaux ombrages,
> Sous ces ombrages nos amants
> Passaient d'agréables moments.

Nature's instrumentality is nevertheless invoked; she provides a cave, and is aided of course by love, who 'guida leurs pas vers ce lieu solitaire'. Of the cave we learn nothing except that it is dark, and seemed especially chosen for amorous delights. Yet we must expect no Rousseauistic impact of nature upon such lovers; although a shower of rain provides them with the final impetus to take refuge in the cave, this is preceded by Hispal's lengthy but persuasive arguments as Alaciel pretends to carve upon the bark of trees:

> Hispal haranguait de façon
> Qu'il aurait échauffé les marbres,
> Tandis qu'Alaciel, à l'aide d'un poinçon,
> Faisait semblant d'écrire sur les arbres.

Later the triumphant swain carves the story of his conquest on every tree in sight, thus making of nature, as La Fontaine put it, a monument.

In the *contes* nature plays a minor role, overshadowed, as in a Poussin painting, by the exploits of man, or by the beauty of woman; which after all, as the poet has said, can surpass 'le printemps et l'aurore...l'éclat des cieux, et les beautés des champs'.

6

Poetic Techniques:
a 'nonchalance savante'

One could almost be grateful to Valéry for proving so wilfully uncom-
prehending about La Fontaine's *contes*. Can one really take seriously
his characterizing their poetry, apparently on the basis of two lines
from 'Belphégor', as 'vers d'une facilité répugnante'?[1] True, the
judgment is only part of a general condemnation of the *contes*, and
great critic though he was, Valéry could be guilty of overstatement
for rhetorical effect. To speak of facility in this connexion, moreover,
suggests in part the very fallacy he had been denouncing: that of the
'rumeur de paresse et de rêverie', that 'première et primitive idée
qu'il avait gardée de La Fontaine'. But whatever its motives or its
foundation, Valéry's diatribe serves as a useful point of departure.
In the course of our examination of the *contes*, I believe that many
quotations have clearly demonstrated this critic's error. In this
chapter I should like to look more closely at La Fontaine's poetic
technique in the *contes*, not so much in an attempt to refute the
accusation of 'facilité' as to demonstrate the sureness of his art.

Vers libres

Various poets before La Fontaine had tried their hand at *vers libres*;
Corneille and Molière with particular success.[2] However, it can be
said at the outset, and without reservation, that La Fontaine shows
unrivalled mastery and inventiveness in the *vers libres* of the *contes*.
Ferdinand Gohin, to whom we owe the most extensive study of
versification in the *fables*, in one of his rare mentions of the *contes*
declares that in them the poet's 'tentative était encore timide'
because the proportion of *vers libres* to decasyllabics in the earlier

---

[1] See above, pp. 32–3.
[2] Cf. Bray, 'L'Introduction des vers mêlés sur la scène classique'.

work was roughly one to five, whereas all but thirteen of the *fables* are in the more varied meter.[1] Yet if we discard numbers of poems as a criterion of boldness, or better, inventiveness, and substitute the variety of line length, we discover that the *vers libre* of the *contes* has a far greater range. In the *fables* over half of the poems in that meter consist of a combination of octosyllabics and alexandrines; in the others these two lines are preponderant. In the *contes*, only two, 'Le Gascon puni' and 'La Matrone d'Ephèse', are restricted to a combination of eight- and ten-syllable lines, and most of the others show a greater variety than the *fables* not so limited. Such a predilection for irregularity should not surprise the reader of the *contes*; what, we must ask ourselves, are the effects of this 'nonchalance savante'?

Of all the poems in *vers libres* 'La Coupe enchantée' displays the most dazzling variety, combining lines of 1, 3, 6, 7, 8, 10 and 12 syllables. As Gohin pointed out for the *fables* in general, in this *conte* the preponderant lines are the octosyllabic and the alexandrine, with 179 of the former and 261 of the latter out of a total of 486 lines. The combination of these two lines produces interesting effects in the 'Defense of Cuckoldry' which forms a part of what the poet calls the prologue of his tale. He organizes this passage in what appear to be four stanzas each ending with a refrain, which gives them an illusory appearance of regularity. In the case of the refrain, it begins as an octosyllabic, 'Cocuage n'est point un mal'; but then, when the poet feels he has proved his point, changes to a six-syllable line, whose brevity underlines his finality: 'Cocuage est un bien.'

Throughout the passage the octosyllabics are abrupt, lending emphasis to the arguments driven forcefully home in the alexandrines:

> Mais je vous veux premièrement,
> Prouver par bon raisonnement,
> Que ce mal dont la peur vous mine et vous consume
> N'est mal qu'en votre idée, et non point dans l'effet.

The following three octosyllabics give examples illustrating that nothing has changed: the three rimes in *-et* emphasize that the cuckold's horns are invisible:

> En mettez-vous votre bonnet
> Moins aisément que de coûtume?
> Cela s'en va -t-il pas tout net?

---

[1] Ferdinand Gohin, *L'Art de La Fontaine dans ses fables* (Paris: Garnier, 1929), p. 144.

The second stanza consists of an exchange between the poet and the 'pauvres gens' who so fear cuckoldry: seven alexandrines followed by the refrain before the two stanzas that prove, not simply that cuckoldry is not an evil, but that it is actually a good. All of these alexandrines make their point with vigor; the firmly ending lines, thrust forth like pointing fingers:

> Quand vous perdez au jeu, l'on vous donne revanche;
> Même votre homme écarte et ses as et ses rois.
> Avez-vous sur le bras quelque monsieur Dimanche,
> Mille bourses vous sont ouvertes à la fois.

Another, final quatrain follows, also in *rimes croisées*, as the argument terminates in the abbreviated refrain:

> Pour toutes ces raisons je persiste en ma thèse,
> Cocuage est un bien.

Thus the four irregular strophic forms separate the 'thesis' from the rest of the narrative.

A similar technique sets the story of the sorceress Nérie apart from the central events that lead to Damon's downfall. To introduce this personage, who encourages Damon's illusions of cuckoldry because she is in love with him, and whose powers include control of the winds, the poet uses the light and graceful seven-syllable line, with frequent *enjambement*:

> L'enchanteresse Nérie
> Fleurissait lors; et Circé
> Au prix d'elle, en diablerie
> N'eût été qu'à l'A B C.
> Car Nérie eut à ses gages
> Les intendants des orages,
> Et tint le destin lié.
> Les Zéphirs étaient ses pages;
> Quand à ses valets de pied,
> C'étaient Messieurs les Borées,
> Qui portaient par les contrées
> Ses mandats souventes fois,
> Gens dispos, mais peu courtois.

There follow two 'stanzas', the first of fourteen, the second of ten lines, combining octosyllabics and alexandrines, but the first, contrary to Gohin's belief that La Fontaine never used the seven-syllable line excepting in series,[1] is linked to the preceding passage by an initial line of the same meter which serves as a transition from the description of the sorceress' powers to the discovery that despite them she has yielded to the forces of love:

> Avec toute sa science,
> Elle ne put trouver de remède à l'amour.

In the *contes* as in the *fables*, the octosyllabic and the alexandrine are the lines most frequently used. A number of effects derive from this combination. Two octosyllabics may follow two alexandrines to express the author's judgment, as a kind of *sententia* drawn from the two preceding lines:

> Damon, de peur de pis, établit des Argus
> A l'entour de sa femme, et la rendit coquette:
> Quand les galants sont défendus,
> C'est alors qu'on les souhaite.

On another occasion the octosyllabic displaces the alexandrine to give an impression of accumulation, for example to depict the rapid swelling of the army of cuckolds. The swift line suits the recital of the burlesque assignments of various ranks:

> Les différents degrés où monte Cocuage
> Règlent le pas et les emplois:
> Ceux qu'il n'a visités seulement qu'une fois
> Sont fantassins pour tout potage:
> On fait les autres cavaliers.
> Quiconque est de ses familiers
> On ne manque pas d'élire
> Ou capitaine ou lieutenant,
> Ou l'on lui donne un régiment:
> Selon qu'entre les mains du sire
> Ou plus ou moins subitement
> La liqueur du vase s'épand.
> Un versa tout en un moment;
> Il fut fait général. Et croyez que l'armée
> De hauts officiers ne manqua:
> Plus d'un intendant se trouva;
> Cette charge fut partagée.

I have quoted this passage at length to demonstrate the subtlety with which La Fontaine uses his two major lines. The metaphor of the

[1] *Ibid.* p. 166.

army is explained in the first two; the alexandrine indicating the basic image of movement upward ('les différents degrés') with the octosyllabic adding the military tone ('Règlent le pas'). The second alexandrine forms the bottom of the pyramid of ascending rank. The list of promotions follows until the last four octosyllabics describe the criterion of rapidity, with the run-on line spilling over onto the following alexandrine like the magic goblet itself. The passage ends with the poet's assurance that the general did not lack company, in a *reprise* of the eight-syllable rhythm.

Similar effects of rapidity can occur when an event is narrated in lines of decreasing length:

> Cela n'était que bien; mais la Parque maudite
> Fut aussi de l'intrigue; et sans perdre de temps
> Le pauvre roi par nos amants
> Fut député vers le Cocyte.
> On le fit trop boire d'un coup:
> Quelquefois, hélas! c'est beaucoup.
> Bientôt un certain breuvage
> Lui fit voir le noir rivage,
> Tandis qu'aux yeux de Gygès
> S'étalaient de blancs objets:
> Car, fût-ce amour, fût-ce rage,
> Bientôt la reine le mit
> Sur le trône et dans son lit.

Here the succession of twelve-, eight- and seven-syllable lines has the effect of forcing gradually into the distance the unfortunate king. The repetition of *Bientôt*, the eclipsing of the *noir rivage* of Hades by the *blancs objets* of the queen's body, are accentuated by the symmetry of the seven lines, each in seven syllables.

The alexandrine may combine with even briefer lines to produce interesting effects. The famous confession of King Lion in 'Les Animaux malades de la peste':

> Même il m'est arrivé quelquefois de manger
> Le berger,

finds numerous counterparts in the *contes*; in 'Le roi Candaule' the device is doubled:

> Parmi ses écoliers, dont il avait toujours
> Longue liste,
> Est un Français moins propre à faire en droit un cours
> Qu'en amours.

The short line may be of one, or two syllables:

> Que doit faire un mari quand on aime sa femme?
> Rien.
>
> ....
>
> Des Grâces, des Vénus, avec un grand concours
> D'Amours.

When, as in the following passage lines of 6, 7, 8, 10 and 12 syllables combine, we note that the narration occurs on a variety of levels: descriptive, reflective, dynamic:

> A la campagne il vivait,
> Loin du commerce et du monde:
> Marié depuis peu; content, je n'en sais rien.
> Sa femme avait de la jeunesse,
> De la beauté, de la délicatesse;
> Il ne tenait qu'à lui qu'il ne s'en trouvât bien.
> Son frère arrive, et lui fait l'ambassade;
> Enfin il le persuade.

In the above quotation from 'Joconde' the decasyllabic, combined with the other principle meters, discreetly supports by its matter-of-factness, the ampler, more philosophic tone for which La Fontaine uses the alexandrine. Here is the description of the preliminaries to taking a castle by night:

> Mainte échelle est portée, et point d'autre embarras,
> Point de tambours, force bons coutelas.
> On part sans bruit, on arrive en silence;
> L'orient vient de s'ouvrir.
> C'est un temps où le somme est dans sa violence,
> Et qui par sa fraîcheur nous contraint de dormir.

One could hardly conceive of a more adroit combination of rhythms to suggest different tones and shadings. The octosyllabic abruptly transports the reader from the details of the attack to the spectacle of the sunrise, whereupon the alexandrines stating a general truth about sleep associate us with the unsuspecting victims.

The decasyllabic

But despite its rather limited role in the *vers libres*, the decasyllabic dominates the *contes*. Pierre Clarac dismisses it with a shrug; La

Fontaine, according to this critic, has simply borrowed 'le décasyllabe... de Maître Clément'.[1] No doubt our poet knew Marot well, but his decasyllabic far surpasses that of the earlier poet. Indeed, had Valéry read beyond 'Belphégor' he might have been impressed at La Fontaine's mastery of the very line that challenged him, by his own account, to write 'Le Cimetière marin'. If we take the couplet he condemned so scathingly,

> Nos deux époux, à ce que dit l'histoire,
> Sans disputer n'étaient pas un moment...

certainly, out of context, it seems lame enough. But if we append to it the four lines that together with it make up the summary of Belphégor's married life, we see how accents and rime send the verse bumping along in the very rhythm of marital discord:

> Souvent leur guerre avait pour fondement
> Le jeu, la juppe ou quelque ameublement
> D'été, d'hiver, d'entretemps, bref un monde
> D'inventions propres à tout gâter.

This uncomfortable jogging stems from the repeated internal and external rimes in -*ment*, and the staccato, unevenly paced rhythm, increased by the *enjambements*. One problem the decasyllabic presents is that if the two accents of the second hemistich fall each on the third syllable, it will tend to lack smoothness, and almost never can approach the calm sonority of which the alexandrine is capable. La Fontaine puts this characteristic to good use in the above lines. Elsewhere, in the same poem, his decasyllabic attains lyric, languorous qualities:

> De votre nom j'orne le frontispice
> Des derniers vers que ma muse a polis.
> Puisse le tout, ô charmante Philis,
> Aller si loin que notre lôs franchisse
> La nuit des temps: nous la saurons dompter,
> Moi par écrire, et vous par réciter.

Thus La Fontaine addresses the beautiful actress La Champmeslé; his lines have nothing 'base' in them; rather a wistful hope for posterity's acclaim, beautifully suggested in the repeated sibilants of *frontispice*, *Puisse*, *Philis* and *franchisse*, demonstrating once again his skill with internal rime, and in the variety of accents. In two of the

---

[1] Pierre Clarac, *La Fontaine* (Paris: Hâtier, 'Connaissance des Lettres', 1959), p. 56.

lines he makes good use of the initial accent, which extends the range of the decasyllabic. Note that of the six, only the third has the 3–3 accent that tends to create jerkiness, and this is avoided by the power of the nasal -*mante*.

The *contes* abound in decasyllabics vigorous, dense, of a deceptive ease and flow, in which the poet seems never to strain for the proper rime, never to need to pad out his line as did even some of his great contemporaries. 'Le Faucon' in particular strikes the reader in this regard. Clitie's remarkable plea[1] owes some of its eloquence to the skilful placing of the accents. I have already quoted this passage, which attains the heights of a dramatic *tirade* in decasyllabics possessing the sweep and sonority of the tragic alexandrine. La Fontaine achieves this quality by maintaining as a firm basis the 2–2–2–4 rhythm, as in 'Ai*mant* d'a*mour* la *chose* la plus *cher*'. Within this pattern, the accent's intensity varies through subtle use of pauses and stress: of the three accents in 'Votre fau*con*. Mais *non*, plutôt pé*risse*', the first two are in strong opposition by position and by internal rime; the third, less marked, runs on to the following line, plunging us into the shocking alternative to the yielding-up of the falcon: 'L'enfant, la mère, avec le demeurant'.

In Clitie's plea the decasyllabic lends itself to pathos, to a dramatic supplication; at the end of 'La Clochette' it beautifully evokes despair and the dangers of solitude, tinging with a touch of the tragic, the tale of a lover's lure:

> A ce discours, la fille toute en transe
> Remplit de cris ces lieux peu fréquentés;
> *Nul* n'accou*rut*. O *bel*les, évi*tez*
> Le *fond* des *bois* et leur *vas*te si*lence*.

The prominence of the four accents, bringing out the full resonance of the nasals, may explain the 'talisman' quality of this line, that Stendhal rather curiously quoted without identifying La Fontaine, in a note stating his enjoyment of Ariosto.[2]

In discussing various meters we have occasionally mentioned rime. The above quotation, forming a quatrain in *rimes embrassées*, offers four examples of La Fontaine's failure to rime for the eye, an important error by the Malherbian standards of his day. Had he obeyed these standards we would have been deprived of the remark-

---

[1] Quoted above, Chapter 2, p. 88.

[2] Stendhal, *Œuvres*, ed. H. Martineau (Paris: Bibliothèque de la Pléiade, 1955), p. 214.

able rime *transe* and *silence*, which he probably included among what he called in the second preface 'mauvaises rimes'. Yet many of his rimes are novel, even startling, especially those involving proper names. In the exotic context of 'La Fiancée du roi de Garbe' we encounter *soudan–Alcoran; Tarvagant–extravagant; essor–Galaor; Mamolin–festin;* in 'Le Petit Chien' *Don–Abandon; Argie–Cajolerie; cruelle–Philomèle; fée–Orphée; dit-elle–Compostelle;* in 'La Mandragore' *celui-ci–Calfucci; iota–Nicia; Callimaque–attaque;* in 'La Matrone d'Ephèse' *matrone* rimes with *Pétrone*.

Licences

Enjambement, one of the *licences* for which La Fontaine expressed contrition in the *mea culpa* of his preface, provides one example of the skill with which he handled this so-called error, which he manipulated with similar ease in the *fables*. The suppleness it provides is of course essential to the 'liberty' of his *vers libres*, as in this emblematic scene from 'La Matrone d'Ephèse':

> Le Dieu qui fait aimer prit son temps; il tira
> Deux traits de son carquois; de l'un il entama
> Le soldat jusqu'au vif; l'autre effleura la dame.

Here the *enjambement* has the effect after *prit son temps* of galvanizing the action; *il tira* following closely upon the accent displaced from its usual position moves with the speed of Cupid's arrow, and that the movement should end with the internal-riming *effleura* before the end of the line helps to suggest the less decisive impact on the mourning widow. Run-on lines in series can also bring about an effect of chatty prosiness, in itself creating a complicity between poet and reader; in the following lines the single word *jugez* is supported by the *enjambements*:

> A ce discours jugez quels étaient les supplices
> Qu'endurait le docteur. Il forme le dessein
> De s'en aller le lendemain
> Au lieu de l'écolier, et sous ce personnage
> Convaincre sa moitié, lui faire un vasselage
> Dont il fût à jamais parlé.

La Fontaine's imperative *jugez* in the preceding quotation offers yet another example of the involvement of the reader in the creative aspect of the work which we have linked to irresponsibility of the 'negligent' poet. Here the versification serves to underline that fusion, projecting us, through the rapidity of the run-on lines, into the mind of the besotted magistrate, and making us, as it were, follow his thoughts to their vainglorious conclusion. And in fact, in addition to his skill with various techniques, La Fontaine succeeds in creating, through his versification, a tone that constitutes still another kind of veil.

If we look at the more lubricious of the tales, we are immediately struck by a counterpointing due in part to the versification. In 'Joconde', to describe the servant-girl's rendezvous with her lover, in the same bed with the king and the hero of the story, the poet skilfully combines octosyllabics and sibilants with a predominant rime:

> La porte ouverte elle laissa:
> Le galant vint et s'approcha
> Des pieds du lit, puis fit en sorte
> Qu'entre les draps il se glissa;
> Et Dieu sait comme il se plaça,
> Et comme enfin tout se passa;
> Et de ceci ni de cela
> Ne se douta le moins du monde
> Ni le roi lombard, ni Joconde.

The indirectness of the language, with its generalizing articles and conjunctions, is reinforced by the whispering insonority of the rimes, with their effect of secretiveness; the sonorous couplet *monde – Joconde* breaks the spell, shifting our glance to the unsuspecting dupes.

On another occasion, variations in line length and the rhythm itself suggest the mock-heroic nature of a suicide threat:

> il forme le dessein
> De se laisser mourir de faim;
> Car de se poignarder, la chose est trop tot faite:
> On n'a pas le temps d'en venir
> Au repentir.

The poet relates Alaciel's decision to submit, in these circumstances, with similar effects of counterpointing; note in particular the prosiness of the decasyllabic 'C'est avoir l'âme un peu trop dure', which is meant to be read with staccato rapidity, after the rather ponderous and moralistic alexandrine:

Le second jour commence à la toucher.
Elle rêve à cette aventure:
Laisser mourir un homme, et pouvoir l'empêcher,
C'est avoir l'âme un peu dure.

Her yielding begins with another decasyllabic punctuated with a flat *donc*, whose accent reinforces the irony. The two alexandrines that terminate the incident could scarcely be more different; the first dances with all the gaiety she brings to her 'difficult' resolution, and the second promptly counteracts the joyous tone by its dry *t* sounds and blunting rhythm:

Par pitié donc elle condescendit
Aux volontés du capitaine,
Et cet office lui rendit
Gaîment, de bonne grâce, et sans montrer de peine:
Autrement le remède eût été sans effet.

In the same poem a series of heptasyllabics produces a similar effect of bluntness. Grifonio's lieutenant is no man to stand on ceremony. He takes the castle, and gives Alaciel extremely short shrift:

Il prend le château d'emblée.
Voilà la fête troublée.
Le jeûneur maudit son sort.
Le corsaire apprend d'abord
L'aventure de la belle;
Et, la tirant à l'ecart,
Il en veut avoir sa part.
Elle fit fort la rebelle.
Il ne s'en etonna pas,
N'étant novice en tels cas.
"Le mieux que vous puissiez faire,
Lui dit tout franc ce corsaire,
C'est de m'avoir pour ami;
Je suis corsaire et demi."

In many such examples, the variety of the lines aids in creating a particular tone. In the above case, the alexandrine following the fourteen heptasyllabics: 'Vous avez fait jeûner un pauvre misérable' acquires both through its sonority and by contrast a particularly minatory tone, strengthened by the blunt alternative he gives her: 'Vous jeûnerez à votre tour/Ou vous me serez favorable.'

This counterpointing effect appears largely confined to *vers libres*, and in the monometric poems the rhythm accentuates if anything the sense. In 'Comment l'esprit vient aux filles' Friar Bonaventure's seduction of the gullible Lise follows a quite obvious cadence:

> Il suit sa pointe, et d'encor en encor.
> Toujours l'esprit s'insinue et s'avance,
> Tant et si bien qu'il arrive à bon port.

Here the rhythm clearly reacts against the euphemistic use of the word *esprit*, reinforcing its fleshly sense by the punctuation of the accents.

So the 'learned nonchalance' of La Fontaine's versification includes not only a unique mastery of *vers libres*, but a wide range of effects through varying line lengths, shifting accents, sonority or its lack, that may both complement and counterpoint a given meaning. One could almost believe that his apologies concerning his prosody were meant, not to deprecate, but to draw the reader's attention to those 'nonchalant' errors from which he drew so much. At any rate there appears no doubt that far from being either 'base' or 'repugnantly facile' the poetry of the *contes* demonstrates an artistry equal to that of 'Adonis' or of the *fables* themselves.

Conclusion

At the close of this study, I am drawn to wonder again, as I hope the reader has been, at the vehemence of critical opposition to the *Contes*. Motives can appear mixed: a Valéry, the admirer of La Fontaine's poetic technique in 'Adonis', fails to recognize the same talent in the *Contes* perhaps because he found their 'libertinage' too repugnant to study them closely. 'Quelles idylles et quelles églogues il était né pour écrire', he exclaims. This amounts first of all to a plain rejection of the subject; Valéry's ideal La Fontaine would have shunned the erotic.

But how futile to deplore the lack of eclogue or idyll, when precisely one of the qualities of the *contes*, is that they embrace so much, and when the reader may find in them the elements, not only of eclogue and idyll, but of elegy as well! Joconde's wife laments his departure for the court in the tones of the eclogue; the story of Friar Philippe's education of his son comes very close to idyll; La Fontaine's asides on his love-life are clearly elegiac. In almost all cases, however, the tone acquires a certain dissonance. This superimposing of one level upon another typifies the *contes* and resolves itself, as I have tried to show, in various kinds of irony, an irony that is, however, benevolent and fraught with the same gentle knowingness concerning human foibles that Molière displays in his scenes of amorous quarrels.

It is true, as one critic has complained, that some of the tales do scarcely more than snigger, lacking the exalted eroticism one may find in such works as the *Thousand and One Nights*.[1] But such a judgment fails once again to take into account the great range of the *contes*. Nor are almost hallucinatory effects of amplification and dynamism lacking, as 'Les Lunettes' attests. In particular to condemn them for their lack of exaltation fails to recognize the joyousness of their attitude toward sex. La Fontaine's paean to the greatest of all 'remedies' in 'L'Abbesse' would alone suffice to refute the charge.

Linked to this joyous sensuality is the play-spirit which imbues the *contes*, where *homo ludens* so frequently plays a role. The amorous

---

[1] Odette de Mourgues, *O muse, fuyante proie...Essai sur la poésie de La Fontaine* (Paris: Corti, 1962), p. 85.

ruse of the Boccaccian tales, the disguises, the *quiproquos*, even the savagely gleeful dance around a burning monastery, partake of the spirit of the game. This spirit has the same function, in La Fontaine's esthetic, of that quality of ceremony Montaigne in 'Sur des vers de Virgile', placed on the level of imagery and metaphor. In general, this kind of dualism, which produces an effect of counterpoint, appears on every level of the *contes*. Just as the play-spirit counteracts the brutality of primitive tales like 'Le Faiseur d'oreilles et le raccommodeur de moules', so the 'ceremony' of the amours of Renaud d'Ast and his hospitable widow refines the scene of seduction like the Virgilian imagery Montaigne so admired.

But it may be that this very process is one source of critical disapproval. One detects a repugnancy based on the attitude that bawdry is all well and good in its proper habitat; that is in the rougher tongues of the *Cent Nouvelles nouvelles* or of Rabelais. Thus, in deploring the waste of time expended on the *contes* the critics may be suggesting that they do not deserve the artistry La Fontaine brought to their re-creation. Yet the whole esthetic process of the *contes*, as I have tried to show, begins with meeting the challenge the subject-matter provokes: 'On m'engage à conter d'une manière honnête/Le sujet d'un de ces tableaux.' The esthetics of negligence involves an artistic coming-to-grips with a recalcitrant theme. To me this joust, like the *gageure* typical of French classicism, is of the highest interest to students of French poetry.

I have spoken above of a central dualism or contrast between subject and form, seriousness and playfulness; a general effect of counterpoint. Yet in the finished product, miraculously these dichotomies are resolved, to produce the fusion that on one level following Montaigne I have called consubstantiality. The author's presence in the work becomes the work; the pose of negligence in life combines with the negligent esthetic, and when La Fontaine declares 'diversité c'est ma devise' we think first of the polyphony of his poetry rather than his professed rakishness.

One by-product of this fusion is that if we set them against the tendencies of popular fiction today, the *contes* appear to civilize sex. To my mind this is a virtue, not a defect. Contemporary novelists frequently spell out in detail the phrase familiar to readers of Zola: 'L'acte fut brutal', reducing the sexual encounter to rape or the degradation of the partner. In so doing they tend to profane a mystery, through which man and woman can become aware of powers greater than themselves. To the objection that by treating sex as a game La Fontaine may trivialize it, one need only instance the exaltation, the range from tranquillity to violence his *contes* possess. What they refuse to do is to brutalize sex. The poet of the *contes* remains human and humane; his amorous fun-making involves partners with a civilized deference for one another, and if his Alaciel and Hispal lack a sense of mystery, they never lack good manners. Even when the sex act in the *contes* represents war between the sexes, it is war fought according to a code.

So I believe that this quality is one reason why we must appreciate the *contes*, for theirs is a sexuality contemplated with the smile of reason. Their art, their admirable structure, the range and variety of their versification, their studied negligence and the 'veil' of their language, all these have become the tools of the civilizing process which is a proper function of art.

Bibliography

(The place of publication is Paris unless stated otherwise)

EDITIONS OF LA FONTAINE'S WORKS

Clarac, Pierre: *Œuvres diverses* (Bibliothèque de la Pléiade, 1948).
Couton, Georges: *Contes et nouvelles en vers* (Garnier, 1961).
Fables choisies mises en vers (Garnier, 1962).
Groos, René and Schiffrin, Jacques: *Fables, contes et nouvelles* (Bibliothèque de la Pléiade, 1954).
Régnier, Henri de: *Œuvres* (Hachette, Les Grands Ecrivains de la France, 1883–92), 11 vols., 1 album.

WORKS CONSULTED

Auerbach, Erich: *Mimesis: The Representation of Reality in Western Literature*, tr. W. Trask (New York: Doubleday, 1957).
Aretino, Pietro: *Raggionamenti*, in *Tutte le opere di Pietro Aretino* (Verona: Mondadori, 1960).
Ariosto, Lodovico: *Orlando Furioso*, ed. L. Casetti (Milan–Naples: Ricciardi, n.d.).
Orlando Furioso, tr. Allen Gilbert (New York: S. F. Vanni, 1954).
Bénichou, Paul: *Morales du grand siècle* (Gallimard, 1948).
Boccaccio, Giovanni: *Le Décaméron de Messire Jehan Boccace Florentin, nouvellement traduict, d'Italien en Françoys par Maistre Anthoine Le Maçon*, ed. Paul Lacroix (Librairie des Bibliophiles, n.d.).
Boileau-Despréaux, Nicolas: *Œuvres complètes*, ed. Charles H. Boudhors (Belles Lettres, 1934–43), 7 vols.
Bray, René: 'L'Introduction des vers mêlés sur la scène classique', *Publications of the Modern Language Association of America*, LXVI (1951), 456–84.
La Formation de la doctrine classique en France (Nizet, 1957).
Brody, Jules: 'Pierre Nicole auteur de la préface du *Recueil des poésies chrétiennes et diverses*', *XVIIe siècle*, LXIV (1964), 31–54.
Cameron, Alice: *The Influence of Ariosto's Epic and Lyric Poetry on Ronsard and his Group* (Baltimore: Johns Hopkins Press, 1930).
Castiglione, Baldesar: *The Book of the Courtier*, tr. Charles Singleton (New York: Anchor Books, 1959).
Catullus: *Priapea*, in *Poésies*, ed. and tr. G. Lafaye (Belles Lettres: 1966).
Cicero: *De oratore* (*De l'orateur*), ed. and tr. E. Courbaud (Belles Lettres, 1957).

Cioranescu, Alexandre: *L'Arioste en France* (Les Presses Modernes, 1939).

Clarac, Pierre: *La Fontaine* (Hâtier, 'Connaissance des Lettres', 1959).

Collinet, J.-P.: *Le Monde littéraire de La Fontaine* (Gap: Imprimerie Louis-Jean, 1970).

Couton, Georges: *La poétique de La Fontaine* (Presses Universitaires de France, 1957).

Croll, Morris W.: 'Juste-Lipse et le mouvement anti-cicéronien à la fin du XVIe et au début du XVIIe siècle', *Revue du XVIe siècle*, II (1914), 200–42.

Curtius, E. R.: *European Literature and the Latin Middle Ages*, tr. W. R. Trask (New York: Harper, 1953).

Diderot, Denis: *Œuvres*, ed. A. Billy (Bibliothèque de la Pléiade, 1962).

Du Bellay, Joachim: *Œuvres poétiques*, ed. H. Chamard (Société des textes français modernes, 1908–39).

Divers jeux rustiques (Didier, 1947).

Durling, Robert: *The Figure of the Poet in Renaissance Epic* (Cambridge, Mass.: Harvard University Press, 1965).

Frame, D. M.: *Montaigne's Discovery of Man* (New York: Columbia University Press, 1955).

Friedrich, Hugo: *Montaigne* (Gallimard, 1968).

Gohin, Ferdinand: *L'Art de La Fontaine dans ses fables* (Garnier, 1929).

Jourda, Pierre, ed.: *Conteurs français du XVIe siècle* (Bibliothèque de la Pléiade, 1965).

Kohn, Renée: *Le Goût de La Fontaine* (Presses Universitaires de France, 1962).

Lafon, Jean: 'La Beauté et la grâce: l'esthétique "platonicienne" des "Amours de Psyché"', *Revue d'histoire littéraire de la France*, LXXX (1969), 475–90.

Lapp, John C.: *Zola before the Rougon-Macquart* (University of Toronto Press, 1964).

'Metamorphosis in Corneille's *Andromède*', *University of Toronto Quarterly*, XXXIX (1970), 164–80.

'Ronsard and La Fontaine: Two Versions of "Adonis"' *L'Esprit créateur*, X (1970), 125–44.

Lewis, C. S.: *The Allegory of Love* (Oxford: Clarendon Press, 1936).

Lucretius: *De rerum natura*, tr. W. H. D. Rouse (Cambridge, Mass.: Harvard University Press, 1959).

De rerum natura, libri sex, ed. D. Lambin (Paris and Lyons: G. Roville, 1563).

Lugli, Vittorio: 'Valéry e Adonis', *La Nuova Italia*, November 1936, 241–5.

Il Prodigio di La Fontaine (Messina–Milano: Principato, 1939).

'La Fontaine, poète de la nature', *Cahier des études littéraires françaises*, VI (1954).

'Amor delle arti e poesia in La Fontaine', *Atti de V^e congresso internationale di lingua e letteratura moderne* (Firenze: Valmartino, 1955).

'La Courtisane amoureuse', *Studi in onore di Italo Siciliano* (Firenze: Leo S. Olschki, 1966).

Marot, Clement: *Œuvres complètes*, ed. C. A. Mayer (London: Athlone Press, 1958–64).

Masters, G. Mallory: *Rabelaisian Dialectic and the Platonic–Hermetic Tradition* (Albany: State University of New York Press, 1969).

May, Georges: *D'Ovide à Racine* (Presses Universitaires de France, 1949).

Michel, Pierre: 'La Fontaine et Montaigne', *Bulletin de la Société des Amis de Montaigne*, juillet–septembre, 1965.

Montaigne, Michel de: *Œuvres complètes*, ed. A. Thibaudet and M. Rat (Bibliothèque de la Pléiade, 1962).

Mourgues, Odette de: *Metaphysical, Baroque and Précieux Poetry* (Oxford University Press, 1953).

O muse, fuyante proie...Essai sur la poésie de La Fontaine (Corti, 1962).

Nims, J. F.: 'Yeats and the Careless Muse', *Learners and Discerners*, ed. R. E. Scholes (Charlottesville: University Press of Virginia, 1964), pp. 31–60.

Ovid: *Ars amatoria* (*L'Art d'aimer*), ed. and tr. H. Bornecque (Belles Lettres, 1929).

Metamorphoseon (*Métamorphoses*), ed. and tr. G. Lafaye (Belles Lettres, 1960).

Remedia amoris (*Remèdes à l'amour*), ed. and tr. H. Bornecque (Belles Lettres, 1961).

Amores, ed. and tr. H. Bornecque (Belles Lettres, 1961).

Pintard, René: *Le Libertinage érudit dans la première moitié du XVIIe siécle* (Boivin, 1943), 2 vols.

Rabelais, François: *Œuvres complètes*, ed. J. Boulenger (Bibliothèque de la Pléiade, 1942).

Œuvres complètes, ed. Pierre Jourda (Garnier, 1962).

Régnier, Mathurin: *Œuvres complètes*, ed. G. Raibaud (Didier, 1958).

Ronsard, *Œuvres*, ed. G. Cohen (Paris: Bibliothèque de la Pléiade, 1950).

Sainte-Beuve, Charles Augustin de: *Causeries du lundi* (Garnier, 1883).

Sorel, Charles: *Histoire comique de Francion*, ed. E. Roy (Hachette, 1924), 5 vols.

Spitzer, Leo: 'Die Kunst des Übergangs bei La Fontaine', *Publications of the Modern Language Association of America*, LIII (1938), 393–433.

Stendhal: *Œuvres*, ed. H. Martineau (Bibliothèque de la Pléiade, 1955).

Terence: *Andria* (*L'Andrienne*), ed. and tr. J. Marouzeau (Belles Lettres, 1963).

Valéry, Paul: *Œuvres*, ed. J. Hytier (Bibliothèque de la Pléiade, 1959–60), 2 vols.

Viau, Théophile de: *Œuvres poétiques*, ed. J. Streicher (Droz, 1951).

Virgil: *Aeneid*, tr. H. R. Fairclough (Cambridge, Mass.: Harvard University Press, 1966).

Wadsworth, Philip: 'La Fontaine as Student and Critic of Malherbe', *Symposium III* (1949), pp. 130–9.

Young La Fontaine: A Study of his Artistic Growth in his Early Poetry and First Fables (Evanston, Ill.: Northwestern University Press, 1952).

Index